MYTHOLOGIES

W. B. YEATS

From a charcoal drawing by John S. Sargent, R.A.

W. B. YEATS

Mythologies

○

THE CELTIC TWILIGHT
THE SECRET ROSE
STORIES OF RED HANRAHAN
ROSA ALCHEMICA
THE TABLES OF THE LAW
THE ADORATION OF THE MAGI
PER AMICA SILENTIA LUNAE

PAPERMAC

First published 1934 by Macmillan

Second edition with additional plays published 1952 by Macmillan

First published in paperback 1982 by Papermac
an imprint of Macmillan Publishers Ltd
25 Eccleston Place London SW1W 9NF
and Basingstoke

Associated companies throughout the world

ISBN 0 333 48894 6

3 5 7 9 8 6 4

A CIP catalogue record for this book is available
from the British Library.

Printed and bound in Malaysia

CONTENTS

Contents

Contents

FRONTISPIECE

NOTE

I HAVE left out a few passages in *The Celtic Twilight*, which was first published in 1893. The *Stories of Red Hanrahan* were published with the stories now called *The Secret Rose* and *Rosa Alchemica* in a book called *The Secret Rose* in 1897, and they owe much of their merit to Lady Gregory. They were, as first published, written in that artificial, elaborate English so many of us played with in the 'nineties, and I had come to hate them. When I was changing the first story in the light of a Sligo tale about 'a wild old man in flannel' who could change a pack of cards into the likeness of a pack of hounds, I asked Lady Gregory's help. We worked together, first upon that tale, and, after, upon all the others, she now suggesting a new phrase or thought, and now I, till all had been put into that simple English she had learned from her Galway countrymen, and the thought had come closer to the life of the people. If their style has merit now, that merit is mainly hers. Dr. Hyde had already founded the first Gaelic play ever performed in a theatre upon one of the stories, and but the other day Lady Gregory made a Hanrahan play upon an incident of her own invention. *The Tables of the Law* and *The Adoration of the Magi* were intended to be part of *The Secret Rose*, but the publisher, A. H. Bullen, took a distaste to them and asked me to leave them out, and then after the book was published liked them and put them into a little volume by themselves. In these, as in most of the other stories, I have left out or rewritten a passage here and there.

W. B. YEATS

1925

THE CELTIC TWILIGHT
1893

A TELLER OF TALES

MANY OF THE TALES in this book were told me by one Paddy Flynn, a little bright-eyed old man, who lived in a leaky and one-roomed cabin in the village of Ballisodare, which is, he was wont to say, 'the most gentle'—whereby he meant faery—'place in the whole of County Sligo.' Others hold it, however, but second to Drumcliff and Dromahair. The first time I saw him he was bent above the fire with a can of mushrooms at his side; the next time he was asleep under a hedge, smiling in his sleep. He was indeed always cheerful, though I thought I could see in his eyes (swift as the eyes of a rabbit, when they peered out of their wrinkled holes) a melancholy which was wellnigh a portion of their joy; the visionary melancholy of purely instinctive natures and of all animals.

And yet there was much in his life to depress him, for in the triple solitude of age, eccentricity, and deafness, he went about much pestered by children. It was for this very reason perhaps that he ever recommended mirth and hopefulness. He was fond, for instance, of telling how Columcille cheered up his mother. 'How are you to-day, mother?' said the saint. 'Worse,' replied the mother. 'May you be worse to-morrow,' said the saint. The next day Columcille came again, and exactly the same conversation took place, but the third day the mother said, 'Better, thank God.' And the saint replied, 'May you be better to-morrow.' He was fond too of telling how the Judge smiles at the Last Day alike when he rewards the good and condemns the lost to unceasing flames. He had many strange sights to keep him cheerful or to make him sad. I asked him had he ever seen the faeries, and got the reply, 'Am I not annoyed with them?' I asked too if he had ever seen the banshee. 'I have seen it,' he said, 'down there by the water, batting the river with its hands.'

BELIEF AND UNBELIEF

THERE are some doubters even in the western villages. One woman told me last Christmas that she did not believe either in Hell or in ghosts. Hell was an invention got up by the priest to keep people good; and ghosts would not be permitted, she held, to go 'trapsin' about the earth' at their own free will; 'but there are faeries and little leprechauns, and water-horses, and fallen angels.' I have met also a man with a Mohawk Indian tattooed upon his arm, who held exactly similar beliefs and unbeliefs. No matter what one doubts, one never doubts the faeries, for, as the man with the Mohawk Indian on his arm said, 'they stand to reason.'

A little girl who was at service in the village of Grange, close under the seaward slopes of Ben Bulben, suddenly disappeared one night about three years ago. There was at once great excitement in the neighbourhood, because it was rumoured that the faeries had taken her. A villager was said to have long struggled to hold her from them, but at last they prevailed, and he found nothing in his hands but a broom-stick. The local constable was applied to, and he at once instituted a house-to-house search, and at the same time advised the people to burn all the *bucalauns* (ragweed) on the field she vanished from, because *bucalauns* are sacred to the faeries. They spent the whole night burning them, the constable repeating spells the while. In the morning the little girl was found wandering in the field. She said the faeries had taken her away a great distance, riding on a faery horse. At last she saw a big river, and

7

the man who had tried to keep her from being carried off was drifting down it—such are the topsyturvy-doms of faery glamour—in a cockle-shell. On the way her companions had mentioned the names of several people who were to die shortly in the village.

MORTAL HELP

ONE hears in the old poems of men taken away to help the gods in a battle, and Cuchulain won the goddess Fand for a while, by helping her married sister and her sister's husband to overthrow another nation of the Land of Promise. I have been told, too, that the people of Faery cannot even play at hurley unless they have on either side some mortal, whose body—or whatever has been put in its place, as the story-teller would say—is asleep at home. Without mortal help they are shadowy and cannot even strike the balls. One day I was walking over some marshy land in Galway with a friend when we found an old, hard-featured man digging a ditch. My friend had heard that this man had seen a wonderful sight of some kind, and at last we got the story out of him. When he was a boy he was working one day with about thirty men and women and boys. They were beyond Tuam and not far from Knocknagur. Presently they saw, all thirty of them, and at a distance of about half a mile, some hundred and fifty of the people of Faery. There were two of them, he said, in dark clothes like people of our own time, who stood about a hundred yards from one another, but the others wore clothes of all colours, 'bracket' or chequered, and some had red waistcoats.

He could not see what they were doing, but all might have been playing hurley, for 'they looked as if it was that.' Sometimes they would vanish, and then he 'would almost swear' they came back out of the bodies of the two men in dark clothes. These two men were of the size of living men, but the others were small. He saw them for about half an hour, and then the old man he and those about him were working for took up a whip and said, 'Get on, get on, or we will have no work done!' I asked if he saw the faeries too. 'O yes, but he did not want work he was paying wages for to be neglected.' He made everybody work so hard that nobody saw what happened to the faeries.

1902

A Visionary

A VISIONARY

A YOUNG man came to see me at my lodgings the other night, and began to talk of the making of the earth and the heavens and much else. I questioned him about his life and his doings. He had written many poems and painted many mystical designs since we met last, but latterly had neither written nor painted, for his whole heart was set upon making his character vigorous and calm, and the emotional life of the artist was bad for him, he feared. He recited his poems readily, however. He had them all in his memory. Some indeed had never been written down. Suddenly it seemed to me that he was peering about him a little eagerly. 'Do you see anything, X——?' I said. 'A shining, winged woman, covered by her long hair, is standing near the doorway,' he answered, or some such words. 'Is it the influence of some living person who thinks of us, and whose thoughts appear to us in that symbolic form?' I said; for I am well instructed in the ways of the visionaries and in the fashion of their speech. 'No,' he replied; 'for if it were the thoughts of a person who is alive I should feel the living influence in my living body, and my heart would beat and my breath would fall. It is a spirit. It is some one who is dead or who has never lived.'

I asked what he was doing, and found he was clerk in a large shop. His pleasure, however, was to wander about upon the hills, talking to half-mad and visionary peasants, or to persuade queer and conscience-stricken persons to deliver up the keeping of their troubles into his care. Another night, when I was with him in his own lodging, more than one turned up to talk over their beliefs and disbeliefs, and sun them as it were in the subtle light of his mind. Sometimes visions come to him as he talks with them, and he is rumoured to have told divers people true matters of their past days and distant friends, and left them hushed with dread of their strange teacher, who seems scarce more than a boy, and is so much more subtle than the oldest among them.

The poetry he recited me was full of his nature and his visions. Sometimes it told of other lives he believes himself to have lived in other centuries, sometimes of people he had talked to, revealing them to their own minds. I told him I would write an article upon him and it, and was told in turn that I might do so if I did not mention his name, for he wished to be always 'unknown, obscure, impersonal.' Next day a bundle of his poems arrived, and with them a note in these words: 'Here are copies of verses you said you liked. I do not think I could ever write or paint any more. I prepare myself for a cycle of other activities in some other life. I will make rigid my roots and branches. It is not now my turn to burst into leaves and flowers.'

The poems were all endeavours to capture some high, impalpable mood in a net of obscure images. There were fine passages in all, but these were often embedded in thoughts which have evidently a special value to his mind, but are to other men the counters of an unknown coinage. At other times the beauty of the thought was obscured by careless writing as though he had suddenly doubted if writing was not a foolish labour. He had frequently illustrated his verses with drawings, in which an imperfect anatomy did not altogether smother a beauty of feeling. The faeries in whom he believes have given him many subjects, notably Thomas of Ercildoune sitting motionless in the twilight while a young and beautiful creature leans softly out of the shadow and whispers in his ear. He had delighted above all in strong effects of colour: spirits who have upon their heads instead of hair the feathers of peacocks; a phantom reaching from a swirl of flame towards a star; a spirit passing with a globe of iridescent crystal—symbol of the soul—half shut within his hand. But always under this largess of colour lay some appeal to human sympathy. This appeal draws to him all those who, like himself, seek for illumination or else mourn for a joy that has gone. One of these especially comes to mind. A winter or two ago he spent much of the night walking up and down upon the mountain talking to an old peasant who, dumb to most men, poured out his cares for him. Both were unhappy: X—— because he had then first decided that art and poetry were not for him, and the old peasant because his life was ebbing out with no achievement remaining and no hope left him. The peasant was wandering in his mind with prolonged sorrow. Once he burst out with, 'God possesses the heavens—God possesses the heavens —but He covets the world'; and once he lamented that his old neighbours were gone, and that all had forgotten him: they used to draw a chair to the fire for him in every cabin, and now they said, 'Who is that old fellow there?' 'The fret' (Irish for doom) 'is over me,' he repeated, and then went on to talk once more of God and Heaven. More than once also he said, waving his arm towards the mountain, 'Only myself knows what happened under the thorn-tree forty years ago'; and as he said it the tears upon his face glistened in the moonlight.

VILLAGE GHOSTS

THE ancient map-makers wrote across unexplored regions, 'Here are lions.' Across the villages of fisher-men and turners of the earth, so different are these from us, we can write but one line that is certain, 'Here are ghosts.'

My ghosts inhabit the village of H——, in Leinster. History has in no manner been burdened by this ancient village, with its crooked lanes, its old abbey church-yard full of long grass, its green background of small fir-trees, and its quay, where lie a few tarry fishing-luggers. In the annals of entomology it is well known. For a small bay lies westward a little, where he who watches night after night may see a certain rare moth fluttering along the edge of the tide, just at the end of evening or the beginning of dawn. A hundred years ago it was carried here from Italy by smugglers in a cargo of silks and laces. If the moth-hunter would throw down his net, and go hunting for ghost tales or tales of those children of Lilith we call faeries, he would have need for far less patience.

To approach the village at night a timid man requires great strategy. A man was once heard complaining, 'By the Cross of Jesus! how shall I go? If I pass by the hill of Dunboy old Captain Burney may look out on me. If I go round by the water, and up by the steps, there is the headless one and another on the quays, and a new one under the old churchyard wall. If I go right round the other way, Mrs. Stewart is appearing at Hill-side Gate, and the Devil himself is in the Hospital Lane.'

I never heard which spirit he braved, but feel sure it was not the one in the Hospital Lane. In cholera times a shed had been there set up to receive patients. When the need had gone by, it was pulled down, but ever since the ground where it stood has broken out in ghosts and demons and faeries. There is a farmer at H——, Paddy B—— by name, a man of great strength, and a teetotaller. His wife and sister-in-law, musing on his great strength, often wonder what he would do if he drank. One night, when passing through the Hospital Lane, he saw what he supposed at first to be a tame rabbit; after a little he found that it was a white cat. When he came near, the creature slowly began to swell larger and larger, and as it grew he felt his own strength ebbing away, as though it were sucked out of him. He turned and ran.

By the Hospital Lane goes the 'Faeries' Path.' Every evening they travel from the hill to the sea, from the sea to the hill. At the sea end of their path stands a cottage. One night Mrs. Arbunathy, who lived there, left her door open, as she was expecting her son. Her husband was asleep by the fire; a tall man came in and sat beside him. After he had been sitting there for a while, the woman said, 'In the name of God, who are you?' He got up and went out, saying, 'Never leave the door open at this hour, or evil may come to you.' She woke her husband and told him. 'One of the Good People has been with us,' said he.

Probably the man braved Mrs. Stewart at Hillside Gate. When she lived she was the wife of the Protestant clergyman. 'Her ghost was never known to harm any one,' say the village people; 'it is only doing penance upon the earth.' Not far from Hillside Gate, where she haunted, appeared for a short time a much more remarkable spirit. Its haunt was the boreen, a green lane leading from the western end of the village. In a cottage at the village end of the boreen lived a house-painter, Jim Montgomery, and his wife. They had several children. He was a little dandy, and came of a higher class than his neighbours. His wife was a very big woman; but he, who had been expelled from the village choir for drink, gave her a beating one day. Her sister heard of it, and came and took down one of the window shutters—Montgomery was neat about everything, and had shutters on the outside of every window—and beat him with it, being big and strong like her sister. He threatened to prosecute her; she answered that she would break every bone in his body if he did. She never spoke to her sister again, because she had allowed herself to be beaten by so small a man. Jim Montgomery grew worse and worse: his wife before long had not enough to eat, but she would tell no one, for she was very proud. Often, too, she would have no fire on a cold night. If any neighbours came in she would say she had let the fire out because she was just going to bed. The people often heard her husband beating her, but she never told any one. She got very thin. At last one Saturday there was no food in the house for herself and the children. She could bear it no longer, and went to the priest and asked him for some money. He gave her thirty shillings. Her husband met her, and took the money, and beat her. On the following

Monday she got very ill, and sent for a Mrs. Kelly. Mrs. Kelly, as soon as she saw her, said, 'My woman, you are dying,' and sent for the priest and the doctor. She died in an hour. After her death, as Montgomery neglected the children, the landlord had them taken to the workhouse. A few nights after they had gone, Mrs Kelly was going home through the boreen when the ghost of Mrs. Montgomery appeared and followed her. It did not leave her until she reached her own house. She told the priest, Father S———, a noted antiquarian, and could not get him to believe her. A few nights afterwards Mrs. Kelly again met the spirit in the same place. She was in too great terror to go the whole way, but stopped at a neighbour's cottage midway, and asked them to let her in. They answered they were going to bed. She cried out, 'In the name of God let me in, or I will break open the door.' They opened, and so she escaped from the ghost. Next day she told the priest again. This time he believed, and said it would follow her until she spoke to it.

She met the spirit a third time in the boreen. She asked what kept it from its rest. The spirit said that its children must be taken from the workhouse, for none of its relations were ever there before, and that three masses were to be said for the repose of its soul. 'If my husband does not believe you,' she said, 'show him that,' and touched Mrs. Kelly's wrist with three fingers. The places where they touched swelled up and blackened. She then vanished. For a time Montgomery would not believe that his wife had appeared. 'She would not show herself to Mrs. Kelly,' he said—'she with respectable people to appear to.' He was convinced by the three marks, and the children were taken from the workhouse. The priest said the masses, and the shade must have been at rest, for it has not since appeared. Some time afterwards Jim Montgomery died in the workhouse, having come to great poverty through drink.

I know some who believe they have seen the headless ghost upon the quay, and one who, when he passes the old cemetery wall at night, sees a woman with white borders to her cap[1] creep out and follow him. The apparition only leaves him at his own door. The villagers imagine that she follows him to avenge some wrong. 'I will haunt you when I die' is a favourite threat. His wife was once half scared to death by what she considers a demon in the shape of a dog.

These are a few of the open-air spirits; the more domestic of their tribe gather within-doors, plentiful as swallows under southern eaves.

One night a Mrs. Nolan was watching by her dying child in Fluddy's Lane. Suddenly there was a sound of knocking heard at the door. She did not open, fearing it was some unhuman thing that knocked. The knocking ceased. After a little the front door and then the back door were burst open, and closed again. Her husband went to see what was wrong. He found both doors bolted. The child died. The doors were again opened

[1] I wonder why she had white borders to her cap. The old Mayo woman, who has told me so many tales, has told me that her brother-in-law saw 'a woman with white borders to her cap going round the stacks in a field, and soon after he got a hurt, and he died in six months.'

and closed as before. Then Mrs. Nolan remembered that she had forgotten to leave window or door open, as the custom is, for the departure of the soul. These strange openings and closings and knockings were warnings and reminders from the spirits who attend the dying.

The house ghost is usually a harmless and well-meaning creature. It is put up with as long as possible. It brings good luck to those who live with it. I remember two children who slept with their mother and sisters and brothers in one small room. In the room was also a ghost. They sold herrings in the Dublin streets, and did not mind the ghost much, because they knew they would always sell their fish easily while they slept in the 'ha'nted' room.

I have some acquaintance among the ghost-seers of western villages. The Connacht tales are very different from those of Leinster. These H—— spirits have a gloomy, matter-of-fact way with them. They come to announce a death, to fulfil some obligation, to revenge a wrong, to pay their bills even—as did a fisherman's daughter the other day—and then hasten to their rest. All things they do decently and in order. It is demons, and not ghosts, that transform themselves into white cats or black dogs. The people who tell the tales are poor, serious-minded fishing-people, who find in the doings of the ghosts the fascination of fear. In the western tales is a whimsical grace, a curious extravagance. The people who recount them live in the most wild and beautiful scenery, under a sky ever loaded and fantastic with flying clouds. They are farmers and labourers, who do a little fishing now and then. They do not fear the spirits too much to feel an artistic and humorous pleasure in their doings. The ghosts themselves share their hilarity. In one western town, on whose deserted wharf the grass grows, these spirits have so much vigour, I have been told, that, when a misbeliever ventured to sleep in a haunted house, they flung him through the window, and his bed after him. In the surrounding villages they adopt strange disguises. A dead old gentleman steals the cabbages of his own garden in the shape of a large rabbit. A wicked sea-captain stayed for years inside the plaster of a cottage wall, in the shape of a snipe, making the most horrible noises. He was only dislodged when the wall was broken down; then out of the solid plaster the snipe rushed away whistling.

'DUST HATH CLOSED HELEN'S EYE'

I

I HAVE been lately to a little group of houses, not many enough to be called a village, in the barony of Kiltartan in County Galway, whose name, Ballylee, is known through all the west of Ireland. There is the old square castle,[1] Ballylee, inhabited by a farmer and his wife, and a cottage where their daughter and their son-in-law live, and a little mill with an old miller, and old ash-trees throwing green shadows upon a little river and great stepping-stones. I went there two or three times last year to talk to the miller about Biddy Early, a wise woman that lived in Clare some years ago, and about her saying, 'There is a cure for all evil between the two mill-wheels of Ballylee,' and to find out from him or another whether she meant the moss between the running waters or some other herb. I have been there this summer, and I shall be there again before it is autumn, because Mary Hynes, a beautiful woman whose name is still a wonder by turf fires, died there sixty years ago; for our feet would linger where beauty has lived its life of sorrow to make us understand that it is not of the world. An old man brought me a little way from the mill and the castle, and down a long, narrow boreen that was nearly lost in brambles and sloe-bushes, and he said, 'That is the little old foundation of the house, but the most of it is taken for building walls, and the goats

[1] Ballylee Castle, or Thoor Ballylee, as I have named it to escape from the too magnificent word 'castle,' is now my property, and I spend my summers or some part of them there. (1924.)

have ate those bushes that are growing over it till
they've got cranky, and they won't grow any more.
They say she was the handsomest girl in Ireland, her
skin was like dribbled snow'—he meant driven snow,
perhaps,—'and she had blushes in her cheeks. She had
five handsome brothers, but all are gone now!' I talked
to him about a poem in Irish, Raftery, a famous poet,
made about her, and how it said, 'There is a strong
cellar in Ballylee.' He said the strong cellar was the
great hole where the river sank underground, and he
brought me to a deep pool, where an otter hurried
away under a grey boulder, and told me that many fish
came up out of the dark water at early morning 'to
taste the fresh water coming down from the hills.'

I first heard of the poem from an old woman who
lives about two miles farther up the river, and who re-
members Raftery and Mary Hynes. She says, 'I never
saw anybody so handsome as she was, and I never will
till I die,' and that he was nearly blind, and had 'no way
of living but to go round and to mark some house to go
to, and then all the neighbours would gather to hear. If
you treated him well he'd praise you, but if you did not,
he'd fault you in Irish. He was the greatest poet in Ire-
land, and he'd make a song about that bush if he chanced
to stand under it. There was a bush he stood under from
the rain, and he made verses praising it, and then when
the water came through he made verses dispraising it.'
She sang the poem to a friend and to myself in Irish, and
every word was audible and expressive, as the words
in a song were always, as I think, before music grew
too proud to be the garment of words, flowing and

changing with the flowing and changing of their energies.
The poem is not as natural as the best Irish poetry of
the last century, for the thoughts are arranged in a too
obviously traditional form, so the old poor half-blind
man who made it has to speak as if he were a rich farmer
offering the best of everything to the woman he loves,
but it has naïve and tender phrases. The friend that was
with me has made some of the translation, but some of
it has been made by the countrypeople themselves. I
think it has more of the simplicity of the Irish verses
than one finds in most translations.

> Going to Mass by the will of God,
> The day came wet and the wind rose;
> I met Mary Hynes at the cross of Kiltartan,
> And I fell in love with her then and there.
>
> I spoke to her kind and mannerly,
> As by report was her own way;
> And she said, 'Raftery, my mind is easy,
> You may come to-day to Ballylee.'
>
> When I heard her offer I did not linger,
> When her talk went to my heart my heart rose.
> We had only to go across the three fields,
> We had daylight with us to Ballylee.
>
> The table was laid with glasses and a quart measure,
> She had fair hair, and she sitting beside me;
> And she said, 'Drink, Raftery, and a hundred welcomes,
> There is a strong cellar in Ballylee.'
>
> O star of light and O sun in harvest,
> O amber hair, O my share of the world,
> Will you come with me upon Sunday
> Till we agree together before all the people?

'Dust hath closed Helen's Eye'

I would not grudge you a song every Sunday evening,
Punch on the table, or wine if you would drink it,
But, O King of Glory, dry the roads before me.
Till I find the way to Ballylee.

There is sweet air on the side of the hill
When you are looking down upon Ballylee;
When you are walking in the valley picking nuts and black-
    berries,
There is music of the birds in it and music of the Sidhe.

What is the worth of greatness till you have the light
Of the flower of the branch that is by your side?
There is no god to deny it or to try and hide it,
She is the sun in the heavens who wounded my heart.

There was no part of Ireland I did not travel,
From the rivers to the tops of the mountains,
To the edge of Lough Greine whose mouth is hidden,
And I saw no beauty but was behind hers.

Her hair was shining, and her brows were shining too;
Her face was like herself, her mouth pleasant and sweet.
She is the pride, and I give her the branch,
She is the shining flower of Ballylee.

It is Mary Hynes, the calm and easy woman,
Has beauty in her mind and in her face.
If a hundred clerks were gathered together,
They could not write down a half of her ways.

An old weaver, whose son is supposed to go away among the Sidhe (the faeries) at night, says, 'Mary Hynes was the most beautiful thing ever made. My mother used to tell me about her, for she'd be at every hurling, and wherever she was she was dressed in white. As many as eleven men asked her in marriage in one day, but she wouldn't have any of them. There was a lot of men up beyond Kilbecanty one night sitting together drinking, and talking of her, and one of them got up and set out to go to Ballylee and see her; but Cloone Bog was open then, and when he came to it he fell into the water, and they found him dead there in the morning. She died of the fever that was before the famine.' Another old man says he was only a child when he saw her, but he remembered that 'the strongest man that was among us, one John Madden, got his death of the head of her, cold he got crossing rivers in the nighttime to get to Ballylee.' This is perhaps the man the other remembered, for tradition gives the one thing many shapes. There is an old woman who remembers her, at Derrybrien among the Echtge hills, a vast desolate place, which has changed little since the old poem said, 'the stag upon the cold summit of Echtge hears the cry of the wolves,' but still mindful of many poems and of the dignity of ancient speech. She says, 'The sun and the moon never shone on anybody so handsome, and her skin was so white that it looked blue, and she had two little blushes on her cheeks.' And an old wrinkled woman who lives close by Ballylee, and has told me many tales of the Sidhe, says, 'I often saw Mary Hynes, she was handsome indeed. She had two bunches of curls beside her cheeks, and they were the colour of silver. I saw Mary Molloy that was drowned in the river beyond, and Mary Guthrie that was in Ardrahan, but she took the sway of them both, a very comely creature. I was at her wake too—she had seen too much of the world. She was a kind creature. One day I was coming home through that field beyond, and I was tired, and who should come out but the Poisin Glegeal (the shining flower), and she gave me a glass of new milk.' This old woman meant no more than some beautiful bright colour by the colour of silver, for though I knew an old man—he is dead now—who thought she might know 'the cure for all the evils in the world,' that the Sidhe knew, she has seen too little gold to know its colour. But a man by the shore at Kinvara, who is too young to remember Mary Hynes, says, 'Everybody says there is no one at all to be seen now so handsome; it is said she had beautiful hair, the colour of gold. She was poor, but her clothes every day were the same as Sunday, she had such neatness. And if she went to any kind of a meeting, they would all be killing one another for a sight of her, and there was a great many in love with her, but she died young. It is said that no one that has a song made about them will ever live long.'

Those who are much admired are, it is held, taken by the Sidhe, who can use ungoverned feeling for their own ends, so that a father, as an old herb-doctor told me once, may give his child into their hands, or a husband his wife. The admired and desired are only safe if one says 'God bless them' when one's eyes are upon them. The old woman that sang the song thinks, too, that Mary Hynes was 'taken,' as the phrase is, 'for they have taken many that are not handsome, and why would they not take her? And people came from all parts to look at her, and maybe there were some that did not say "God bless her."' An old man who lives by the sea at Duras has as little doubt that she was taken, 'for there are some living yet can remember her coming to the pattern[1] there beyond, and she was said to be the handsomest girl in Ireland.' She died young because the gods loved her, for the Sidhe are the gods, and it may be that the old saying, which we forget to understand literally, meant her manner of death in old times. These poor countrymen and countrywomen in their beliefs, and in their emotions, are many years nearer to that old Greek world, that set beauty beside the fountain of things, than are our men of learning. She 'had seen too much of the world'; but these old men and women, when they tell of her, blame another and not her, and though they can be hard, they grow gentle as the old men of Troy grew gentle when Helen passed by on the walls.

The poet who helped her to so much fame has himself a great fame throughout the west of Ireland. Some think that Raftery was half blind, and say, 'I saw Raftery, a dark man, but he had sight enough to see her,' or the like, but some think he was wholly blind, as he may have been at the end of his life. Fable makes all things perfect in their kind, and her blind people must never look on the world and the sun. I asked a man I met one day, when I was looking for a pool *na mna Sidhe* where women of Faery have been seen, how Raftery could have admired Mary Hynes so much if he had been altogether blind. He said, 'I think Raftery was altogether blind, but those that are blind have a way of seeing things, and have the power to know more, and

[1] A 'pattern,' or 'patron,' is a festival in honour of a saint.

to feel more, and to do more, and to guess more than those that have their sight, and a certain wit and a certain wisdom is given to them.' Everybody, indeed, will tell you that he was very wise, for was he not not only blind but a poet? The weaver, whose words about Mary Hynes I have already given, says, 'His poetry was the gift of the Almighty, for there are three things that are the gift of the Almighty—poetry and dancing and principles. That is why in the old times an ignorant man coming down from the hillside would be better behaved and have better learning than a man with education you'd meet now, for they got it from God'; and a man at Coole says, 'When he put his finger to one part of his head, everything would come to him as if it was written in a book'; and an old pensioner at Kiltartan says, 'He was standing under a bush one time, and he talked to it, and it answered him back in Irish. Some say it was the bush that spoke, but it must have been an enchanted voice in it, and it gave him the knowledge of all the things of the world. The bush withered up afterwards, and it is to be seen on the roadside now between this and Rahasine.' There is a poem of his about a bush, which I have never seen, and it may have come out of the cauldron of Fable in this shape.

A friend of mine met a man once who had been with him when he died, but the people say that he died alone, and one Maurteen Gillane told Dr. Hyde that all night long a light was seen streaming up to heaven from the roof of the house where he lay, and 'that was the angels who were with him'; and all night long there was a

great light in the hovel, 'and that was the angels who
were waking him. They gave that honour to him be-
cause he was so good a poet, and sang such religious
songs.' It may be that in a few years Fable, who changes
mortalities to immortalities in her cauldron, will have
changed Mary Hynes and Raftery to perfect symbols
of the sorrow of beauty and of the magnificence and
penury of dreams.

1900

II

When I was in a northern town a while ago I had a
long talk with a man who had lived in a neighbouring
country district when he was a boy. He told me that
when a very beautiful girl was born in a family that had
not been noted for good looks, her beauty was thought
to have come from the Sidhe, and to bring misfortune
with it. He went over the names of several beautiful
girls that he had known, and said that beauty had never
brought happiness to anybody. It was a thing, he said,
to be proud of and afraid of. I wish I had written out
his words at the time, for they were more picturesque
than my memory of them.

1902

A Knight of the Sheep

A KNIGHT OF THE SHEEP

Away to the north of Ben Bulben and Cope's mountain lives 'a strong farmer,' a knight of the sheep they would have called him in the Gaelic days. Proud of his descent from one of the most fighting clans of the Middle Ages, he is a man of force alike in his words and in his deeds. There is but one man that swears like him, and this man lives far away upon the mountain. 'Father in Heaven, what have I done to deserve this?' he says when he has lost his pipe; and no man but he who lives on the mountain can rival his language on a fair-day over a bargain.

One day I was dining with him when the servant-maid announced a certain Mr. O'Donnell. A sudden silence fell upon the old man and upon his two daughters. At last the eldest daughter said somewhat severely to her father, 'Go and ask him to come in and dine.' The old man went out, and then came in looking greatly relieved, and said, 'He says he will not dine with us.' 'Go out,' said the daughter, 'and ask him into the back parlour, and give him some whiskey.' Her father, who had just finished his dinner, obeyed sullenly, and I heard the door of the back parlour—a little room where the daughters sat and sewed during the evening —shut to behind the men. The daughter then turned to me and said, 'Mr. O'Donnell is the tax-gatherer, and last-year he raised our taxes, and my father was very angry, and when he came, brought him into the dairy, and sent the dairy-woman away on a message, and then swore at him a great deal. "I will teach you, sir,"

O'Donnell replied, "that the law can protect its officers"; but my father reminded him that he had no witness. At last my father got tired, and sorry too, and said he would show him a short way home. When they were half-way to the main road they came on a man of my father's who was ploughing, and this somehow brought back remembrance of the wrong. He sent the man away on a message, and began to swear at the tax-gatherer again. When I heard of it I was disgusted that he should have made such a fuss over a miserable creature like O'Donnell; and when I heard a few weeks ago that O'Donnell's only son had died and left him heart-broken, I resolved to make my father be kind to him next time he came.'

She then went out to see a neighbour, and I sauntered towards the back parlour. When I came to the door I heard angry voices inside. The two men were evidently getting on to the tax again, for I could hear them bandying figures to and fro. I opened the door; at sight of my face the farmer was reminded of his peaceful intentions, and asked me if I knew where the whiskey was. I had seen him put it into the cupboard, and was able therefore to find it and get it out, looking at the thin, grief-struck face of the tax-gatherer. He was rather older than my friend, and very much more feeble and worn, and of a very different type. He was not, like him, a robust, successful man, but rather one of those whose feet find no resting-place upon the earth. 'You are doubtless of the stock of the old O'Donnells,' I said. 'I know well the hole in the river where their treasure lies buried under the guard of a serpent with many heads.' 'Yes, sir,' he replied, 'I am the last of a line of princes.'

We then fell to talking of many commonplace things, and when at last the gaunt old tax-gatherer got up to go, my friend said, 'I hope we will have a glass together next year.' 'No, no,' was the answer, 'I shall be dead next year.' 'I too have lost sons,' said the other, in quite a gentle voice. 'But your sons were not like my son.' And then the two men parted, with an angry flush and bitter hearts, and had I not cast between them some common words or other, might not have parted, but have fallen rather into an angry discussion of the value of their dead sons.

The knight of the sheep would have had the victory. He was indeed but once beaten; and this is his tale of how it was. He and some farm-hands were playing at cards in a small cabin that stood against the end of a big barn. A wicked woman had once lived in this cabin. Suddenly one of the players threw down an ace and began to swear without any cause. His swearing was so dreadful that the others stood up, and my friend said, 'All is not right here; there is a spirit in him.' They ran to the door that led into the barn to get away as quickly as possible. The wooden bolt would not move, so the knight of the sheep took a saw which stood against the wall near at hand, and sawed through the bolt, and at once the door flew open with a bang, as though some one had been holding it, and they fled through.

AN ENDURING HEART

ONE day a friend of mine was making a sketch of my knight of the sheep. The old man's daughter was sitting by, and, when the conversation drifted to love and love-making, she said, 'O, father, tell him about your love affair.' The old man took his pipe out of his mouth and said, 'Nobody ever marries the woman he loves,' and then, with a chuckle, 'There were fifteen of them I liked better than the woman I married,' and he repeated many women's names. He went on to tell how when he was a lad he had worked for his grandfather, his mother's father, and was called (my friend has forgotten why) by his grandfather's name, which we will say was Doran. He had a great friend, whom I shall call John Byrne; and one day he and his friend went to Queenstown to await an emigrant ship, that was to take John Byrne to America. When they were walking along the quay, they saw a girl sitting on a seat, crying miserably, and two men standing up in front of her quarrelling with one another. Doran said, 'I think I know what is wrong. *That* man will be her brother, and *that* man will be her lover, and the brother is sending her to America to get her away from the lover. How she is crying! but I think I could console her myself.' Presently the lover and brother went away, and Doran began to walk up and down before her, saying, 'Mild weather, Miss,' or the like. She answered him in a little while, and the three began to talk together. The emigrant ship did not arrive for some days; and the three drove about on outside cars very innocently and happily, seeing everything that was to be seen. When at last the ship came, and Doran had to break it to her that he was not going to America, she cried more after him than after the first lover. Doran whispered to Byrne as he went aboard ship, 'Now, Byrne, I don't grudge her to you, but don't marry young.'

When the story got to this, the farmer's daughter joined in mockingly with, 'I suppose you said that for Byrne's good, father.' But the old man insisted that he *had* said it for Byrne's good; and went on to tell how, when he got a letter telling of Byrne's engagement to the girl, he wrote him the same advice. Years passed by, and he heard nothing; and though he was now married, he could not keep from wondering what she was doing. At last he went to America to find out, and though he asked many people for tidings, he could get none. More years went by, and his wife was dead, and he well on in years, and a rich farmer with not a few great matters on his hands. He found an excuse in some vague business to go out to America again, and to begin his search again. One day he fell into talk with an Irish-man in a railway carriage, and asked him, as his way was, about emigrants from this place and that, and at last, 'Did you ever hear of the miller's daughter from Innis Rath?' and he named the woman he was looking for. 'O yes,' said the other, 'she is married to a friend of mine, John MacEwing. She lives at such-and-such a street in Chicago.' Doran went to Chicago and knocked at her door. She opened the door herself, and was 'not a bit changed.' He gave her his real name, which he had taken again after his grandfather's death, and the name of the man he had met in the train. She did not recognise him, but asked him to stay to dinner, saying that her husband would be glad to meet anybody who knew that old friend of his. They talked of many things, but for all their talk, I do not know why, and perhaps he did not know why, he never told her who he was. At dinner he asked her about Byrne, and she put her head down on the table and began to cry, and she cried so he was afraid her husband might be angry. He was afraid to ask what had happened to Byrne, and left soon after, never to see her again.

When the old man had finished the story, he said, 'Tell that to Mr. Yeats, he will make a poem about it, perhaps.' But the daughter said, 'O no, father. Nobody could make a poem about a woman like that.' Alas! I never made the poem, perhaps because my own heart, which has loved Helen and all the lovely and fickle women of the world, would be too sore. There are things it is well not to ponder over too much, things that bare words are the best suited for.

1902

THE SORCERERS

IN Ireland we hear but little of the darker powers,[1] and come across any who have seen them even more rarely, for the imagination of the people dwells rather upon the fantastic and capricious, and fantasy and caprice would lose the freedom which is their breath of life, were they to unite them either with evil or with good. I have indeed come across very few persons in Ireland who try to communicate with evil powers, and the few I have met keep their purpose and practice wholly hidden from those among whom they live. They are mainly small clerks, and meet for the purpose of their art in a room hung with black hangings, but in what town that room is I shall not say. They would not admit me into this room, but finding me not altogether ignorant of the arcane science, showed elsewhere what they could do. 'Come to us,' said their leader, 'and we will show you spirits who will talk to you face to face, and in shapes as solid and heavy as our own.'

I had been talking of the power of communicating in states of trance with the angelical and faery beings,— the children of the day and of the twilight,—and he had been contending that we should only believe in what we can see and feel when in our ordinary everyday state of mind. 'Yes,' I said, 'I will come to you,' or some such words; 'but I will not permit myself to

[1] I know better now. We have the dark powers much more than I thought, but not as much as the Scottish, and yet I think the imagination of the people does dwell chiefly upon the fantastic and capricious.

become entranced, and will therefore know whether these shapes you talk of are any the more to be touched and felt by the ordinary senses than are those I talk of.' I was not denying the power of other beings to take upon themselves a clothing of mortal substance, but only that simple invocations, such as he spoke of, seemed unlikely to do more than cast the mind into trance.

'But,' he said, 'we have seen them move the furniture hither and thither, and they go at our bidding, and help or harm people who know nothing of them.' I am not giving the exact words, but as accurately as I can the substance of our talk.

On the night arranged I turned up about eight, and found the leader sitting alone in almost total darkness in a small back room. He was dressed in a black gown, like an inquisitor's dress in an old drawing, that left nothing of him visible except his eyes, which peered out through two small round holes. Upon the table in front of him was a brass dish of burning herbs, a large bowl, a skull covered with painted symbols, two crossed daggers, and certain implements, whose use I failed to discover, shaped like quern-stones. I also put on a black gown, and remember that it did not fit perfectly, and that it interfered with my movements considerably. The sorcerer then took a black cock out of a basket, and cut its throat with one of the daggers, letting the blood fall into the large bowl. He opened a book and began an invocation, which was neither English nor Irish, and had a deep guttural sound. Before he had finished, another of the sorcerers, a man of about twenty-five, came in, and having put on a black gown also, seated himself at my left hand. I had the invoker directly in front of me, and soon began to find his eyes, which glittered through the small holes in his hood, affecting me in a curious way. I struggled hard against their influence, and my head began to ache. The invocation continued, and nothing happened for the first few minutes. Then the invoker got up and extinguished the light in the hall, so that no glimmer might come through the slit under the door. There was now no light except from the herbs on the brass dish, and no sound except from the deep guttural murmur of the invocation.

Presently the man at my left swayed himself about, and cried out, 'O God! O God!' I asked him what ailed him, but he did not know he had spoken. A moment after he said he could see a great serpent moving about the room, and became considerably excited. I saw nothing with any definite shape, but thought that black clouds were forming about me. I felt I must fall into a trance if I did not struggle against it, and that the influence which was causing this trance was out of harmony with itself, in other words, evil. After a struggle I got rid of the black clouds, and was able to observe with my ordinary senses again. The two sorcerers now began to see black and white columns moving about the room, and finally a man in a monk's habit, and they became greatly puzzled because I did not see these things also, for to them they were as solid as the table before them. The invoker appeared to be gradually increasing in power, and I began to feel as if a tide of darkness was pouring from him and concentrating itself about me; and now too I noticed that the man on my left hand had passed into a death-like trance. With a last great effort I drove off the black clouds; but feeling them to be the only shapes I should see without passing into a trance, and having no great love for them, I asked for lights, and after the needful exorcism returned to the ordinary world.

I said to the more powerful of the two sorcerers, 'What would happen if one of your spirits had over-powered me?' 'You would go out of this room,' he answered, 'with his character added to your own.' I asked about the origin of his sorcery, but got little of importance, except that he had learned it from his father, and that one word which he had repeated several times was Arabic. He would not tell me more, for he had, it appeared, taken a vow of secrecy.

The Devil

THE DEVIL

My old Mayo woman told me one day that something very bad had come down the road and gone into the house opposite, and though she would not say what it was, I knew quite well. Another day she told me of two friends of hers who had been made love to by one whom they believed to be the Devil. One of them was standing by the roadside when he came by on horseback, and asked her to mount up behind him, and go riding. When she would not he vanished. The other was out on the road late at night waiting for her young man, when something came flapping and rolling along the road up to her feet. It had the likeness of a newspaper, and presently it flapped up into her face, and she knew by the size of it that it was the *Irish Times*. All of a sudden it changed into a young man, who asked her to go walking with him. She would not, and he vanished.

I know of an old man too, on the slopes of Ben Bulben, who found the Devil ringing a bell under his bed, and he went off and stole the chapel bell and rang him out.

HAPPY AND UNHAPPY THEOLOGIANS

I

A MAYO woman once said to me, 'I knew a servant-girl who hung herself for the love of God. She was lonely for the priest and her society,[1] and hung herself to the banisters with a scarf. She was no sooner dead than she became white as a lily, and if it had been murder or suicide she would have become black as black. They gave her Christian burial, and the priest said she was no sooner dead than she was with the Lord. So nothing matters that you do for the love of God.' I do not wonder at the pleasure she has in telling this story, for she herself loves all holy things with an ardour that brings them quickly to her lips. She told me once that she never hears anything described in a sermon that she does not afterwards see with her eyes. She has described to me the gates of Purgatory as they showed themselves to her eyes, but I remember nothing of the description except that she could not see the souls in trouble but only the gates. Her mind continually dwells on what is pleasant and beautiful. One day she asked me what month and what flower were the most beautiful. When I answered that I did not know, she said, 'The month of May, because of the Virgin, and the lily of the valley, because it never sinned, but came pure out of the rocks,' and then she asked, 'What is the cause of the three cold months of winter?' I did not know even that, and so she said, 'The sin of man and

[1] The religious society she had belonged to.

the vengeance of God.' Christ Himself was not only blessed, but perfect in all manly proportions in her eyes, so much do beauty and holiness go together in her thoughts. He alone of all men was exactly six feet high, all others are a little more or a little less.

Her thoughts and her sights of the people of Faery are pleasant and beautiful too, and I have never heard her call them the Fallen Angels. They are people like ourselves, only better-looking, and many and many a time she has gone to the window to watch them drive their wagons through the sky, wagon behind wagon in long line, or to the door to hear them singing and dancing in the forth. They sing chiefly, it seems, a song called 'The Distant Waterfall', and though they once knocked her down she never thinks badly of them. She saw them most easily when she was in service in King's County, and one morning a little while ago she said to me, 'Last night I was waiting up for the master and it was a quarter-past eleven. I heard a bang right down on the table. "King's County all over," says I, and I laughed till I was near dead. It was a warning I was staying too long. They wanted the place to them-selves.' I told her once of somebody who saw a faery and fainted, and she said, 'It could not have been a faery, but some bad thing, nobody could faint at a faery. It was a demon. I was not afraid when they near put me, and the bed under me, out through the roof. I wasn't afraid either when you were at some work and I heard a thing coming flop-flop up the stairs like an eel, and squealing. It went to all the doors. It could not get in where I was. I would have sent it through the

universe like a flash of fire. There was a man in my
place, a tearing fellow, and he put one of them down.
He went out to meet it on the road, but he must have
been told the words. But the faeries are the best neigh-
bours. If you do good to them they will do good to
you, but they don't like you to be on their path.'
Another time she said to me, 'They are always good to
the poor.'

II

There is, however, a man in a Galway village who
can see nothing but wickedness. Some think him very
holy, and others think him a little crazed, but some of
his talk reminds one of those old Irish visions of the
Three Worlds, which are supposed to have given
Dante the plan of the *Divine Comedy*. But I could not
imagine this man seeing Paradise. He is especially angry
with the people of Faery, and describes the faun-like
feet that are so common among them, who are indeed
children of Pan, to prove them children of Satan. He
will not grant that 'they carry away women, though
there are many that say so,' but he is certain that they
are 'as thick as the sands of the sea about us, and they
tempt poor mortals.'

He says, 'There is a priest I know of was looking
along the ground like as if he was hunting for some-
thing, and a voice said to him, "If you want to see them
you'll see enough of them," and his eyes were opened
and he saw the ground thick with them. Singing they
do be sometimes, and dancing, but all the time they
have cloven feet.' Yet he was so scornful of unchristian

beings for all their dancing and singing that he thinks that 'you have only to bid them begone and they will go. It was one night,' he says, 'after walking back from Kinvara and down by the wood beyond I felt one coming beside me, and I could feel the horse he was riding on and the way he lifted his legs, but they do not make a sound like the hoofs of a horse. So I stopped and turned around and said, very loud, "Be off!" and he went and never troubled me after. And I knew a man who was dying, and one came on his bed, and he cried out to it, "Get out of that, you unnatural animal!" and it left him. Fallen angels they are, and after the fall God said, "Let there be Hell," and there it was in a moment.' An old woman who was sitting by the fire joined in as he said this with 'God save us, it's a pity He said the word, and there might have been no Hell the day,' but the seer did not notice her words. He went on, 'And then he asked the Devil what would he take for the souls of all the people. And the Devil said nothing would satisfy him but the blood of a virgin's son, so he got that, and then the gates of Hell were opened.' He understood the story, it seems, as if it were some riddling old folk-tale.

'I have seen Hell myself. I had a sight of it one time in a vision. It had a very high wall around it, all of metal, and an archway, and a straight walk into it, just like what 'ud be leading into a gentleman's orchard, but the edges were not trimmed with box, but with red-hot metal. And inside the wall there were cross-walks, and I'm not sure what there was to the right, but to the left there were five great furnaces, and they full of souls kept there with great chains. So I turned short and went away, and in turning I looked again at the wall, and I could see no end to it.

'And another time I saw Purgatory. It seemed to be in a level place, and no walls around it, but it all one bright blaze, and the souls standing in it. And they suffer near as much as in Hell, only there are no devils with them there, and they have the hope of Heaven.

'And I heard a call to me from there, "Help me to come out o' this!" And when I looked it was a man I used to know in the Army, an Irishman, and from this county, and I believe him to be a descendant of King O'Connor of Athenry.

'So I stretched out my hand first, but then I called out, "I'd be burned in the flames before I could get within three yards of you." So then he said, "Well, help me with your prayers," and so I do.

'And Father Connellan says the same thing, to help the dead with your prayers, and he's a very clever man to make a sermon, and has a great deal of cures made with the Holy Water he brought back from Lourdes.'

1902

THE LAST GLEEMAN

MICHAEL MORAN was born about 1794 off Black Pitts, in the Liberties of Dublin, in Faddle Alley. A fortnight after birth he went stone blind from illness, and became thereby a blessing to his parents, who were soon able to send him to rhyme and beg at street corners and at the bridges over the Liffey. They may well have wished that their quiver were full of such as he, for, free from the interruption of sight, his mind turned every movement of the day and every change of public passion into rhyme or quaint saying. By the time he had grown to manhood he was the admitted rector of all the ballad-mongers of the Liberties, of Madden, the weaver, Kearney, the blind fiddler from Wicklow, Martin from Meath, M'Bride from Heaven knows where, and that M'Grane, who in after days, when the true Moran was no more, strutted in borrowed plumes, or rather in borrowed rags, and gave out that there had never been any Moran but himself, and many another. Nor despite his blindness did he find any difficulty in getting a wife, but rather was able to pick and choose, for he was just that mixture of ragamuffin and of genius which is dear to the heart of woman, who, however conventional in herself, loves the unexpected, the crooked, the bewildering. Nor did he lack, despite his rags, many excellent things, for it is remembered that he ever loved caper sauce, and upon one occasion when his wife had forgotten it, he flung a leg of mutton at her head. He was not, certainly, much to look at, with his coarse frieze coat with its cape and scalloped edge, his old

47

corduroy trousers and great brogues, and his stout stick made fast to his wrist by a thong of leather: and he would have been a woeful shock to the gleeman MacCoinglinne, could that friend of kings have beheld him in prophetic vision from the pillar stone at Cork. And yet though the short cloak and the leather wallet were no more, he was a true gleeman, being alike poet, jester, and newsman of the people. In the morning when he had finished his breakfast, his wife or some neighbour would read the newspaper to him, and read on and on until he interrupted with, 'That'll do—I have me meditations'; and from these meditations would come the day's store of jest and rhyme. He had the whole Middle Ages under his frieze coat.

He had not, however, MacCoinglinne's hatred of the Church and clergy, for when the fruit of his meditations did not ripen well, or when the crowd called for something more solid, he would recite or sing a metrical tale or ballad of saint or martyr or some Biblical adventure. He would stand at a street corner, and when a crowd had gathered would begin in some such fashion as follows (I copy the record of one who knew him):— 'Gather round me, boys, gather round me. Boys, am I standin' in puddle? am I standin' in wet?' Thereon several boys would cry, 'Ah, no! yez not! yer in a nice dry place. Go on with *Saint Mary*; go on with *Moses*'— each calling for his favourite tale. Then Moran, with a wriggle of his body and a clutch at his rags, would burst out with, 'All me buzzim friends are turned backbiters'; and after a final warning to the boys, 'If yez don't drop your coddin' and diversion I'll lave some

of yez a case,' begin his recitation, or perhaps still de-
lay, to ask, 'Is there a crowd round me now? Any
blaguard heretic around me?' Or he would, it may
be, start by singing:—

> Gather round me, boys, will yez
> Gather round me?
> And hear what I have to say
> Before ould Sally brings me
> My bread and jug of tay.

The best-known of his religious tales was *Saint Mary of
Egypt*, a long poem of exceeding solemnity, condensed
from the much longer work of a certain Bishop Coyle.
It told how an Egyptian harlot, Mary by name, fol-
lowed pilgrims to Jerusalem in pursuit of her trade, and
then, on finding herself withheld from entering the
Temple by supernatural interference, turned penitent,
fled to the desert and spent the remainder of her life in
solitary penance. When at last she was at the point of
death, God sent Bishop Zosimus to hear her confession,
give her the last sacrament, and with the help of a lion,
whom He sent also, dig her grave. The poem has the
intolerable cadence of the eighteenth century at its
worst, but was so popular and so often called for that
Moran was nicknamed Zosimus, and by that name is
he remembered. He had also a poem of his own called
Moses, which went a little nearer poetry without going
very near. But he could ill brook solemnity, and before
long parodied his own verses in the following raga-
muffin fashion:—

> In Egypt's land, contagious to the Nile,
> King Pharoah's daughter went to bathe in style.

She tuk her dip, then walked unto the land,
To dry her royal pelt she ran along the strand.
A bulrush tripped her, whereupon she saw
A smiling babby in a wad o' straw.
She tuk it up, and said with accents mild,
' 'Tare-and-agers, girls, which av yez owns the child?'

His humorous rhymes were, however, more often quips and cranks at the expense of his contemporaries. It was his delight, for instance, to remind a shoemaker, noted alike for display of wealth and for personal uncleanness, of his inconsiderable origin in a song of which but the first stanza has come down to us:—

At the dirty end of Dirty Lane,
Liv'd a dirty cobbler, Dick Maclane;
His wife was in the old King's reign
    A stout brave orange-woman.
On Essex Bridge she strained her throat,
And six-a-penny was her note.
But Dickey wore a bran-new coat
    He got among the yeomen.
He was a bigot, like his clan,
And in the streets he wildly sang,
O Roly, toly, toly raid, with his old jade.

He had troubles of divers kinds, and numerous interlopers to face and put down. Once an officious peeler arrested him as a vagabond, but was triumphantly routed amid the laughter of the court, when Moran reminded his worship of the precedent set by Homer, who was also, he declared, a poet, and a blind man, and a beggar-man. He had to face a more serious difficulty as his fame grew. Various imitators started up upon all sides. A certain actor, for instance, made as many guineas as Moran did shillings by mimicking his sayings and his songs and his get-up upon the stage. One night this actor was at supper with some friends, when dispute arose as to whether his mimicry was overdone or not. It was agreed to settle it by an appeal to the mob. A forty-shilling supper at a famous coffee-house was to be the wager. The actor took up his station at Essex Bridge, a great haunt of Moran's, and soon gathered a small crowd. He had scarce got through 'In Egypt's land, contagious to the Nile,' when Moran himself came up, followed by another crowd. The crowds met in great excitement and laughter. 'Good Christians,' cried the pretender, 'is it possible that any man would mock the poor dark man like that?'

'Who's that? It's some imposhterer,' replied Moran.

'Begone, you wretch! it's you'se the imposhterer. Don't you fear the light of heaven being struck from your eyes for mocking the poor dark man?'

'Saints and angels, is there no protection against this? You're a most inhuman blaguard to try to deprive me of my honest bread this way,' replied poor Moran.

'And you, you wretch, won't let me go on with the beautiful poem? Christian people, in your charity won't you beat this man away? he's taking advantage of my darkness.'

The pretender, seeing that he was having the best of it, thanked the people for their sympathy and protection, and went on with the poem, Moran listening for a time in bewildered silence. After a while Moran protested again with:—

'Is it possible that none of yez can know me? Don't yez see it's myself; and that's some one else?'

'Before I can proceed any further in this lovely story,' interrupted the pretender, 'I call on yez to contribute your charitable donations to help me to go on.'

'Have you no sowl to be saved, you mocker of Heaven?' cried Moran, put completely beside himself by this last injury. 'Would you rob the poor as well as desave the world? O, was ever such wickedness known?'

'I leave it to yourselves, my friends,' said the pretender, 'to give to the real dark man, that you all know so well, and save me from that schemer,' and with that he collected some pennies and halfpence. While he was doing so, Moran started his *Mary of Egypt*, but the indignant crowd seizing his stick were about to belabour him, when they fell back bewildered anew by his close resemblance to himself. The pretender now called to them to 'just give him a grip of that villain, and he'd soon let him know who the imposhterer was!' They led him over to Moran, but instead of closing with him he thrust a few shillings into his hand, and turning to the crowd explained to them he was indeed but an actor, and that he had just gained a wager, and so departed amid much enthusiasm, to eat the supper he had won.

In April 1846 word was sent to the priest that Michael Moran was dying. He found him at 15 (now 14½) Patrick Street, on a straw bed, in a room full of ragged ballad-singers come to cheer his last moments. After his death the ballad-singers, with many fiddles and the like, came again and gave him a fine wake, each adding to the merriment whatever he knew in the way of rann, tale, old saw, or quaint rhyme. He had had his day, had said his prayers and made his confession, and why should they not give him a hearty send-off? The funeral took place the next day. A good party of his admirers and friends got into the hearse with the coffin, for the day was wet and nasty. They had not gone far when one of them burst out with, 'It's cruel cowld, isn't it?' 'Garra',' replied another, 'we'll all be as stiff as the corpse when we get to the berrin'-ground.' 'Bad cess to him,' said a third; 'I wish he'd held out another month until the weather got dacent.' A man called Carroll thereupon produced a half-pint of whiskey, and they all drank to the soul of the departed. Unhappily, however, the hearse was overweighted, and they had not reached the cemetery before the spring broke, and the bottle with it.

REGINA, REGINA PIGMEORUM, VENI [1]

ONE night a middle-aged man, who had lived all his life far from the noise of cab-wheels, a young girl, a relation of his, who was reported to be enough of a seeress to catch a glimpse of unaccountable lights moving over the fields among the cattle, and myself, were walking along a far western sandy shore. We talked of the Forgetful People, as the faery people are sometimes called, and came in the midst of our talk to a notable haunt of theirs, a shallow cave amidst black rocks, with its reflection under it in the wet sea sand. I asked the young girl if she could see anything, for I had quite a number of things to ask the Forgetful People. She stood still for a few minutes, and I saw that she was passing into a kind of waking trance, in which the cold sea breeze no longer troubled her, nor the dull boom of the sea distracted her attention. I then called aloud the names of the great faeries, and in a moment or two she said that she could hear music far inside the rocks, and then a sound of confused talking, and of people stamping their feet as if to applaud some unseen performer. Up to this my other friend had been walking to and fro some yards off, but now he passed close to us, and as he did so said suddenly that we were going to be interrupted, for he heard the laughter of children somewhere beyond the rocks. We were, however, quite alone. The spirits of the place had begun to cast their influence over him also. In a moment he was corroborated by the girl, who said

[1] These words were used as an evocation in Windsor Forest by Lilly, the astrologer. (1924.)

that bursts of laughter had begun to mingle with the music, the confused talking, and the noise of feet. She next saw a bright light streaming out of the cave, which seemed to have grown much deeper, and a quantity of little people,[1] in various coloured dresses, red predominating, dancing to a tune which she did not recognise.

I then bade her call out to the queen of the little people to come and talk with us. There was, however, no answer to her command. I therefore repeated the words aloud myself, and in a moment she described a very beautiful tall woman, who came out of the cave. I too had by this time fallen into a kind of trance,[2] in which what we call the unreal had begun to take upon itself a masterful reality, and I had an impression, not anything I could call an actual vision, of gold ornaments and dark hair. I then bade the girl tell this tall queen to marshal her followers according to their natural divisions, that we might see them. I found as before that I had to repeat the command myself. The beings then came out of the cave, and drew themselves up, if I remember rightly, in four bands. One of these bands,

[1] The people and faeries in Ireland are sometimes as big as we are, sometimes bigger, and sometimes, as I have been told, about three feet high. The old Mayo woman I so often quote thinks that it is something in our eyes that makes them seem big or little.

[2] The word 'trance' gives a wrong impression. I had learned from MacGregor Mathers and his pupils to so suspend the will that the imagination moved of itself. The girl was, however, fully entranced, and the man so affected by her that he heard the children's voices as if with his physical ears. On two occasions, later on, her trance so affected me that I also heard or saw some part of what she did as if with physical eyes and ears. (1924.)

according to her description, carried boughs of mountain-ash in their hands, and another had necklaces made apparently of serpents' scales, but their dress I cannot remember. I asked their queen to tell the seeress whether these caves were the greatest faery haunts in the neighbourhood. Her lips moved, but the answer was inaudible. I bade the seeress lay her hand upon the breast of the queen, and after that she heard every word quite distinctly. No, this was not the greatest faery haunt, for there was a greater one a little farther ahead. I then asked her whether it was true that she and her people carried away mortals, and if so, whether they put another soul in the place of the one they had taken. 'We change the bodies,' was her answer. 'Are any of you ever born into mortal life?' 'Yes.' 'Do I know any who were among your people before birth?' 'You do.' 'Who are they?' 'It would not be lawful for you to know.' I then asked whether she and her people were not 'dramatisations of our moods'? 'She does not understand,' said my friend, 'but says that her people are much like human beings, and do most of the things human beings do.' I asked her other questions, as to her nature, and her purpose in the universe, but only seemed to puzzle her. At last she appeared to lose patience, for she wrote this message for me upon the sands—the sands of vision—'Be careful, and do not seek to know too much about us.' Seeing that I had offended her, I thanked her for what she had shown and told, and let her depart again into her cave. In a little while the young girl awoke out of her trance, and felt the cold wind from the sea, and began to shiver.

'And Fair, Fierce Women'

'AND FAIR, FIERCE WOMEN'

ONE day a woman that I know came face to face with heroic beauty, that highest beauty which Blake says changes least from youth to age, a beauty which has been fading out of the arts, since that decadence we call progress set voluptuous beauty in its place. She was standing at the window, looking over to Knocknarea where Queen Maeve is thought to be buried, when she saw, as she has told me, 'the finest woman you ever saw, travelling right across from the mountains and straight to her.' The woman had a sword by her side and a dagger lifted up in her hand, and was dressed in white, with bare arms and feet. She looked 'very strong, but not wicked,' that is, not cruel. The old woman had seen the Irish giant, and 'though he was a fine man,' he was nothing to this woman, 'for he was round, and could not have stepped out so soldierly'; 'she was like Mrs.——' (a stately lady of the neighbourhood) 'but she had no stomach on her, and was slight and broad in the shoulders, and was handsomer than any one you ever saw; she looked about thirty.' The old woman covered her eyes with her hands, and when she uncovered them the apparition had vanished. The neighbours were 'wild with her,' she told me, because she did not wait to find out if there was a message, for they were sure it was Queen Maeve, who often shows herself to the pilots. I asked the old woman if she had seen others like Queen Maeve, and she said, 'Some of them have their hair down, but they look quite different, like the sleepy-looking ladies one sees in the papers. Those with their hair up are like this one. The others have long white dresses, but those with their hair up have short dresses, so that you can see their legs right up to the calf.' After some careful questioning I found that they wore what might very well be a kind of buskin; she went on, 'They are fine and dashing looking, like the men one sees riding their horses in twos and threes on the slopes of the mountains with their swords swinging.' She repeated over and over, 'There is no such race living now, none so finely proportioned,' or the like, and then said, 'The present Queen[1] is a nice, pleasant-looking woman, but she is not like her. What makes me think so little of the ladies is that I see none as they be,' meaning as the spirits. 'When I think of her and of the ladies now, they are like little children running about without knowing how to put their clothes on right. Is it the ladies? Why, I would not call them women at all.' The other day a friend of mine questioned an old woman in a Galway workhouse about Queen Maeve, and was told that 'Queen Maeve was handsome, and overcame all her enemies with a hazel stick, for the hazel is blessed, and the best weapon that can be got. You might walk the world with it,' but she grew 'very disagreeable in the end—O very disagreeable. Best not to be talking about it. Best leave it between the book and the hearer.' My friend thought the old woman had got some scandal about Fergus son of Rogh and Maeve in her head.

And I myself met once with a young man in the Burren Hills who remembered an old poet who made his poems in Irish and had met when he was young, the

[1] Queen Victoria.

young man said, one who called herself Maeve, and said she was a queen 'among them', and asked him if he would have money or pleasure. He said he would have pleasure, and she gave him her love for a time, and then went from him, and ever after he was very mournful. The young man had often heard him sing the poem of lamentation that he made, but could only remember that it was 'very mournful', and that he called her 'beauty of all beauties'.

1902

ENCHANTED WOODS

I

LAST summer, whenever I had finished my day's work, I used to go wandering in certain roomy woods, and there I would often meet an old countryman, and talk to him about his work and about the woods, and once or twice a friend came with me to whom he would open his heart more readily than to me. He had spent all his life lopping away the witch-elm and the hazel and the privet and the hornbeam from the paths, and had thought much about the natural and supernatural creatures of the wood. He has heard the hedgehog— 'grainne oge,' he calls him—'grunting like a Christian,' and is certain that he steals apples by rolling about under an apple-tree until there is an apple sticking to every quill. He is certain too that the cats, of whom there are many in the woods, have a language of their own—some kind of old Irish. He says, 'Cats were serpents, and they were made into cats at the time of some great change in the world. That is why they are hard to kill, and why it is dangerous to meddle with them. If you annoy a cat it might claw or bite you in a way that would put poison in you, and that would be the serpent's tooth.' Sometimes he thinks they change into wild cats, and then a nail grows on the end of their tails; but these wild cats are not the same as the marten cats, who have been always in the woods. The foxes were once tame, as the cats are now, but they ran away and became wild. He talks of all wild creatures except squirrels—whom he hates—with what seems an affectionate interest, though at times his eyes will twinkle with pleasure as he remembers how he made hedgehogs unroll themselves when he was a boy, by putting a wisp of burning straw under them.

I am not certain that he distinguishes between the natural and supernatural very clearly. He told me the other day that foxes and cats like, above all, to be in the 'forths' and lisses after nightfall; and he will certainly pass from some story about a fox to a story about a spirit with less change of voice than when he is going to speak about a marten cat—a rare beast nowadays. Many years ago he used to work in the garden, and once they put him to sleep in a garden-house where there was a loft full of apples, and all night he could hear people rattling plates and knives and forks over his head in the loft. Once, at any rate, he has seen an unearthly sight in the woods. He says, 'One time I was out cutting timber over in Inchy, and about eight o'clock one morning when I got there I saw a girl picking nuts, with her hair hanging down over her shoulders, brown hair, and she had a good, clean face, and she was tall and nothing on her head, and her dress no way gaudy but simple, and when she felt me coming she gathered herself up and was gone as if the earth had swallowed her up. And I followed her and looked for her, but I never could see her again from that day to this, never again.' He used the word clean as we would use words like fresh or comely.

Others too have seen spirits in the Enchanted Woods. A labourer told us of what a friend of his had seen in a part of the woods that is called Shan-walla, from some old village that was before the wood. He said, 'One evening I parted from Lawrence Mangan in the yard, an' he went away through the path in Shan-walla, an' bid me good-night. And two hours after, there he was back again in the yard, an' bid me light a candle that was in the stable. An' he told me that when he got into Shan-walla, a little fellow about as high as his knee, but having a head as big as a man's body, came beside him and led him out of the path an' round about, and at last it brought him to the lime-kiln, and then it vanished and left him.'

A woman told me of a sight that she and others had seen by a certain deep pool in the river. She said, 'I came over the stile from the chapel, and others along with me; and a great blast of wind came and two trees were bent and broken and fell into the river, and the splash of water out of it went up to the skies. And those that were with me saw many figures, but myself I only saw one, sitting there by the bank where the trees fell. Dark clothes he had on, and he was headless.'

A man told me that one day, when he was a boy, he and another boy went to catch a horse in a certain field, full of boulders and bushes of hazel and creeping juniper and rock-roses, that is where the lake-side is for a little clear of the woods. He said to the boy that was with him, 'I bet a button that if I fling a pebble on to that bush it will stay on it,' meaning that the bush was so matted the pebble would not be able to go through it. So he took up 'a pebble of cow-dung, and as soon as it hit the bush there came out of it the most beautiful music that ever was heard.' They ran away, and when they had gone about two hundred yards they looked back and saw a woman dressed in white, walking round and round the bush. 'First it had the form of a woman, and then of a man, and it was going round the bush.'

II

I often entangle myself in arguments more complicated than even those paths of Inchy as to what is the true nature of apparitions. But at other times I say as Socrates said when they told him a learned opinion about a nymph of the Ilissus, 'The common opinion is enough for me'; and believe that all nature is full of invisible people, and that some of these are ugly or grotesque, some wicked or foolish, many beautiful beyond any one we have ever seen, and that the beautiful are not far away when we are walking in pleasant and quiet places. Even when I was a boy I could never walk in a wood without feeling that at any moment I might find before me somebody or something I had long looked for without knowing what I looked for. And now I will at times explore every little nook of some poor coppice with almost anxious footsteps, so deep a hold has this imagination upon me. You too meet with a like imagination, doubtless, somewhere, wherever your ruling stars will have it, Saturn driving you to the woods, or the Moon, it may be, to the edges of the sea. I will not of a certainty believe that there is nothing in the sunset, where our forefathers imagined the dead following their shepherd the sun, or nothing but some vague presence as little moving as nothing. If beauty is not a gateway out of the net we were taken in at our birth, it will not long be beauty, and we will find it better to sit at home by the fire and fatten a lazy body or to run hither and thither in some foolish sport than to look at the finest show that light and shadow ever made among green leaves. I say to myself, when I am well out of that thicket of argument, that they are surely there, the divine people, for only we who have neither simplicity nor wisdom have denied them, and the simple of all times and the wise men of ancient times have seen them and even spoken to them. They live out their passionate lives not far off, as I think, and we shall be among them when we die if we but keep our natures simple and passionate. May it not even be that death shall unite us to all romance, and that some day we shall fight dragons among blue hills, or come to that whereof all romance is but

> Foreshadowings mingled with the images
> Of man's misdeeds in greater days than these,

as the old men thought in *The Earthly Paradise* when they were in good spirits?

1902

MIRACULOUS CREATURES

THERE are marten cats and badgers and foxes in the Enchanted Woods, but there are, it seems, mightier creatures, and the lake may hide what neither net nor line can take. These creatures are of the race of the white stag that flits in and out of the tales of Arthur, and of the evil pig that slew Diarmuid where Ben Bulben mixes with the sea wind. They are, as I conceive it, the wizard creatures of hope and fear, they are of them that fly and of them that follow among the thickets that are about the Gates of Death. A man I know remembers that his father was one night in the wood of Inchy, 'where the lads of Gort used to be stealing rods. He was sitting by the wall, and the dog beside him, and he heard something come running from Owbawn Weir, and he could see nothing, but the sound of its feet on the ground was like the sound of the feet of a deer. And when it passed him, the dog got between him and the wall and scratched at it there as if it was afraid, but still he could see nothing but only hear the sound of hoofs. So when it was past he turned and came away home.' 'Another time,' the man says, 'my father told me he was in a boat out on the lake with two or three men from Gort, and one of them had an eel-spear, and he thrust it into the water, and it hit something, and the man fainted and they had to carry him out of the boat to land, and when he came to himself he said that what he struck was like a calf, but whatever it was, it was not fish!'

1902

ARISTOTLE OF THE BOOKS

THE friend who can get the wood-cutter to talk more readily than he will to anybody else went lately to see his old wife. She lives in a cottage not far from the edge of the woods, and is as full of old talk as her husband. This time she began to talk of Goban, the legendary mason, and his wisdom, but said presently, 'Aristotle of the Books, too, was very wise, and he had a great deal of experience, but did not the bees get the better of him in the end? He wanted to know how they packed the comb, and he wasted the better part of a fortnight watching them, and he could not see them doing it. Then he made a hive with a glass cover on it and put it over them, and he thought to see. But when he went and put his eyes to the glass, they had it all covered with wax so that it was as black as the pot; and he was as blind as before. He said he was never rightly kilt till then. They had him that time surely!'

1902

The Swine of the Gods

THE SWINE OF THE GODS

A FEW years ago a friend of mine told me of something that happened to him when he was a young man and out drilling with some Connacht Fenians. They were but a carful, and drove along a hillside until they came to a quiet place. They left the car and went farther up the hill with their rifles, and drilled for a while. As they were coming down again they saw a very thin, long-legged pig of the old Irish sort, and the pig began to follow them. One of them cried out as a joke that it was a faery pig, and they all began to run to keep up the joke. The pig ran too, and presently, how nobody knew, this mock terror became real terror, and they ran as for their lives. When they got to the car they made the horse gallop as fast as possible, but the pig still followed. Then one of them put up his rifle to fire, but when he looked along the barrel he could see nothing. Presently they turned a corner and came to a village. They told the people of the village what had happened, and the people of the village took pitchforks and spades and the like, and went along the road with them to drive the pig away. When they turned the corner they could not find anything.

1902

A VOICE

ONE day I was walking over a bit of marshy ground close to Inchy Wood when I felt, all of a sudden, and only for a second, an emotion which I said to myself was the root of Christian mysticism. There had swept over me a sense of weakness, of dependence on a great personal Being somewhere far off yet near at hand. No thought of mine had prepared me for this emotion, for I had been pre-occupied with Aengus and Edain, and with Manannan, Son of the Sea. That night I awoke lying upon my back and hearing a voice speaking above me and saying, 'No human soul is like any other human soul, and therefore the love of God for any human soul is infinite, for no other soul can satisfy the same need in God.' A few nights after this I awoke to see the loveliest people I have ever seen. A young man and a young girl dressed in olive-green raiment, cut like old Greek raiment, were standing at my bedside. I looked at the girl and noticed that her dress was gathered about her neck into a kind of chain, or perhaps into some kind of stiff embroidery which represented ivy-leaves. But what filled me with wonder was the miraculous mildness of her face. There are no such faces now. It was beautiful as few faces are beautiful, but it had not, one would think, the light that is in desire or in hope or in fear or in speculation. It was peaceful like the faces of animals, or like mountain pools at evening, so peaceful that it was a little sad. I thought for a moment that she might be the beloved of Aengus, but how could that hunted, alluring, happy, immortal wretch have a face like this?

1902

KIDNAPPERS

A LITTLE north of the town of Sligo, on the southern side of Ben Bulben, some hundreds of feet above the plain, is a small white square in the limestone. No mortal has ever touched it with his hand; no sheep or goat has ever browsed grass beside it. There is no more inaccessible place upon the earth, and to an anxious consideration few more encircled by terror. It is the door of Faeryland. In the middle of night it swings open, and the unearthly troop rushes out. All night the gay rabble sweep to and fro across the land, invisible to all, unless perhaps where, in some more than commonly 'gentle' place—Drumcliff or Dromahair, the night-capped heads of 'faery-doctors' or 'cow-doctors' may be thrust from their doors to see what mischief the 'gentry' are doing. To their trained eyes and ears doubtless the fields are covered by red-hatted riders, and the air is full of shrill voices—a sound like whistling, as an ancient Scottish seer has recorded, and wholly different from the talk of the angels, who 'speak much in the throat, like the Irish,' as Lilly, the astrologer, has wisely said. If there be a new-born baby or new-wed bride in the neighbourhood, the 'doctors' will peer with more than common care, for the unearthly troop do not always return empty-handed. Sometimes a new-wed bride or a new-born baby goes with them into their mountains; the door swings to behind, and the new-born or the new-wed moves henceforth in the blood-less land of Faery; happy, the story has it, but doomed to melt at the Last Judgment like bright vapour, for the soul cannot live without sorrow. Through this door of white stone, and the other doors of that land where *geabheadh tu an sonas aer pingin* ('you can buy joy for a penny'), have gone those kings, queens, and princes whose stories are in our old Gaelic literature.

There suddenly appeared at the western corner of Market Street, Sligo, where the butcher's shop now is, as did a palace in Keats's *Lamia*, an apothecary's shop, ruled over by a certain unaccountable Dr. Opendon. Where he came from, none ever knew. There also was in Sligo, in those days, a woman, Ormsby by name, whose husband had fallen mysteriously sick. The doctors could make nothing of him. Nothing seemed wrong with him, yet weaker and weaker he grew. Away went the wife to Dr. Opendon. She was shown into the shop parlour. A black cat was sitting straight up before the fire. She had just time to see that the sideboard was covered with fruit, and to say to herself, 'Fruit must be wholesome when the doctor has so much,' before Dr. Opendon came in. He was dressed all in black, the same as the cat, and his wife walked behind him dressed in black likewise. She gave him a guinea, and got a little bottle in return. Her husband recovered that time. Meanwhile the black doctor cured many people; but one day a rich patient died, and cat, wife, and doctor all vanished the night after. In a year the man Ormsby fell sick once more. Now he was a good-looking man, and his wife felt sure the 'gentry' were coveting him. She went and called on the 'faery-doctor' at Cairnsfoot. As soon as he had heard her tale, he went behind the back door and began muttering spells. Her husband got well this time also. But after a while he sickened again, the fatal third time, and away went she once more to Cairnsfoot, and out went the 'faery-doctor' behind his back door and began muttering, but soon he came in and told her it was no use—her husband would die; and sure enough the man died, and ever after when she spoke of him Mrs. Ormsby shook her head saying she knew well where he was, and it wasn't in Heaven or Hell or Purgatory either. She probably believed that a log of wood was left behind in his place, but so bewitched that it seemed the dead body of her husband.

She is dead now herself, but many still living remember her. She was, I believe, for a time a servant or else a kind of pensioner of some relations of my own.

Sometimes those who are carried off are allowed after many years—seven usually—a final glimpse of their friends. Many years ago a woman vanished suddenly from a Sligo garden where she was walking with her husband. When her son, who was then a baby, had grown up he received word in some way, not handed down, that his mother was glamoured by faeries, and imprisoned for the time in a house in Glasgow and longing to see him. Glasgow in those days of sailing-ships seemed to the peasant mind almost over the edge of the known world, yet he, being a dutiful son, started away. For a long time he walked the streets of Glasgow; at last down in a cellar he saw his mother working. She was happy, she said, and had the best of good eating, and would he not eat? and therewith laid all kinds of food on the table; but, he knowing well that she was trying to cast on him the glamour by giving him faery food, that she might keep him with her, refused and came home to his people in Sligo.

Some five miles southward of Sligo is a gloomy and tree-bordered pond, a great gathering-place of water-fowl, called, because of its form, the Heart Lake. Out of this lake, as from the white square stone in Ben Bulben, issues an unearthly troop. Once men began to drain it; suddenly one of them raised a cry that he saw his house in flames. They turned round, and every man there saw his own house burning. They hurried home to find it was but faery glamour. To this hour on the border of the lake is shown a half-dug trench—the signet of their impiety. A little way from this lake I heard a beautiful and mournful history of faery kidnapping. I heard it from a little old woman in a white cap, who sings in Gaelic, and moves from one foot to the other as though she remembered the dancing of her youth.

A young man going at nightfall to the house of his just-married bride, met on the way a jolly company, and with them his bride. They were faeries and had stolen her as a wife for the chief of their band. To him they seemed only a company of merry mortals. His bride, when she saw her old love, bade him welcome, but was most fearful lest he should eat the faery food, and so be glamoured out of the earth into that bloodless dim nation, wherefore she set him down to play cards with three of the cavalcade; and he played on, realising nothing until he saw the chief of the band carrying his bride away in his arms. Immediately he started up, and knew that they were faeries, for all that jolly company melted into shadow and night. He hurried to his house, and as he drew near heard the cry of the keeners and knew that his wife was dead. Some noteless Gaelic poet had made this into a forgotten ballad, some odd verses of which my white-capped friend remembered and sang for me.[1]

Sometimes one hears of stolen people acting as good genii to the living, as in this tale, heard also close by the haunted pond, of John Kirwan of Castle Hackett. The Kirwans[2] are a family much rumoured of in peasant stories, and believed to be the descendants of a man and a spirit. They have ever been famous for beauty, and I have read that the mother of the present Lord Cloncurry was of their tribe.

John Kirwan was a great horse-racing man, and once landed in Liverpool with a fine horse, going racing somewhere in middle England. That evening, as he walked by the docks, a slip of a boy came up and asked where he was stabling his horse. In such-and-such a place, he answered. 'Don't put him there,' said the slip of a boy; 'that stable will be burnt to-night.' He took his horse elsewhere, and sure enough the stable was burnt down. Next day the boy came and asked as re-

[1] There is a ballad in my *Wind among the Reeds* on this theme. (1924.)

[2] I have since heard that it was not the Kirwans, but their predecessors at Castle Hackett, the Hacketts themselves, I think, who were descended from a man and a spirit, and were notable for beauty. I imagine that the mother of Lord Cloncurry was descended from the Hacketts. It may well be that all through these stories the name of Kirwan has taken the place of the older name. (1902.) Castle Hackett was burned by incendiaries during our civil war. (1924.)

ward to ride as his jockey in the coming race, and then was gone. The race-time came round. At the last moment the boy ran forward and mounted, saying, 'If I strike him with the whip in my left hand I will lose, but if in my right hand bet all you are worth.' For, said Paddy Flynn, who told me the tale, 'the left arm is good for nothing. I might go on making the sign of the cross with it, and all that, come Christmas, and a Banshee would no more mind than if it was that broom.' Well, the slip of a boy struck the horse with his right hand, and John Kirwan cleared the field out. When the race was over, 'What can I do for you now?' said he. 'Nothing but this,' said the boy: 'my mother has a cottage on your land—they stole me from the cradle. Be good to her, John Kirwan, and wherever your horses go I will watch that no ill follows them; but you will never see me more.' With that he made himself air, and vanished.

Sometimes animals are carried off — apparently drowned animals more than others. In Claremorris, Mayo, Paddy Flynn told me, lived a poor widow with one cow and its calf. The cow fell into the river and was washed away. There was a man thereabouts who went to a red haired woman—for such are supposed to be wise in these things—and she told him to take the calf down to the edge of the river, and hide himself and watch. He did as she had told him, and as evening came on the calf began to low, and after a while the cow came along the edge of the river and commenced suckling it. Then, as he had been told, he caught the cow's tail. Away they went at a great pace, across hedges and ditches, till they came to a royalty—Paddy Flynn's name for a rath. Therein he saw walking or sitting all the people who had died out of his village in his time. A woman was sitting on the edge with a child on her knees, and she called out to him to mind what the red-haired woman had told him, and he remembered she had said, 'Bleed the cow.' So he stuck his knife into the cow and drew blood. That broke the spell, and he was able to turn her homeward. 'Do not forget the spancel,' said the woman with the child on her knees; 'take the inside one.' There were three spancels on a bush; he took one, and the cow was driven safely home to the widow.

There is hardly a valley or mountain-side where they cannot tell you of some one pillaged from amongst them. Two or three miles from the Heart Lake lives an old woman who was stolen away in her youth. After seven years she was brought home again for some reason or other, but she had no toes left. She had danced them off.

The Untiring Ones

THE UNTIRING ONES

IT is one of the great troubles of life that we cannot have any unmixed emotions. There is always something in our enemy that we like, and something in our sweetheart that we dislike. It is this entanglement of moods which makes us old, and puckers our brows and deepens the furrows about our eyes. If we could love and hate with as good heart as the Sidhe do, we might grow to be long-lived like them. But until that day their untiring joys and sorrows must ever be one-half of their fascination. Love with them never grows weary, nor can the circles of the stars tire out their dancing feet. The Donegal peasants remember this when they bend over the spade, or sit full of the heaviness of the fields beside the griddle at nightfall, and they tell stories about it that it may not be forgotten. A short while ago, they say, two little creatures, one like a young man, one like a young woman, came to a farmer's house, and spent the night sweeping the hearth and setting all tidy. The next night they came again, and while the farmer was away, brought all the furniture upstairs into one room, and having arranged it round the walls, for the greater grandeur, it seems, they began to dance. They danced on and on, and days and days went by, and all the countryside came to look at them, but still their feet never tired. The farmer did not dare to live at home the while; and after three months he made up his mind to stand it no more, and went and told them that the priest was coming. The little creatures when they heard this went back to their own country, and there their joy shall last as long as the points of the rushes are brown, the people say, and this is until God shall burn up the world with a kiss.

But it is not merely the Sidhe who know untiring days, for there have been men and women who, falling under their enchantment, have attained, perhaps by the right of their God-given spirits, an even more than faery abundance of life and feeling. Such a mortal was born long ago at a village in the south of Ireland. She lay asleep in a cradle, and her mother sat by rocking her, when a woman of the Sidhe came in, and said that the child was chosen to be the bride of the prince of the dim kingdom, but that as it would never do for his wife to grow old and die while he was still in the first ardour of his love, she would be gifted with a faery life. The mother was to take the glowing log out of the fire and bury it in the garden, and her child would live as long as it remained unconsumed. The mother buried the log, and the child grew up, became a beauty, and married the prince, who came to her at nightfall. After seven hundred years the prince died, and another prince ruled in his stead and married the beautiful peasant girl in his turn; and after another seven hundred years he died also, and another prince and another husband came in his stead, and so on until she had had seven husbands. At last one day the priest of the parish called upon her, and told her that she was a scandal to the whole neighbourhood with her seven husbands and her long life. She was very sorry, she said, but she was not to blame, and then she told him about the log, and he went straight out and dug until he found it, and then they burned it, and she died, and was buried like a Christian, and everybody was pleased. Such a mortal too was Clooth-na-Bare,[1] who went all over the world seeking a lake deep enough to drown her faery life, of which she had grown weary, leaping from hill to lake and lake to hill, and setting up a cairn of stones wherever her feet lighted, until at last she found the deepest water in the world in little Lough Ia, on the top of the Birds' Mountain at Sligo.

The two little creatures may well dance on, and the woman of the log and Clooth-na-Bare sleep in peace, for they have known untrammelled hate and unmixed love, and have never wearied themselves with 'yes' and 'no,' or entangled their feet with the sorry net of 'maybe' and 'perhaps.' The great winds came and took them up into themselves.

[1] Doubtless Clooth-na-Bare should be Cailleac Beare, which would mean the old Woman Beare. Beare or Bere or Verah or Dera or Dhera was a very famous person, perhaps the Mother of the Gods herself. Standish O'Grady found her, as he thinks, frequenting Lough Leath, or the Grey Lake on a mountain of the Fews. Perhaps Lough Ia is my mishearing, or the story-teller's mispronunciation of Lough Leath, for there are many Lough Leaths.

EARTH, FIRE AND WATER

SOME French writer that I read when I was a boy said that the desert went into the heart of the Jews in their wanderings and made them what they are. I cannot remember by what argument he proved them to be even yet the indestructible children of earth, but it may well be that the elements have their children. If we knew the Fire-Worshippers better we might find that their centuries of pious observance have been rewarded, and that the fire has given them a little of its nature; and I am certain that the water, the water of the seas and of lakes and of mist and rain, has all but made the Irish after its image. Images form themselves in our minds perpetually as if they were reflected in some pool. We gave ourselves up in old times to mythology, and saw the gods everywhere. We talked to them face to face, and the stories of that communion are so many that I think they outnumber all the like stories of all the rest of Europe. Even to-day our countrypeople speak with the dead and with some who perhaps have never died as we understand death; and even our educated people pass without great difficulty into the condition of quiet that is the condition of vision. We can make our minds so like still water that beings gather about us that they may see, it may be, their own images, and so live for a moment with a clearer, perhaps even with a fiercer life because of our quiet. Did not the wise Porphyry think that all souls come to be born because of water, and that 'even the generation of images in the mind is from water'?

1902

The Old Town

THE OLD TOWN

I FELL, one night some fifteen years ago, into what seemed the power of Faery.

I had gone with a young man and his sister—friends and relations of my own—to pick stories out of an old countryman; and we were coming home talking over what he had told us. It was dark, and our imaginations were excited by his stories of apparitions, and this may have brought us, unknown to us, to the threshold, between sleeping and waking, where Sphinxes and Chimeras sit open-eyed and where there are always murmurings and whisperings. We had come under some trees that made the road very dark, when the girl saw a bright light moving slowly across the road. Her brother and myself saw nothing, and did not see anything until we had walked for about half an hour along the edge of the river and down a narrow lane to some fields where there were a ruined church covered with ivy, and the foundations of what was called 'the Old Town,' which had been burned down, it was said, in Cromwell's day. We had stood for some few minutes, so far as I can recollect, looking over the fields full of stones and brambles and elder-bushes, when I saw a small bright light on the horizon, as it seemed, mounting up slowly towards the sky; then we saw other faint lights for a minute or two, and at last a bright flame like the flame of a torch moving rapidly over the river. We saw it all in such a dream, and it seems all so unreal, that I have never written of it until now, and hardly ever spoken of it, and even when thinking, because of some unreasonable impulse, I have avoided giving it weight in the argument. Perhaps I have felt that my recollections of things seen when the sense of reality was weakened must be untrustworthy. A few months ago, however, I talked it over with my two friends, and compared their somewhat meagre recollections with my own. That sense of unreality was all the more wonderful because the next day I heard sounds as unaccountable as were those lights, and without any emotion of unreality, and I remember them with perfect distinctness and confidence. The girl was sitting reading under a large old-fashioned mirror, and I was reading and writing a couple of yards away, when I heard a sound as if a shower of peas had been thrown against the mirror, and while I was looking at it I heard the sound again, and presently, while I was alone in the room, I heard a sound as if something much bigger than a pea had struck the wainscoting beside my head. And after that for some days came other sights and sounds, not to me but to the girl, her brother, and the servants. Now it was a bright light, now it was letters of fire that vanished before they could be read, now it was a heavy foot moving about in the seemingly empty house. One wonders whether creatures who live, the countrypeople believe, wherever men and women have lived in earlier times, followed us from the ruins of the old town? or did they come from the banks of the river by the trees where the first light had shone for a moment?

1902

The Man and His Boots

THE MAN AND HIS BOOTS

THERE was a doubter in Donegal, and he would not hear of ghosts or faeries, and there was a house in Donegal that had been haunted as long as man could remember, and this is the story of how the house got the better of the man. The man came into the house and lighted a fire in the room under the haunted one, and took off his boots and set them on the hearth, and stretched out his feet and warmed himself. For a time he prospered in his unbelief; but a little while after the night had fallen, and everything had got very dark, one of his boots began to move. It got up off the floor and gave a kind of slow jump towards the door, and then the other boot did the same, and after that the first boot jumped again. And thereupon it occurred to the man that an invisible being had got into his boots, and was now going away in them. When the boots reached the door they went upstairs slowly, and then the man heard them go tramp, tramp round the haunted room over his head. A few minutes passed, and he could hear them again upon the stairs, and after that in the passage outside, and then one of them came in at the door, and the other gave a jump past it and came in too. They jumped along towards him, and then one got up and hit him, and afterwards the other hit him, and then again the first hit him, and so on, until they drove him out of the room, and finally out of the house. In this way he was kicked out by his own boots, and Donegal was avenged upon its doubter. It is not recorded whether the invisible being was a ghost or one of the Sidhe, but the fantastic nature of the vengeance is like the work of the Sidhe who live in the heart of fantasy.

A Coward

A COWARD

ONE day I was at the house of my friend the strong farmer, who lives beyond Ben Bulben and Cope's mountain, and met there a young lad who seemed to be disliked by the two daughters. I asked why they disliked him, and was told he was a coward. This interested me, for some whom robust children of Nature take to be cowards are but men and women with a nervous system too finely made for their life and work. I looked at the lad; but no, that pink-and-white face and strong body had nothing of undue sensibility. After a little he told me his story. He had lived a wild and reckless life, until one day, two years before, he was coming home late at night, and suddenly felt himself sinking in, as it were, upon the ghostly world. For a moment he saw the face of a dead brother rise up before him, and then he turned and ran. He did not stop till he came to a cottage nearly a mile down the road. He flung himself against the door with so much of violence that he broke the thick wooden bolt and fell upon the floor. From that day he gave up his wild life, but was a hopeless coward. Nothing could ever bring him to look, either by day or night, upon the spot where he had seen the face, and he often went two miles round to avoid it; nor could, he said, 'the prettiest girl in the country' persuade him to see her home after a party if he were alone.

THE THREE O'BYRNES AND THE EVIL FAERIES

IN the dim kingdom there is a great abundance of all excellent things. There is more love there than upon the earth; there is more dancing there than upon the earth; and there is more treasure there than upon the earth. In the beginning the earth was perhaps made to fulfil the desire of man, but now it has got old and fallen into decay. What wonder if we try and pilfer the treasures of that other kingdom!

A friend was once at a village near Slieve League. One day he was straying about a rath called 'Cashel Nore.' A man with a haggard face and unkempt hair, and clothes falling in pieces, came into the rath and began digging. My friend turned to a peasant who was working near and asked who the man was. 'That is the third O'Byrne,' was the answer. A few days after he learned this story: A great quantity of treasure had been buried in the rath in pagan times, and a number of evil faeries set to guard it; but some day it was to be found and belong to the family of the O'Byrnes. Before that day three O'Byrnes must find it and die. Two had already done so. The first had dug and dug until at last he got a glimpse of the stone coffin that contained it, but immediately a thing like a huge hairy dog came down the mountain and tore him to pieces. The next morning the treasure had again vanished deep into the earth. The second O'Byrne came and dug and dug until he found the coffin, and lifted the lid and saw the gold shining within. He saw some horrible sight the next moment, and went raving mad and soon died. The treasure again sank out of sight. The third O'Byrne is now digging. He believes that he will die in some terrible way the moment he finds the treasure, but that the spell will be broken, and the O'Byrne family made rich for ever, as they were of old.

A peasant of the neighbourhood once saw the treasure. He found the shin-bone of a hare lying on the grass. He took it up; there was a hole in it; he looked through the hole, and saw the gold heaped up under the ground. He hurried home to bring a spade, but when he got to the rath again he could not find the spot where he had seen it.

DRUMCLIFF AND ROSSES

DRUMCLIFF and Rosses were, are, and ever shall be, please Heaven! places of unearthly resort. I have lived near by them and in them, time after time, and thereby gathered much faery lore. Drumcliff is a wide green valley, lying at the foot of Ben Bulben, whereon the great Saint Columba himself, the builder of many of the old ruins in the valley, climbed one day to get near Heaven with his prayers. Rosses is a little sea-dividing, sandy plain, covered with short grass, like a green table-cloth, and lying in the foam midway between the round cairn-headed Knocknarea and 'Ben Bulben, famous for hawks':

> But for Ben Bulben and Knocknarea
> Many a poor sailor 'd be cast away,

as the rhyme goes.

At the northern corner of Rosses is a little promontory of sand and rocks and grass: a mournful, haunted place. Few countrymen would fall asleep under its low cliff, for he who sleeps here may wake 'silly', the Sidhe having carried off his soul. There is no more ready short-cut to the dim kingdom than this plovery headland, for, covered and smothered now from sight by mounds of sand, a long cave goes thither 'full of gold and silver, and the most beautiful parlours and drawing-rooms.' Once, before the sand covered it, a dog strayed in, and was heard yelping helplessly deep underground in a fort far inland. These forts or raths, made before modern history had begun, cover all Rosses and all Columcille. The one where the dog yelped has, like most others, an underground beehive chamber in the midst. Once when I was poking about there, an unusually intelligent and 'reading' countryman who had come with me, and waited outside, knelt down by the opening, and whispered in a timid voice, 'Are you all right, sir?' I had been some little while underground, and he feared I had been carried off like the dog.

This fort or rath is on the ridge of a small hill, on whose northern slope lie a few stray cottages. One night a farmer's young son came from one of them and saw it all flaming, and ran towards it, but the 'glamour' fell on him, and he sprang on to a fence, cross-legged, and commenced beating it with a stick, for he imagined the fence was a horse. In the morning he was still beating his fence, still riding across country as it seemed to him, and they carried him home, where he remained a simpleton for three years before he came to himself again. A little later a farmer tried to level the fort. His cows and horses died, and all manner of trouble overtook him, and finally he himself was led home, and left useless with 'his head on his knees by the fire to the day of his death.'

A few hundred yards southwards of the northern angle of Rosses is another angle having also its cave, though this one is not covered with sand. About twenty years ago a brig was wrecked near by, and three or four fishermen were put to watch the deserted hulk through the darkness. At midnight they saw sitting on a stone at the cave's mouth two red-capped fiddlers fiddling with all their might. The men fled. A great crowd of villagers rushed down to the cave to see the fiddlers, but the creatures had gone.

To the wise peasant the green hills and woods round him are full of never-fading mystery. When the aged countrywoman stands at her door in the evening, and, in her own words, 'looks at the mountains and thinks of the goodness of God,' God is all the nearer, because the pagan powers are not far: because northward in Ben Bulben, famous for hawks, the white square door swings open at sundown, and those wild unchristian riders rush forth upon the fields, while southward the White Lady, who is doubtless Maeve herself, wanders under the broad cloud nightcap of Knocknarea. How may she doubt these things, even though the priest shakes his head at her? Did not a herd-boy, no long while since, see the White Lady? She passed so close that the skirt of her dress touched him. 'He fell down, and was dead three days.'

One night as I sat eating Mrs. H——'s soda-bread, her husband told me a longish story, much the best of all I heard in Rosses. Many a poor man from Finn mac Cumhal to our own days has had some such adventure to tell of, for the 'Good People' love to repeat themselves. At any rate the story-tellers do. 'In the times when we used to travel by the canal,' he said, 'I was coming down from Dublin. When we came to Mullingar the canal ended, and I began to walk, and stiff and fatigued I was after the slowness. I had some friends with me, and now and then we walked, now and then we rode in a cart. So on till we saw some girls milking cows, and stopped to joke with them. After a while we asked them for a drink of milk. "We have nothing to put it in here," they said, "but come to the house with us." We went home with them, and sat round the fire talking. After a while the others went, and left me, loath to stir from the good fire. I asked the girls for something to eat. There was a pot on the fire, and they took the meat out and put it on a plate, and told me to eat only the meat that came off the head. When I had eaten, the girls went out, and I did not see them again. It grew darker and darker, and there I still sat, loath as ever to leave the good fire, and after a while two men came in, carrying between them a corpse. When I saw them coming I hid behind the door. Says one to the other, putting the corpse on the spit, "Who'll turn the meat?" Says the other, "Michael H——, come out of that and turn the meat." I came out all of a tremble, and began turning the corpse. "Michael H——," says the one who spoke first, "if you let it burn we'll have to put you on the spit instead"; and on that they went out. I sat there trembling and turning the corpse till towards midnight. The men came again, and the one said it was burnt, and the other said it was done right. But having fallen out over it, they both said they would do me no harm that time; and, sitting by the fire, one of them cried out: "Michael H——, can you tell me a story?" "Divil a one," said I. On which he caught me by the shoulder, and put me out like a shot. It was a wild blowing night. Never in all my born days did I see such a night—the darkest night that ever came out of the heavens. I did not know where I was for the life of me. So when one of the men came after me and touched me on the shoulder, with a "Michael H——, can you tell a story now?" "I can," says I. In he brought me; and putting me by the fire, says, "Begin." "I have no story but the one," says I, "that I was sitting here, and you two men brought in a corpse and put it on the spit, and set me turning it." "That will do," says he; "ye may go in there and lie down on the bed." And I went, nothing loath; and in the morning where was I but in the middle of a green field!'

Drumcliff is a great place for omens. Before a prosperous fishing season a herring-barrel appears in the midst of a storm-cloud; and at a place called Columcille's Strand, a place of marsh and mire, an ancient boat, with Saint Columba himself, comes floating in from sea on a moonlight night; a portent of a brave harvesting. They have their dread portents too. Some few seasons ago a fisherman saw, far on the horizon, renowned Hy Brazil, where he who touches shall find no more labour or care, nor cynic laughter, but shall go walking about under shadiest boscage, and enjoy the conversation of Cuchulain and his heroes. A vision of Hy Brazil forebodes national troubles.

Drumcliff and Rosses are choke-full of ghosts. By bog, road, rath, hillside, sea-border they gather in all shapes: headless women, men in armour, shadow hares, fire-tongued hounds, whistling seals, and so on. A whistling seal sank a ship the other day. At Drumcliff there is a very ancient graveyard. *The Annals of the Four Masters* have this verse about a soldier named Denadhach, who died in 871: 'A pious soldier of the race of Conn lies under hazel crosses at Drumcliff.' Not very

Drumcliff and Rosses

long ago an old woman, turning to go into the church-yard at night to pray, saw standing before her a man in armour, who asked her where she was going. It was the 'pious soldier of the race of Conn,' says local wisdom, still keeping watch, with his ancient piety, over the graveyard. Again, the custom is still common hereabouts of sprinkling the doorstep with the blood of a chicken on the death of a very young child, thus (as the belief is) drawing into the blood the evil spirits from the too weak soul. Blood is a great gatherer of evil spirits. To cut your hand on a stone on going into a fort is said to be very dangerous.

There is no more curious ghost in Drumcliff or Rosses than the snipe-ghost. There is a bush behind a house in a village that I know well: for excellent reasons I do not say whether in Drumcliff or Rosses or on the slope of Ben Bulben, or even on the plain round Knock-narea. There is a history concerning the house and the bush. A man once lived there who found on the quay of Sligo a package containing three hundred pounds in notes. It was dropped by a foreign sea-captain. This my man knew, but said nothing. It was money for freight, and the sea-captain, not daring to face his owners, committed suicide in mid-ocean. Shortly afterwards my man died. His soul could not rest. At any rate, strange sounds were heard round his house. The wife was often seen by those still alive out in the garden praying at the bush I have spoken of, for the shade of the dead man appeared there at times. The bush remains to this day: once portion of a hedge, it now stands by itself, for no one dare put spade or pruning-knife about it. As to the strange sounds and voices, they did not cease till a few years ago, when, during some repairs, a snipe flew out of the solid plaster and away; the troubled ghost, say the neighbours, of the note-finder was at last dislodged.

My forebears and relations have lived near Rosses and Drumcliff these many years. A few miles northward I am wholly a stranger, and can find nothing. When I ask for stories of the faeries, my answer is some such as was given me by a woman who lives near a white stone fort—one of the few stone ones in Ireland —under the seaward angle of Ben Bulben: 'They always mind their own affairs and I always mind mine': for it is dangerous to talk of them. Only friendship for yourself or knowledge of your forebears will loosen these cautious tongues. One friend of mine (I do not give his name for fear of gaugers) has the science of unpacking the stubbornest heart, but then he supplies the potheen-makers with grain from his own fields. Besides, he is descended from a noted Gaelic magician, and he has a kind of prescriptive right to hear tell of all kinds of other-world creatures. They are relations of his, if all people say concerning the parentage of magicians be true.

THE THICK SKULL OF THE FORTUNATE

I

ONCE a number of Icelandic peasantry found a very thick skull in the cemetery where the poet Egil was buried. Its great thickness made them feel certain it was the skull of a great man, doubtless of Egil himself. To be doubly sure they put it on a wall and hit it hard blows with a hammer. It got white where the blows fell, but did not break, and they were convinced that it was in truth the skull of the poet, and worthy of every honour. In Ireland we have much kinship with the Icelanders, or 'Danes' as we call them, and all other dwellers in the Scandinavian countries. In some of our mountainous and barren places, and in our seaboard villages, we still test each other in much the same way the Icelanders tested the head of Egil. We may have acquired the custom from those ancient Danish pirates, whose descendants, the people of Rosses tell me, still remember every field and hillock in Ireland which once belonged to their forebears, and are able to describe Rosses itself as well as any native. There is one seaboard district known as Roughley, where the men are never known to shave or trim their wild red beards, and where there is a fight ever on foot. I have seen them at a boat-race fall foul of each other, and after much loud Gaelic, strike each other with oars. The first boat had gone aground, and by dint of hitting out with the long oars kept the second boat from passing, only to give the victory to the third. One day, the Sligo people say, a man from Roughley was tried in Sligo for breaking a skull in a row, and made the defence, not unknown in Ireland, that some heads are so thin you cannot be responsible for them. Having turned with a look of passionate contempt towards the solicitor who was prosecuting, and cried, 'That little fellow's skull if ye were to hit it would go like an egg-shell,' he beamed upon the judge, and said in a wheedling voice, 'but a man might wallop away at your lordship's for a fortnight.'

II

I wrote all this years ago, out of what were even then old memories. I was in Roughley the other day, and found it much like other desolate places. I may have been thinking of Moughorow, a much wilder place, for the memories of one's childhood are brittle things to lean upon.

1902

The Religion of a Sailor

THE RELIGION OF A SAILOR

A SEA-CAPTAIN when he stands upon the bridge, or looks out from his deck-house, thinks much about God and about the world. Away in the valley yonder among the corn and the poppies men may well forget all things except the warmth of the sun upon the face, and the kind shadow under the hedge; but he who journeys through storm and darkness must needs think and think. One July a couple of years ago I took my supper with a Captain Moran on board the s.s. *Margaret*, that had put into a western river from I know not where. I found him a man of many notions all flavoured with his personality, as is the way with sailors.

'Sur,' said he, 'did you ever hear tell of the sea-captain's prayer?'

'No,' said I; 'what is it?'

'It is,' he replied, ' "O Lord, give me a stiff upper lip." '

'And what does that mean?'

'It means,' he said, 'that when they come to me some night and wake me up, and say, "Captain, we're going down," that I won't make a fool o' meself. Why, sur, we war in mid Atlantic, and I standin' on the bridge, when the third mate comes up to me lookin' mortial bad. Says he, "Captain, all's up with us." Says I, "Didn't you know when you joined that a certain percentage go down every year?" "Yes, sur," says he; and says I, "Aren't you paid to go down?" "Yes, sur," says he; and says I, "Then go down like a man, and be damned to you!" '

CONCERNING THE NEARNESS TOGETHER OF HEAVEN, EARTH, AND PURGATORY

IN Ireland this world and the world we go to after death are not far apart. I have heard of a ghost that was many years in a tree and many years in the archway of a bridge, and my old Mayo woman says, 'There is a bush up at my own place, and the people do be saying that there are two souls doing their penance under it. When the wind blows one way the one has shelter, and when it blows from the north the other has shelter. It is twisted over with the way they be rooting under it for shelter. I don't believe it, but there is many a one would not pass by it at night.' Indeed there are times when the worlds are so near together that it seems as if our earthly chattels were no more than the shadows of things beyond. A lady I knew once saw a village child running about with a long trailing petticoat upon her, and asked why she did not have it cut short. 'It was my grandmother's,' said the child; 'would you have her going about yonder with her petticoat up to her knees, and she dead but four days?' I have read a story of a woman whose ghost haunted her people because they had made her grave-clothes so short that the fires of Purgatory burned her knees. The peasantry expect to have beyond the grave houses much like their earthly houses, only there the thatch will never grow leaky, nor the white walls lose their lustre, nor shall the dairy be at any time

empty of good milk and butter. But now and then a landlord or an agent or a gauger will go by begging for bread, to show how God divides the righteous from the unrighteous.

1892 and 1902

THE EATERS OF PRECIOUS STONES

SOMETIMES when I have been shut off from common interests, and have for a little forgotten to be restless, I get waking dreams, now faint and shadow-like, now vivid and solid-looking, like the material world under my feet. Whether they be faint or vivid, they are ever beyond the power of my will to alter in any way. They have their own will, and sweep hither and thither, and change according to its commands. One day I saw faintly an immense pit of blackness, round which went a circular parapet, and on this parapet sat innumerable apes eating precious stones out of the palms of their hands. The stones glittered green and crimson, and the apes devoured them with an insatiable hunger. I knew that I saw my own Hell there, the Hell of the artist, and that all who sought after beautiful and wonderful things with too avid a thirst, lost peace and form and became shapeless and common. I have seen into other people's Hells also, and saw in one an infernal Peter, who had a black face and white lips, and who weighed on a curious double scales not only the evil deeds committed, but the good deeds left undone, of certain invisible shades. I could see the scales go up and down, but I could not see the shades who were, I knew, crowding about him. I saw on another occasion a quantity of demons of all kinds of shapes—fish-like, serpent-like, ape-like, and dog-like—sitting about a black pit such as that in my own Hell, and looking at the moon-like reflection of the heavens which shone up from the depths of the pit.

OUR LADY OF THE HILLS

WHEN we were children we did not say 'at such a distance from the post-office,' or 'so far from the butcher's or the grocer's,' but measured things by the covered well in the wood, or by the burrow of the fox in the hill. We belonged then to God and to His works, and to things come down from the ancient days. We would not have been greatly surprised had we met the shining feet of an angel among the white mushrooms upon the mountains, for we knew in those days immense despair, unfathomed love—every eternal mood,—but now the draw-net is about our feet. A few miles eastward of Lough Gill, a young Protestant girl, who was both pretty herself and prettily dressed in blue and white, wandered up among those mountain mushrooms, and I have a letter of hers telling how she met a troop of children, and became a portion of their dream. When they first saw her they threw themselves face down in a bed of rushes, as if in a great fear; but after a little other children came about them, and they got up and followed her almost bravely. She noticed their fear, and presently stood still and held out her arms. A little girl threw herself into them with the cry, 'Ah, you are the Virgin out o' the picture!' 'No,' said another, coming near also, 'she is a sky faery, for she has the colour of the sky.' 'No,' said a third, 'she is the faery out of the foxglove grown big.' The other children, however, would have it that she was indeed the Virgin, for she wore the Virgin's colours. Her good Protestant heart was greatly troubled, and she got the children to sit down about her, and tried to explain who she was, but they would have none of her explanation. Finding explanation of no avail, she asked had they ever heard of Christ? 'Yes,' said one; 'but we do not like Him, for He would kill us if it were not for the Virgin.' 'Tell Him to be good to me,' whispered another into her ear. 'He would not let me near Him, for dad says I am a divil,' burst out a third.

She talked to them a long time about Christ and the apostles, but was finally interrupted by an elderly woman with a stick, who, taking her to be some adventurous hunter for converts, drove the children away, despite their explanation that here was the great Queen of Heaven come to walk upon the mountain and be kind to them. When the children had gone she went on her way, and had walked about half a mile, when the child who was called 'a divil' jumped down from the high ditch by the lane, and said she would believe her 'an ordinary lady' if she had 'two skirts,' for 'ladies always had two skirts.' The 'two skirts' were shown, and the child went away crestfallen, but a few minutes later jumped down again from the ditch, and cried angrily, 'Dad's a divil, mum's a divil, and I'm a divil, and you are only an ordinary lady,' and having flung a handful of mud and pebbles ran away sobbing. When my pretty Protestant had come to her own home she found that she had dropped the tassels of her parasol. A year later she was by chance upon the mountain, but wearing now a plain black dress, and met the child who had first called her the Virgin out o' the picture, and saw the tassels hanging about the child's neck, and said, 'I am the lady you met last year, who told you about Christ.' 'No, you are not! no, you are not! no, you are not!' was the passionate reply.

THE GOLDEN AGE

A WHILE ago I was in the train, and getting near Sligo. The last time I had been there something was troubling me, and I had longed for a message from those beings or bodiless moods, or whatever they be, who inhabit the world of spirits. The message came, for one night I saw with blinding distinctness, as I lay between sleeping and waking, a black animal, half weasel, half dog, moving along the top of a stone wall, and presently the black animal vanished, and from the other side came a white weasel-like dog, his pink flesh shining through his white hair and all in a blaze of light; and I remembered a peasant belief about two faery dogs who go about representing day and night, good and evil, and was comforted by the excellent omen. But now I longed for a message of another kind, and chance, if chance there is, brought it, for a man got into the carriage and began to play on a fiddle made apparently of an old blacking-box, and though I am quite unmusical the sounds filled me with the strangest emotions. I seemed to hear a voice of lamentation out of the Golden Age. It told me that we are imperfect, incomplete, and no more like a beautiful woven web, but like a bundle of cords knotted together and flung into a corner. It said that the world was once all perfect and kindly, and that still the kindly and perfect world existed, but buried like a mass of roses under many spadefuls of earth. The faeries and the more innocent of the spirits dwelt within it, and lamented over our fallen world in the lamentation of the wind-tossed reeds, in the song of the birds, in the moan of the waves, and in the sweet cry of the fiddle. It said that with us the beautiful are not clever and the clever are not beautiful, and that the best of our moments are marred by a little vulgarity, or by a needle-prick out of sad recollection, and that the fiddle must ever lament about it all. It said that if only they who live in the Golden Age could die we might be happy, for the sad voices would be still; but they must sing and we must weep until the eternal gates swing open.

A REMONSTRANCE WITH SCOTSMEN FOR HAV-
ING SOURED THE DISPOSITION OF THEIR
GHOSTS AND FAERIES

Not only in Ireland is faery belief still extant. It was
only the other day I heard of a Scottish farmer who be-
lieved that the lake in front of his house was haunted
by a water-horse. He was afraid of it, and dragged the
lake with nets, and then tried to pump it empty. It
would have been a bad thing for the water-horse had he
found him. An Irish peasant would have long since
come to terms with the creature. For in Ireland there is
something of timid affection between men and spirits.
They only ill-treat each other in reason; each admits the
other to have feelings. There are points beyond which
neither will go. No Irish peasant would treat a captured
faery as did the man Campbell tells of. He caught a
kelpie, and tied her behind him on his horse. She was
fierce, but he kept her quiet by driving an awl and a
needle into her. They came to a river, and she grew
very restless, fearing to cross the water. Again he drove
the awl and needle into her. She cried out, 'Pierce me
with the awl, but keep that slender, hair-like slave (the
needle) out of me.' They came to an inn. He turned the
light of a lantern on her; immediately she dropped down
'like a falling star', and changed into a lump of jelly. She
was dead. Nor would they treat the faeries as one is
treated in an old Highland poem. A faery loved a little
child who used to cut turf at the side of a faery hill.
Every day the faery put out his hand from the hill with
an enchanted knife. The child used to cut the turf with

the knife. It did not take long, the knife being charmed. Her brothers wondered why she was done so quickly. At last they resolved to watch, and find out who helped her. They saw the small hand come out of the earth, and the little child take from it the knife. When the turf was all cut, they saw her make three taps on the ground with the handle. The small hand came out of the hill. Snatching the knife from the child, they cut the hand off with a blow. The faery was never again seen. He drew his bleeding arm into the earth, thinking, as it is recorded, he had lost his hand through the treachery of the child.

In Scotland you are too theological, too gloomy. You have made even the Devil religious. 'Where do you live, good-wyf, and how is the minister?' he said to the witch when he met her on the high-road, as it came out in the trial. You have burnt all the witches. In Ireland we have left them alone. To be sure, the 'loyal minority' knocked out the eye of one with a cabbage-stump on the 31st of March 1711, in the town of Carrickfergus. But then the 'loyal minority' is half Scottish. You have discovered the faeries to be pagan and wicked. You would like to have them all up before the magistrate. In Ireland warlike mortals have gone among them, and helped them in their battles, and they in turn have taught men great skill with herbs, and permitted some few to hear their tunes. Carolan slept upon a faery rath. Ever after their tunes ran in his head, and made him the great musician he was. In Scotland you have denounced them from the pulpit. In Ireland they have been permitted by the priests to consult them on the state of their souls. Unhappily the priests have decided that they have no souls, that they will dry up like so much bright vapour at the last day; but more in sadness than in anger. The Catholic religion likes to keep on good terms with its neighbours.

These two different ways of looking at things have influenced in each country the whole world of sprites and goblins. For their gay and graceful doings you must go to Ireland; for their deeds of terror to Scotland. Our Irish faery terrors have about them something of make-believe. When a countryman strays into an enchanted hovel, and is made to turn a corpse all night on a spit before the fire, we do not feel anxious; we know he will wake in the midst of a green field, the dew on his old coat. In Scotland it is altogether different. You have soured the naturally excellent disposition of ghosts and goblins. The piper M'Crimmon of the Hebrides shouldered his pipes and marched into a sea cavern, playing loudly, and followed by his dog. For a long time the people could hear the pipes. He must have gone nearly a mile, when they heard the sound of a struggle. Then the piping ceased suddenly. Some time went by, and then his dog came out of the cavern completely flayed, too weak even to howl. Nothing else ever came out of the cavern. Then there is the tale of the man who dived into a lake where treasure was thought to be. He saw a great coffer of iron. Close to the coffer lay a monster, who warned him to return whence he came. He rose to the surface; but the bystanders, when they heard he had seen the treasure, persuaded him to dive again. He dived. In a little while his heart and liver floated up, reddening the water. No man ever saw the rest of his body.

These water-goblins and water-monsters are common in Scottish folk-lore. We have them too, but take them much less dreadfully. A hole in the Sligo river is haunted by one of these monsters. He is ardently believed in by many, but that does not prevent the country-people playing with the subject, and surrounding it with deliberate fantasy. When I was a small boy I fished one day for congers in the monster's hole. Returning home, a great eel on my shoulder, his head flapping down in front, his tail sweeping the ground behind, I met a fisherman of my acquaintance. I began a tale of an immense conger, three times larger than the one I carried, that had broken my line and escaped. 'That was him,' said the fisherman. 'Did you ever hear how he made my brother emigrate? My brother was a diver, as you know, and grubbed stones for the Harbour Board. One day the beast comes up to him, and says, "What are you after?" "Stones, sur," says he. "Don't you think you had better be going?" "Yes, sur," says he. And that's why my brother emigrated.'

WAR

WHEN there was a rumour of war with France a while ago, I met a poor Sligo woman, a soldier's widow, that I know, and I read her a sentence out of a letter I had just had from London: 'The people here are mad for war, but France seems inclined to take things peacefully,' or some like sentence. Her mind ran a good deal on war, which she imagined partly from what she had heard from soldiers, and partly from tradition of the rebellion of '98, but the word London doubled her interest, for she knew there were a great many people in London, and she herself had once lived in 'a congested district.' 'There are too many over one another in London. They are getting tired of the world. It is killed they want to be. It will be no matter; but sure the French want nothing but peace and quietness. The people here don't mind the war coming. They could not be worse than they are. They may as well die soldierly before God. Sure they will get quarters in Heaven.' Then she began to say that it would be a hard thing to see children tossed about on bayonets, and I knew her mind was running on traditions of the great rebellion. She said presently, 'I never knew a man that was in a battle that liked to speak of it after. They'd sooner be throwing hay down from a hayrick.' She told me how she and her neighbours used to be sitting over the fire when she was a girl, talking of the war that was coming, and now she was afraid it was coming again, for she had dreamed that all the bay was 'stranded and covered with seaweed.' I asked her if it was in the

War

Fenian times that she had been so much afraid of war coming. But she cried out, 'Never had I such fun and pleasure as in the Fenian times. I was in a house where some of the officers used to be staying, and in the day-time I would be walking after the soldiers' band, and at night I'd be going down to the end of the garden watching a soldier, with his red coat on him, drilling the Fenians in the field behind the house. One night the boys tied the liver of an old horse, that had been dead three weeks, to the knocker, and I found it when I opened the door in the morning.' And presently our talk of war shifted, as it had a way of doing, to the battle of the Black Pig, which seems to her a battle between Ireland and England, but to me an Armageddon which shall quench all things in the Ancestral Darkness again, and from this to sayings about war and vengeance. 'Do you know,' she said, 'what the curse of the Four Fathers is? They put the man-child on the spear, and somebody said to them, "You will be cursed in the fourth generation after you," and that is why disease or anything always comes in the fourth generation.'

1902

THE QUEEN AND THE FOOL

I HAVE heard one Hearne, a witch-doctor, who is on the border of Clare and Galway, say that in 'every household' of Faery 'there is a queen and a fool,' and that if you are 'touched' by either you never recover, though you may from the touch of any other in Faery. He said of the fool that he was 'maybe the wisest of all,' and spoke of him as dressed like one of 'the mummers that used to be going about the country.' I remember seeing a long, lank, ragged man sitting by the hearth in the cottage of an old miller not far from where I am now writing, and being told that he was a fool; and from the stories that a friend has gathered for me I find that he is believed to go to Faery in his sleep; but whether he becomes an *Amadán-na-Breena*, a fool of the forth, and is attached to a household there, I cannot tell. It was an old woman that I know well, and who has been in Faery herself, that spoke to my friend about him. She said, 'There are fools amongst them, and the fools we see, like that *Amadán* of Ballylee, go away with them at night, and so do the woman fools that we call *Oinseachs* (apes).' A woman who is related to the witch-doctor on the border of Clare, and who can cure people and cattle by spells, said, 'There are some cures I can't do. I can't help any one that has got a stroke from the queen or the fool of the forth. I knew of a woman that saw the queen one time, and she looked like any Christian. I never heard of any that saw the fool but one woman that was walking near Gort, and she said, "There is the fool of the forth coming after me." So her friends that were with her called out, though they could see nothing, and I suppose he went away at that, for she got no harm. He was like a big strong man, she said, and half naked, and that is all she said about him. I have never seen any myself, but I am a cousin of Hearne, and my uncle was away twenty-one years.' The wife of the old miller said, 'It is said they are mostly good neighbours, but the stroke of the fool is what there is no cure for; any one that gets that is gone. The *Amadán-na-Breena* we call him!' And an old woman who lives in the Bog of Kiltartan, and is very poor, said, 'It is true enough, there is no cure for the stroke of the *Amadán-na-Breena*. There was an old man I knew long ago, he had a tape, and he could tell what diseases you had with measuring you; and he knew many things. And he said to me one time, "What month of the year is the worst?" and I said, "The month of May, of course." "It is not," he said; "but the month of June, for that's the month that the *Amadán* gives his stroke!" They say he looks like any other man, but he's leathan (wide), and not smart. I knew a boy one time got a great fright, for a lamb looked over the wall at him with a beard on it, and he knew it was the *Amadán*, for it was the month of June. And they brought him to that man I was telling about, that had the tape, and when he saw him he said, "Send for the priest, and get a Mass said over him." And so they did, and what would you say but he's living yet and has a family! A certain Regan said, "They, the other sort of people, might be passing you close here and they might touch you. But any that gets the touch of the *Amadán-na-Breena* is done for." It's true enough that it's in the month of June he's most likely to give the touch. I knew one that got it, and he told me about it himself. He was a boy I knew well, and he told me that one night a gentleman came to him, that had been his landlord, and that was dead. And he told him to come along with him, for he wanted him to fight another man. And when he went he found two great troops of them, and the other troop had a living man with them too, and he was put to fight him. And they had a great fight, and he got the better of the other man, and then the troop on his side gave a great shout, and he was let home again. But about three years after that he was cutting bushes in a wood and he saw the *Amadán* coming at him. He had a big vessel in his arms, and it was shining, so that the boy could see nothing else; but he put it behind his back then and came running, and the boy said he looked wild and wide, like the side of the hill. And the boy ran, and he threw the vessel after him, and it broke with a great noise, and whatever came out of it, his head was gone there and then. He lived for a while after, and used to tell us many things, but his wits were gone. He thought they mightn't have liked him to beat the other man, and he used to be afraid something would come on him.' And an old woman in Galway workhouse, who had some little knowledge of Queen Maeve, said the other day, 'The *Amadán-na-Breena* changes his shape every two days. Sometimes he comes like a youngster, and then he'll come like the worst of beasts, trying to give the touch he used to be. I heard it said of late he was shot, but I think myself it would be hard to shoot him.'

The Queen and the Fool

I knew a man who was trying to bring before his mind's eye an image of Aengus, the old Irish god of love and poetry and ecstasy, who changed four of his kisses into birds, and suddenly the image of a man with a cap and bells rushed before his mind's eye, and grew vivid and spoke and called itself 'Aengus' messenger.' And I knew another man, a truly great seer, who saw a white fool in a visionary garden, where there was a tree with peacocks' feathers instead of leaves, and flowers that opened to show little human faces when the white fool had touched them with his cockscomb, and he saw at another time a white fool sitting by a pool and smiling and watching images of beautiful women floating up from the pool.

What else can death be but the beginning of wisdom and power and beauty? and foolishness may be a kind of death. I cannot think it wonderful that many should see a fool with a shining vessel of some enchantment or wisdom or dream too powerful for mortal brains in 'every household of them.' It is natural, too, that there should be a queen to every household of them, and that one should hear little of their kings, for women come more easily than men to that wisdom which ancient peoples, and all wild peoples even now, think the only wisdom. The self, which is the foundation of our knowledge, is broken in pieces by foolishness, and is forgotten in the sudden emotions of women, and therefore fools may get, and women do get of a certainty, glimpses of much that sanctity finds at the end of its painful journey. The man who saw the white fool said of a certain woman, not a peasant woman, 'If I had her power of vision I would know all the wisdom of the gods, and her visions do not interest her.' And I know of another woman, also not a peasant woman, who would pass in sleep into countries of an unearthly beauty, and who never cared for anything but to be busy about her house and her children; and presently a herb doctor cured her, as he called it. Wisdom and beauty and power may sometimes, as I think, come to those who die every day they live, though their dying may not be like the dying Shakespeare spoke of. There is a war between the living and the dead, and the Irish stories keep harping upon it. They will have it that when the potatoes or the wheat or any other of the fruits of the earth decay, they ripen in Faery, and that our dreams lose their wisdom when the sap rises in the trees, and that our dreams can make the trees wither, and that one hears the bleating of the lambs of Faery in November, and that blind eyes can see more than other eyes. Because the soul always believes in these, or in like things, the cell and the wilderness shall never be long empty, or lovers come into the world who will not understand the verse:—

> Heardst thou not sweet words among
> That heaven-resounding minstrelsy?
> Heardst thou not that those who die
> Awake in a world of ecstasy?
> That love, when limbs are interwoven,
> And sleep, when the night of life is cloven,
> And thought, to the world's dim boundaries clinging,
> And music, when one beloved is singing,
> Is death?

1901

THE FRIENDS OF THE PEOPLE OF FAERY

THOSE that see the people of Faery most often, and so have the most of their wisdom, are often very poor, but often, too, they are thought to have a strength beyond that of man, as though one came, when one has passed the threshold of trance, to those sweet waters where Maeldun saw the dishevelled eagles bathe and become young again.

There was an old Martin Roland, who lived near a bog a little out of Gort, who saw them often from his young days, and always towards the end of his life, though I would hardly call him their friend. He told me a few months before his death that 'they' would not let him sleep at night with crying things at him in Irish, and with playing their pipes. He had asked a friend of his what he should do, and the friend had told him to buy a flute, and play on it when they began to shout or to play on their pipes, and maybe they would give up annoying him; and he did, and they always went out into the field when he began to play. He showed me the pipe, and blew through it, and made a noise, but he did not know how to play; and then he showed me where he had pulled his chimney down, because one of them used to sit up on it and play on the pipes. A friend of his and mine went to see him a little time ago, for she heard that 'three of them' had told him he was to die. He said they had gone away after warning him, and that the children (children they had 'taken,' I suppose) who used to come with them, and play about the house with them, had 'gone to some other place,' because 'they found the house too cold for them, maybe'; and he died a week after he had said these things.

His neighbours were not certain that he really saw anything in his old age, but they were all certain that he saw things when he was a young man. His brother said, 'Old he is, and it's all in his brain the things he sees. If he was a young man we might believe in him.' But he was improvident, and never got on with his brothers. A neighbour said, 'The poor man! They say they are mostly in his head now, but sure he was a fine fresh man twenty years ago the night he saw them linked in two lots, like young slips of girls walking together. It was the night they took away Fallon's little girl.' And she told how Fallon's little girl had met a woman 'with red hair that was as bright as silver,' who took her away. Another neighbour, who was herself 'clouted over the ear' by one of them for going into a fort where they were, said, 'I believe it's mostly in his head they are; and when he stood in the door last night I said, "The wind does be always in my ears, and the sound of it never stops," to make him think it was the same with him; but he says, "I hear them singing and making music all the time, and one of them is after bringing out a little flute, and it's on it he's playing to them." And this I know, that when he pulled down the chimney where he said the piper used to be sitting and playing, he lifted up stones, and he an old man, that I could not have lifted when I was young and strong.'

A friend has sent me from Ulster an account of one who was on terms of true friendship with the people of Faery. It has been taken down accurately, for my friend,

118

who had heard the old woman's story some time before I heard of it, got her to tell it over again, and wrote it out at once. She began by telling the old woman that she did not like being in the house alone because of the ghosts and faeries; and the old woman said, 'There's nothing to be frightened about in faeries, Miss. Many's the time I talked to a woman myself that was a faery, or something of the sort, and no less and more than mortal anyhow. She used to come about your grandfather's house—your mother's grandfather, that is—in my young days. But you'll have heard all about her.' My friend said that she had heard about her, but a long time before, and she wanted to hear about her again; and the old woman went on, 'Well, dear, the very first time ever I heard word of her coming about was when your uncle—that is, your mother's uncle—Joseph married, and was building a house for his wife, for he brought her first to his father's, up at the house by the Lough. My father and us were living nigh-hand to where the new house was to be built, to overlook the men at their work. My father was a weaver, and brought his looms and all there into a cottage that was close by. The foundations were marked out, and the building stones lying about, but the masons had not come yet; and one day I was standing with my mother fornent the house, when we sees a smart wee woman coming up the field over the burn to us. I was a bit of a girl at the time, playing about and sporting myself, but I mind her as well as if I saw her there now!' My friend asked how the woman was dressed, and the old woman said, 'It was a grey cloak she had on, with a green cashmere skirt and a black silk handkercher tied round her head, like the countrywomen did use to wear in them times.' My friend asked, 'How wee was she?' And the old woman said, 'Well, now, she wasn't wee at all when I think of it, for all we called her the Wee Woman. She was bigger than many a one, and yet not tall as you would say. She was like a woman about thirty, brown-haired and round in the face. She was like Miss Betty, your grandmother's sister, and Betty was like none of the rest, not like your grandmother, nor any of them. She was round and fresh in the face, and she never was married, and she never would take any man; and we used to say that the Wee Woman—her being like Betty—was, maybe, one of their own people that had been took off before she grew to her full height, and for that she was always following us and warning and foretelling. This time she walks straight over to where my mother was standing. "Go over to the Lough this minute!"—ordering her like that—"Go over to the Lough, and tell Joseph that he must change the foundation of this house to where I'll show you fornent the thorn-bush. That is where it is to be built, if he is to have luck and prosperity, so do what I'm telling ye this minute." The house was being built on "the path," I suppose—the path used by the people of Faery in their journeys, and my mother brings Joseph down and shows him, and he changes the foundation, the way he was bid, but didn't bring it exactly to where was pointed, and the end of that was, when he come to the house, his own wife lost her life with an accident that come to a horse that hadn't room to turn right with a harrow between the bush and the wall. The Wee Woman was queer and angry when next she come, and says to us, "He didn't do as I bid him, but he'll see what he'll see." ' My friend asked where the woman came from this time, and if she was dressed as before, and the woman said, 'Always the same way, up the field beyant the burn. It was a thin sort of shawl she had about her in summer, and a cloak about her in winter; and many and many a time she came, and always it was good advice she was giving to my mother, and warning her what not to do if she would have good luck. There was none of the other children of us ever seen her unless me; but I used to be glad when I seen her coming up the burn, and would run out and catch her by the hand and the cloak, and call to my mother, "Here's the Wee Woman!" No man-body ever seen her. My father used to be wanting to, and was angry with my mother and me, thinking we were telling lies and talking foolish-like. And so one day when she had come, and was sitting by the fireside talking to my mother, I slips out to the field where he was digging. "Come up," says I, "if ye want to see her. She's sitting at the fireside now, talking to mother." So in he comes with me and looks round angry-like and sees nothing, and he up with a broom that was near hand and hits me a crig with it. "Take that now!" says he, "for making a fool of me!" and away with him as fast as he could, and queer and angry with me. The Wee Woman says to me then, "Ye got that now for bringing people to see me. No man-body ever seen me, and none ever will."

'There was one day, though, she gave him a queer

fright anyway, whether he had seen her or not. He was in among the cattle when it happened, and he comes up to the house all trembling-like. "Don't let me hear you say another word of your Wee Woman. I have got enough of her this time." Another time, all the same, he was up Gortin to sell horses, and before he went off, in steps the Wee Woman and says she to my mother, holding out a sort of a weed, "Your man is gone up by Gortin, and there's a bad fright waiting him coming home, but take this and sew it in his coat, and he'll get no harm by it." My mother takes the herb, but thinks to herself, "Sure, there's nothing in it," and throws it on the fire, and lo and behold, and sure enough! coming home from Gortin, my father got as bad a fright as ever he got in his life. What it was I don't right mind, but anyway he was badly damaged by it. My mother was in a queer way, frightened of the Wee Woman, after what she done, and sure enough the next time she was angry. "Ye didn't believe me," she said, "and ye threw the herb I gave ye in the fire, and I went far enough for it." There was another time she came and told how William Hearne was dead in America. "Go over," she says, "to the Lough, and say that William is dead, and he died happy, and this was the last Bible chapter ever he read," and with that she gave the verse and chapter. "Go," she says, "and tell them to read them at the next class-meeting, and that I held his head while he died." And sure enough word came after that how William had died on the day she named. And, doing as she bid about the chapter and hymn, they never had such a prayer-meeting as that. One day she and me and my mother was standing talking, and she was warning her about something, when she says of a sudden, "Here comes Miss Letty in all her finery, and it's time for me to be off." And with that she gave a swirl round on her feet, and raises up in the air, and round and round she goes, and up and up, as if it was a winding stairs she went up, only far swifter.[1] She went up and up, till she was no bigger than a bird up against the clouds, singing and singing the whole time the loveliest music I ever heard in my life from that day to this. It wasn't a hymn she was singing, but poetry, lovely poetry, and me and my mother stands gaping up, and all of a tremble. "What is she at all, mother?" says I. "Is it an angel she is, or a faery woman, or what?" With that up come Miss Letty, that was your grandmother, dear, but Miss Letty she was then, and no word of her being anything else, and she wondered to see us gaping up that way, till me and my mother told her of it. She went on gay-dressed then, and was lovely-looking. She was up the lane where none of us could see her coming forward when the Wee Woman rose up in that queer way, saying, "Here comes Miss Letty in all her finery." Who knows to what far country she went, or to see whom dying?

'It was never after dark she came, but daylight always, as far as I mind, but wanst, and that was on a Hallow Eve night. My mother was by the fire, making ready the supper; she had a duck down and some apples.

[1] A countryman near Coole told me of a spirit so ascending. Swedenborg, in his *Spiritual Diary*, speaks of gyres of spirits, and Blake painted Jacob's Ladder as an ascending gyre.   1924.

In slips the Wee Woman. "I'm come to pass my Hallow Eve with you," says she. "That's right," says my mother, and thinks to herself, "I can give her her supper nicely." Down she sits by the fire a while. "Now I'll tell you where you'll bring my supper," says she. "In the room beyond there beside the loom—set a chair in and a plate." "When ye're spending the night, mayn't ye as well sit by the table and eat with the rest of us?" "Do what you're bid, and set whatever you give me in the room beyant. I'll eat there and nowhere else." So my mother sets her a plate of duck and some apples, whatever was going, in where she bid, and we gòt to our supper and she to hers; and when we rose I went in, and there, lo and behold ye, was her supper-plate a bit ate of each portion, and she clean gone!'

1897

DREAMS THAT HAVE NO MORAL

THE friend who heard about Maeve and the hazel-stick went to the workhouse another day. She found the old people cold and wretched, 'like flies in winter,' she said; but they forgot the cold when they began to talk. A man had just left them who had played cards in a rath with the people of Faery, who had played 'very fair'; and one old man had seen an enchanted black pig one night, and there were two old people my friend had heard quarrelling as to whether Raftery or Callanan was the better poet. One had said of Raftery, 'He was a big man, and his songs have gone through the whole world. I remember him well. He had a voice like the wind'; but the other was certain 'that you would stand in the snow to listen to Callanan.' Presently an old man began to tell my friend a story, and all listened delightedly, bursting into laughter now and then. The story, which I am going to tell just as it was told, was one of those old rambling moralless tales, which are the delight of the poor and the hard-driven, wherever life is left in its natural simplicity. They tell of a time when nothing had consequences, when even if you were killed, if only you had a good heart, somebody would bring you to life again with a touch of a rod, and when if you were a prince and happened to look exactly like your brother, you might go to bed with his queen, and have only a little quarrel afterwards. We too, if we were so weak and poor that everything threatened us with misfortune, might remember every old dream that has been strong enough to fling the weight of the world from its shoulders.

There was a king one time who was very much put out because he had no son, and he went at last to consult his chief adviser. And the chief adviser said, 'It's easy enough managed if you do as I tell you. Let you send someone,' says he, 'to such a place to catch a fish. And when the fish is brought in, give it to the queen, your wife, to eat.'

So the king sent as he was told, and the fish was caught and brought in, and he gave it to the cook, and bade her put it before the fire, but to be careful with it, and not to let any blob or blister rise on it. But it is impossible to cook a fish before the fire without the skin of it rising in some place or other, and so there came a blob on the skin, and the cook put her finger on it to smooth it down, and then she put her finger into her mouth to cool it, and so she got a taste of the fish. And then it was sent up to the queen, and she ate it, and what was left of it was thrown out into the yard and there were a mare in the yard and a greyhound, and they ate the bits that were thrown out.

And before a year was out, the queen had a young son, and the cook had a young son, and the mare had two foals, and the greyhound had two pups.

And the two young sons were sent out for a while to some place to be cared, and when they came back they were so much like one another no person could know which was the queen's son and which was the cook's. And the queen was vexed at that, and she went to the chief adviser and said, 'Tell me some way that I can know which is my own son, for I don't like to be giving the same eating and drinking to the cook's son as to my own.' 'It is easy to know that,' said the chief adviser, 'if you will do as I tell you. Go you outside, and stand at the door they will be coming in by, and when they see you, your own son will bow his head, but the cook's son will only laugh.'

So she did that, and when her own son bowed his head, her servants put a mark on him that she would know him again. And when they were all sitting at their dinner after that, she said to Jack, that was the cook's son, 'It is time for you to go away out of this, for you are not my son.' And her own son, that we will call Bill, said, 'Do not send him away, are we not brothers?' But Jack said, 'I would have been long ago out of this house if I knew it was not my own father and mother owned it.' And for all Bill could say to him, he would not stop. But before he went, they were by the well that was in the garden, and he said to Bill, 'If harm ever happens to me, that water on the top of the well will be blood, and the water below will be honey.'

Then he took one of the pups, and one of the two horses that were foaled after the mare eating the fish, and the wind that was after him could not catch him, and he caught the wind that was before him. And he went on till he came to a weaver's house, and he asked him for a lodging, and he gave it to him. And then he went on till he came to a king's house, and he sent in at the door to ask, 'Did he want a servant?' 'All I want,' said the king, 'is a boy that will drive out the cows to the field every morning, and bring them in at night to be milked.' 'I will do that for you,' said Jack; so the king engaged him.

In the morning Jack was sent out with the four-and-twenty cows, and the place he was told to drive them to had not a blade of grass in it for them, but was full of stones. So Jack looked about for some place where there would be better grass, and after a while he saw a field with good green grass in it, and it belonging to a giant. So he knocked down a bit of the wall and drove them in, and he went up himself into an apple-tree and began to eat the apples. Then the giant came into the field. 'Fee-faw-fum,' says he, 'I smell the blood of an Irishman. I see you where you are, up in the tree,' he said; 'you are too big for one mouthful, and too small for two mouthfuls, and I don't know what I'll do with you if I don't grind you up and make snuff for my nose.' 'As you are strong, be merciful,' says Jack up in the tree. 'Come down out of that, you little dwarf,' said the giant, 'or I'll tear you and the tree asunder.' So Jack came down. 'Would you sooner be driving red-hot knives into one another's hearts,' said the giant, 'or would you sooner be fighting one another on red-hot flags?' 'Fighting on red-hot flags is what I'm used to at home,' said Jack, 'and your dirty feet will be sinking in them and my feet will be rising.' So then they began the fight. The ground that was hard they made soft, and the ground that was soft they made hard, and they made spring wells come up through the green flags. They were like that all through the day, no one getting the upper hand of the other, and at last a little bird came and sat on the bush and said to Jack, 'If you don't make an end of him by sunset, he'll make an end of you.' Then Jack put out his strength, and he brought the giant down on his knees. 'Give me my life,' says the giant, 'and I'll give you the best gift that I have.' 'What is that?' said Jack. 'A sword that nothing can stand against.' 'Where is it to be found?' said Jack. 'In that red door you see there in the hill.' So Jack went and got it out. 'Where will I try the sword?' says he. 'Try it on that ugly black stump of a tree,' says the giant. 'I see nothing blacker or uglier than your own head,' says Jack. And with that he made one stroke, and cut off the giant's head that it went into the air, and he caught it on the sword as it was coming down, and made two halves of it. 'It is well for you I did not join the body again,' said the head, 'or you would have never been able to strike it off again.' 'I did not give you the chance of that,' said Jack.

So he brought the cows home at evening, and every one wondered at all the milk they gave that night. And when the king was sitting at dinner with the princess, his daughter, and the rest, he said, 'I think I only hear two roars from beyond to-night in place of three.'

The next morning Jack went out again with the cows, and he saw another field full of grass, and he knocked down the wall and let the cows in. All happened the same as the day before, but the giant that came this time had two heads, and they fought together, and the little bird came and spoke to Jack as before. And when Jack had brought the giant down, he said, 'Give me my life, and I'll give you the best thing I have.' 'What is that?' says Jack. 'It's a suit that you can put on, and you will see every one but no one can see you.' 'Where is it?' said Jack. 'It's inside that little red door at the side of the hill.' So Jack went and brought out the suit. And then he cut off the giant's two heads, and caught them coming down and made four halves of them. And they said it was well for him he had not given them time to join the body.

That night when the cows came home they gave so much milk that all the vessels that could be found were filled up.

The next morning Jack went out again, and all happened as before, and the giant this time had four heads, and Jack made eight halves of them. And the giant had told him to go to a little blue door in the side of the hill, and there he got a pair of shoes that when you put them on would go faster than the wind.

That night the cows gave so much milk that there were not vessels enough to hold it, and it was given to tenants and to poor people passing the road, and the rest was thrown out at the windows. I was passing that way myself, and I got a drink of it.

That night the king said to Jack, 'Why is it the cows are giving so much milk these days? Are you bringing them to any other grass?' 'I am not,' said Jack, 'but I have a good stick, and whenever they would stop still or lie down, I give them blows of it, that they jump and leap over walls and stones and ditches; that's the way to make cows give plenty of milk.'

And that night at the dinner, the king said, 'I hear no roars at all.'

The next morning, the king and the princess were watching at the window to see what would Jack do when he got to the field. And Jack knew they were there, and he got a stick, and began to batter the cows, that they went leaping and jumping over stones, and walls, and ditches. 'There is no lie in what Jack said,' said the king then.

Now there was a great serpent at that time used to come every seven years, and he had to get a king's daughter to eat, unless she would have some good man to fight for her. And it was the princess at the place Jack was had to be given to it that time, and the king had been feeding a bully underground for seven years, and you may believe he got the best of everything, to be ready to fight it.

And when the time came, the princess went out and the bully with her down to the shore, and when they got there what did he do, but to tie the princess to a tree, the way the serpent would be able to swallow her easy with no delay, and he himself went and hid up in an ivy-tree. And Jack knew what was going on, for the princess had told him about it, and had asked would he help her, but he said he would not. But he came out now, and he put on the sword he had taken from the first giant, and he came by the place the princess was, but she didn't know him. 'Is that right for a princess to be tied to a tree?' said Jack. 'It is not, indeed,' said she, and she told him what had happened, and how the serpent was coming to take her. 'If you will let me sleep for a while with my head in your lap,' said Jack, 'you could wake me when it is coming.' So he did that, and she awakened him when she saw the serpent coming, and Jack got up and fought with it, and drove it back into the sea. And then he cut the rope that fastened her, and he went away. The bully came down then out of the tree, and he brought the princess to where the king was, and he said, 'I got a friend of mine to come and fight the serpent to-day, when I was a little timorous after being so long shut up underground, but I'll do the fighting myself to-morrow.'

The next day they went out again, and the same thing happened; the bully tied up the princess where the serpent could come at her fair and easy, and went up himself to hide in the ivy-tree. Then Jack put on the suit he had taken from the second giant, and he walked out, and the princess did not know him, but she told him all that had happened yesterday, and how some young gentleman she did not know had come and saved her. So Jack asked might he lie down and take a sleep with his head in her lap, the way she could awake him. And all happened the same way as the day before. And the bully gave her up to the king, and said he had brought another of his friends to fight for her that day.

The next day she was brought down to the shore as before, and a great many people gathered to see the serpent that was coming to bring the king's daughter away. And Jack and the princess had talked as before. But when he was asleep this time, she thought she would make sure of being able to find him again, and she took out her scissors and cut off a piece of his hair, and made a little packet of it and put it away. And she did another thing, she took off one of the shoes that were on his feet.

And when she saw the serpent coming she woke him, and he said, 'This time I will put the serpent in a way that he will eat no more kings' daughters.' So he took out the sword he had got from the giant, and he put it in at the back of the serpent's neck, the way blood and water came spouting out that went for fifty miles inland, and made an end of him. And then he made off, and no one saw what way he went, and the bully brought the princess to the king, and claimed to have saved her, and it is he who was made much of, and was the right-hand man after that.

But when the feast was made ready for the wedding, the princess took out the bit of hair she had, and she said she would marry no one but the man whose hair would match that, and she showed the shoe and said that she would marry no one whose foot would not fit that shoe as well. And the bully tried to put on the shoe, but so much as his toe would not go into it, and as to his hair, it didn't match at all to the bit of hair she had cut from the man that saved her.

So then the king gave a great ball, to bring all the chief men of the country together to try would the shoe fit any of them. And they were all going to carpenters and joiners getting bits of their feet cut off to try could they wear the shoe, but it was no use, not one of them could get it on.

Then the king went to his chief adviser and asked what could he do. And the chief adviser bade him to give another ball, and this time he said, 'Give it to poor as well as rich.'

So the ball was given, and many came flocking to it, but the shoe would not fit any one of them. And the chief adviser said, 'Is every one here that belongs to the house?' 'They are all here,' said the king, 'except the boy that minds the cows, and I would not like him to be coming up here.'

Jack was below in the yard at the time, and he heard what the king said, and he was very angry, and he went and got his sword and came running up the stairs to strike off the king's head, but the man that kept the gate met him on the stairs before he could get to the king, and quieted him down, and when he got to the top of the stairs and the princess saw him, she gave a cry and ran into his arms. And they tried the shoe and it fitted him, and his hair matched to the piece that had been cut off. So then they were married, and a great feast was given for three days and three nights.

And at the end of that time, one morning there came a deer outside the window, with bells on it, and they ringing. And it called out, 'Here is the hunt, where are the huntsmen and the hounds?' So when Jack heard that he got up and took his horse and his hound and went hunting the deer. When it was in the hollow he was on the hill, and when it was on the hill he was in the hollow, and that went on all through the day, and when night fell it went into a wood. And Jack went into the wood after it, and all he could see was a mud-wall cabin, and he went in, and there he saw an old woman, about two hundred years old, and she sitting over the fire. 'Did you see a deer pass this way?' says Jack. 'I did not,' says she, 'but it's too late now for you to be following a deer, let you stop the night here.' 'What will I do with my horse and my hound?' said Jack. 'Here are two ribs of hair,' says she, 'and let you tie them up with them.' So Jack went out and tied up the horse and the hound, and when he came in again the old woman said, 'You killed my three sons, and I'm going to kill you now,' and she put on a pair of boxing-gloves, each one of them nine stone weight, and the nails in them fifteen inches long. Then they began to fight, and Jack was getting the worst of it. 'Help, hound!' he cried out, then 'Squeeze, hair!' cried out the old woman, and the rib of hair that was about the hound's neck squeezed him to death. 'Help, horse!' Jack called out, then 'Squeeze, hair!' called out the old woman, and the rib of hair that was about the horse's neck began to tighten and squeeze him to death. Then the old woman made an end of Jack and threw him outside the door.

To go back now to Bill. He was out in the garden one day, and he took a look at the well, and what did he see but the water at the top was blood, and what was underneath was honey. So he went into the house again, and he said to his mother, 'I will never eat a second meal at the same table, or sleep a second night in the same bed, till I know what is happening to Jack.'

So he took the other horse and hound then, and set off, over hills where cock never crows and horn never sounds, and the Devil never blows his bugle. And at last he came to the weaver's house, and when he went in, the weaver says, 'You are welcome, and I can give you better treatment than I did the last time you came in to me,' for he thought it was Jack who was there, they were so much like one another. 'That is good,' said Bill to himself, 'my brother has been here.' And he gave the weaver the full of a basin of gold in the morning before he left.

Then he went on till he came to the king's house, and when he was at the door the princess came running down the stairs, and said, 'Welcome to you back again.' And all the people said, 'It is a wonder you have gone hunting three days after your marriage, and to stop so long away.' So he stopped that night with the princess, and she thought it was her own husband all the time.

And in the morning the deer came, and bells ringing on it, under the windows, and called out, 'The hunt is here, where are the huntsmen and the hounds?' Then Bill got up and got his horse and his hound, and followed it over hills and hollows till they came to the wood, and there he saw nothing but the mud-wall cabin and the old woman sitting by the fire, and she bade him stop the night there, and gave him two ribs of hair to tie his horse and his hound with. But Bill was wittier than Jack was, and before he went out, he threw the ribs of hair into the fire secretly. When he came in the old woman said, 'Your brother killed my three sons, and I killed him, and I'll kill you along with him.' And she put her gloves on, and they began the fight, and then Bill called out, 'Help, horse!' 'Squeeze, hair!' called the old woman. 'I can't squeeze, I'm in the fire,' said the hair. And the horse came in and gave her a blow of his hoof. 'Help, hound!' said Bill then. 'Squeeze, hair!' said the old woman. 'I can't, I'm in the fire,' said the second hair. Then the hound put his teeth in her, and Bill brought her down, and she cried for mercy. 'Give me my life,' she said, 'and I'll tell you where you'll get your brother again, and his hound and horse.' 'Where's that?' said Bill. 'Do you see that rod over the fire?' said she; 'take it down and go outside the door where you'll see three green stones, and strike them with the rod, for they are your brother, and his horse and hound, and they'll come to life again.' 'I will, but I'll make a green stone of you first,' said Bill, and he cut off her head with his sword.

Then he went out and struck the stones, and sure enough there were Jack and his horse and hound, alive and well. And they began striking other stones around, and men came from them, that had been turned to stones, hundreds and thousands of them.

Then they set out for home, but on the way they had some dispute or some argument together, for Jack was not well pleased to hear he had spent the night with his wife, and Bill got angry, and he struck Jack with the rod, and turned him to a green stone. And he went home, but the princess saw he had something on his mind, and he said then, 'I have killed my brother.' And he went back then and brought him to life, and they lived happy ever after, and they had children by the basketful, and threw them out by the shovelful. I was passing one time myself, and they called me in and gave me a cup of tea.

1902

BY THE ROADSIDE

LAST night I went to a wide place on the Kiltartan road to listen to some Irish songs. While I waited for the singers an old man sang about that country beauty who died so many years ago, and spoke of a singer he had known who sang so beautifully that no horse would pass him, but must turn its head and cock its ears to listen. Presently a score of men and boys and girls, with shawls over their heads, gathered under the trees to listen. Somebody sang *Sa Muirnín Díles*, and then somebody else *Jimmy Mo Mílestór*, mournful songs of separation, of death, and of exile. Then some of the men stood up and began to dance, while another lilted the measure they danced to, and then somebody sang *Eiblín a Rúin*, that glad song of meeting which has always moved me more than other songs, because the lover who made it sang it to his sweetheart under the shadow of a mountain I looked at every day through my childhood. The voices melted into the twilight, and were mixed into the trees, and when I thought of the words they too melted away, and were mixed with the generations of men. Now it was a phrase, now it was an attitude of mind, an emotional form, that had carried my memory to older verses, or even to forgotten mythologies. I was carried so far that it was as though I came to one of the four rivers, and followed it under the wall of Paradise to the roots of the Trees of Knowledge and of Life. There is no song or story handed down among the cottages that has not words and thoughts to carry one as far, for though one can know but a little of their ascent, one knows that they ascend like mediaeval genealogies through unbroken dignities to the beginning of the world. Folk-art is, indeed, the oldest of the aristocracies of thought, and because it refuses what is passing and trivial, the merely clever and pretty, as certainly as the vulgar and insincere, and because it has gathered into itself the simplest and most unforgettable thoughts of the generations, it is the soil where all great art is rooted. Wherever it is spoken by the fireside, or sung by the roadside, or carved upon the lintel, appreciation of the arts that a single mind gives unity and design to, spreads quickly when its hour is come.

In a society that has cast out imaginative tradition, only a few people—three or four thousand out of millions—favoured by their own characters and by happy circumstance, and only then after much labour, have understanding of imaginative things, and yet 'the imagination is the man himself.' The Churches in the Middle Ages won all the arts into their service because men understood that when imagination is impoverished, a principal voice—some would say the only voice—for the awakening of wise hope and durable faith, and understanding charity, can speak but in broken words, if it does not fall silent. And so it has always seemed to me that we, who would re-awaken imaginative tradition by making old songs live again, or by gathering old stories into books, take part in the quarrel of Galilee. Those who are Irish and would spread foreign ways, which, for all but a few, are ways of spiritual poverty, take part also. Their part is with those who were of Jewry, and yet cried out, 'If thou let this man go thou art not Caesar's friend.'

1901

Into the Twilight

Out-worn heart, in a time out-worn,
Come clear of the nets of wrong and right;
Laugh, heart, again in the grey twilight;
Sigh, heart, again in the dew of the morn.

Your mother Eire is always young,
Dew ever shining and twilight grey;
Though hope fall from you and love decay,
Burning in fires of a slanderous tongue.

Come, heart, where hill is heaped upon hill:
For there the mystical brotherhood
Of sun and moon and hollow and wood
And river and stream work out their will;

And God stands winding His lonely horn,
And time and the world are ever in flight;
And love is less kind than the grey twilight,
And hope is less dear than the dew of the morn.

THE END

THE SECRET ROSE
1897

'*As for living, our servants will do that for us.*'—VILLIERS DE L'ISLE-ADAM

'*Helen, when she looked in her mirror, and saw there the wrinkles of old age, wept, and wondered that she had twice been carried away.*'—A quotation from Ovid in one of LEONARDO DA VINCI'S note-books

To the Secret Rose

Far-off, most secret, and inviolate Rose,
Enfold me in my hour of hours; where those
Who sought thee in the Holy Sepulchre,
Or in the wine-vat, dwell beyond the stir
And tumult of defeated dreams; and deep
Among pale eyelids, heavy with the sleep
Men have named beauty. Thy great leaves enfold
The ancient beards, the helms of ruby and gold
Of the crowned Magi; and the king whose eyes
Saw the Pierced Hands and Rood of elder rise
In Druid vapour and make the torches dim;
Till vain frenzy awoke and he died; and him
Who met Fand walking among flaming dew
By a grey shore where the wind never blew,
And lost the world and Emer for a kiss;
And him who drove the gods out of their liss,
And till a hundred morns had flowered red
Feasted, and wept the barrows of his dead;
And the proud dreaming king who flung the crown
And sorrow away, and calling bard and clown
Dwelt among wine-stained wanderers in deep woods;
And him who sold tillage, and house, and goods,
And sought through lands and islands numberless years,
Until he found, with laughter and with tears,
A woman of so shining loveliness
That men threshed corn at midnight by a tress,
A little stolen tress. I, too, await
The hour of thy great wind of love and hate.

When shall the stars be blown about the sky,
Like the sparks blown out of a smithy, and die?
Surely thine hour has come, thy great wind blows,
Far-off, most secret, and inviolate Rose?

THE CRUCIFIXION OF THE OUTCAST

A MAN, WITH THIN BROWN HAIR and a pale face, half ran, half walked, along the road that wound from the south to the town of Sligo. Many called him Cumhal, the son of Cormac, and many called him the Swift Wild Horse; and he was a gleeman, and he wore a short parti-coloured doublet, and had pointed shoes, and a bulging wallet. Also he was of the blood of the Ernaans, and his birthplace was the Field of Gold; but his eating and sleeping places were in the five kingdoms of Eri, and his abiding-place was not upon the ridge of the earth. His eyes strayed from the tower of what was later the Abbey of the White Friars to a row of crosses which stood out against the sky upon a hill a little to the eastward of the town, and he clenched his fist, and shook it at the crosses. He knew they were not empty, for the birds were fluttering about them; and he thought how, as like as not, just such another vagabond as himself had been mounted on one of them; and he muttered: 'If it were hanging or bow-stringing, or stoning or beheading, it would be bad enough. But to have the birds pecking your eyes and the wolves eating your feet! I would that the red wind of the Druids had withered in his cradle the soldier of Dathi who brought the tree of death out of barbarous lands, or that the lightning, when it smote Dathi at the foot of the mountain, had smitten him also, or that his grave had been dug by the green-haired and green-toothed merrows deep at the roots of the deep sea.'

While he spoke, he shivered from head to foot, and the sweat came out upon his face, and he knew not why, for he had looked upon many crosses. He passed over two hills and under the battlemented gate, and then round by a left-hand way to the door of the Abbey. It was studded with great nails, and when he knocked at it he roused the lay brother who was the porter, and of him he asked a place in the guest-house. Then the lay brother took a glowing turf on a shovel, and led the way to a big and naked outhouse strewn with very dirty rushes; and lighted a rush-candle fixed between two of the stones of the wall, and set the glowing turf upon the hearth and gave him two unlighted sods and a wisp of straw, and showed him a blanket hanging from a nail, and a shelf with a loaf of bread and a jug of water, and a tub in a far corner. Then the lay brother left him and went back to his place by the door. And Cumhal the son of Cormac began to blow upon the glowing turf that he might light the two sods and the wisp of straw; but the sods and the straw would not light, for they were damp. So he took off his pointed shoes, and drew the tub out of the corner with the thought of washing the dust of the highway from his feet; but the water was so dirty that he could not see the bottom. He was very hungry, for he had not eaten all that day, so he did not waste much anger upon the tub, but took up the black loaf, and bit into it, and then spat out the bite, for the bread was hard and mouldy. Still he did not give way to his anger, for he had not drunken these many hours; having a hope of heath beer or wine at his day's end, he had left the brooks untasted, to make his supper the more delightful. Now he put the jug to his lips, but he flung it from him straightway, for the water was bitter and ill-smelling. Then he gave the jug a kick, so that it broke against the opposite wall, and he took down the blanket to wrap it about him for the night. But no sooner did he touch it than it was alive with skipping fleas. At this, beside himself with anger, he rushed to the door of the guest-house, but the lay brother, being well accustomed to such outcries, had locked it on the outside; so he emptied the tub and began to beat the door with it, till the lay brother came to the door and asked what ailed him, and why he woke him out of sleep. 'What ails me!' shouted Cumhal; 'are not the sods as wet as the sands of the Three Rosses? and are not the fleas in the blanket as many as the waves of the sea and as lively? and is not the bread as hard as the heart of a lay brother who has forgotten God? and is not the water in the jug as bitter and as ill-smelling as his soul? and is not the foot-water the colour that shall be upon him when he has been charred in the Undying Fires?' The lay brother saw that the lock was fast, and went back to his niche, for he was too sleepy to talk with comfort. And Cumhal went on beating at the door, and presently he heard the lay brother's foot once more, and cried out at him, 'O cowardly and tyrannous race of monks, persecutors of the bard and the gleeman, haters of life and joy! O race that does not draw the sword and tell the truth! O race that melts the bones of the people with cowardice and with deceit!'

'Gleeman,' said the lay brother, 'I also make rhymes; I make many while I sit in my niche by the door, and I sorrow to hear the bards railing upon the monks. Brother, I would sleep, and therefore I make known to you that it is the head of the monastery, our gracious abbot, who orders all things concerning the lodging of travellers.'

'You may sleep,' said Cumhal. 'I will sing a bard's curse on the abbot.' And he set the tub upside-down under the window, and stood upon it, and began to sing in a very loud voice. The singing awoke the abbot, so that he sat up in bed and blew a silver whistle until the lay brother came to him. 'I cannot get a wink of sleep with that noise,' said the abbot. 'What is happening?'

'It is a gleeman,' said the lay brother, 'who complains of the sods, of the bread, of the water in the jug, of the foot-water, and of the blanket. And now he is singing a bard's curse upon you, O brother abbot, and upon your father and your mother, and your grandfather and your grandmother, and upon all your relations.'

'Is he cursing in rhyme?'

'He is cursing in rhyme, and with two assonances in every line of his curse.'

The abbot pulled his night-cap off and crumpled it in his hands, and the circular grey patch of hair in the middle of his bald head looked like the cairn upon Knocknarea, for in Connacht they had not yet abandoned the ancient tonsure. 'Unless we do somewhat,' he said, 'he will teach his curses to the children in the street, and the girls spinning at the doors, and to the robbers upon Ben Bulben.'

'Shall I go, then,' said the other, 'and give him dry sods, a fresh loaf, clean water in a jug, clean foot-water, and a new blanket, and make him swear by the blessed Saint Benignus, and by the sun and moon, that no bond be lacking, not to tell his rhymes to the children in the street, and the girls spinning at the doors, and the robbers upon Ben Bulben?'

'Neither our Blessed Patron nor the sun and moon would avail at all,' said the abbot; 'for to-morrow or the next day the mood to curse would come upon him, or a pride in those rhymes would move him, and he would teach his lines to the children, and the girls, and the robbers. Or else he would tell another of his craft how he fared in the guest-house, and he in his turn would begin to curse, and my name would wither. For learn, there is no steadfastness of purpose upon the roads, but only under roofs and between four walls. Therefore I bid you go and awaken Brother Kevin, Brother Dove, Brother Little Wolf, Brother Bald Patrick, Brother Bald Brandon, Brother James, and Brother Peter. And they shall take the man, and bind him with ropes, and dip him in the river that he shall cease to sing. And in the morning, lest this but make him curse the louder, we will crucify him.'

'The crosses are all full,' said the lay brother.

'Then we must make another cross. If we do not make an end of him another will, for who can eat and sleep in peace while men like him are going about the world? We would stand shamed indeed before blessed Saint Benignus, and sour would be his face when he comes to judge us at the Last Day, were we to spare an enemy of his when we had him under our thumb! Brother, there is not one of these bards and gleemen who has not scattered his bastards through the five kingdoms, and if they slit a purse or a throat, and it is always one or the other, it never comes into their heads to confess and do penance. Can you name one that is not heathen in his heart, always longing after the Son of Lir, and Aengus, and Bridget, and the Dagda, and Dana the Mother, and all the false gods of the old days; always making poems in praise of those kings and queens of the demons, Finvaragh, whose home is under Cruachmaa, and Red Aodh of Cnoc-na-Sidha, and Cliona of the Wave, and Aoibheal of the Grey Rock, and him they call Donn of the Vats of the Sea; and railing against God and Christ and the blessed Saints?' While he was speaking he crossed himself, and when he had finished he drew the night-cap over his ears to shut out the noise, and closed his eyes and composed himself to sleep.

The lay brother found Brother Kevin, Brother Dove, Brother Little Wolf, Brother Bald Patrick, Brother Bald Brandon, Brother James, and Brother Peter sitting up in bed, and he made them get up. Then they bound Cumhal, and they dragged him to the river, and they dipped him in it at the place which was afterwards called Buckley's Ford.

'Gleeman,' said the lay brother, as they led him back to the guest-house, 'why do you ever use the wit which God has given you to make blasphemous and immoral tales and verses? For such is the way of your craft. I have, indeed, many such tales and verses wellnigh by rote, and so I know that I speak true! And why do you praise with rhyme those demons, Finvaragh, Red

Aodh, Cliona, Aoibheal and Donn? I, too, am a man of great wit and learning, but I ever glorify our gracious abbot, and Benignus our Patron, and the princes of the province. My soul is decent and orderly, but yours is like the wind among the salley gardens. I said what I could for you, being also a man of many thoughts, but who could help such a one as you?'

'Friend,' answered the gleeman, 'my soul is indeed like the wind, and it blows me to and fro, and up and down, and puts many things into my mind and out of my mind, and therefore am I called the Swift Wild Horse.' And he spoke no more that night, for his teeth were chattering with the cold.

The abbot and the monks came to him in the morning, and bade him get ready to be crucified, and led him out of the guest-house. And while he still stood upon the step a flock of great grass-barnacles passed high above him with clanking cries. He lifted his arms to them and said, 'O great grass-barnacles, tarry a little, and mayhap my soul will travel with you to the waste places of the shore and to the ungovernable sea!' At the gate a crowd of beggars gathered about them, being come there to beg from any traveller or pilgrim who might have spent the night in the guest-house. The abbot and the monks led the gleeman to a place in the woods at some distance, where many straight young trees were growing, and they made him cut one down and fashion it to the right length, while the beggars stood round them in a ring, talking and gesticulating. The abbot then bade him cut off another and shorter piece of wood, and nail it upon the first. So there was his cross for him; and they put it upon his shoulder, for his crucifixion was to be on the top of the hill where the others were. A half-mile on the way he asked them to stop and see him juggle for them; for he knew, he said, all the tricks of Aengus the Subtle-hearted. The old monks were for pressing on, but the young monks would see him: so he did many wonders for them, even to the drawing of live frogs out of his ears. But after a while they turned on him, and said his tricks were dull and a little unholy, and set the cross on his shoulders again. Another half-mile on the way and he asked them to stop and hear him jest for them, for he knew, he said, all the jests of Conan the Bald, upon whose back a sheep's wool grew. And the young monks, when they had heard his merry tales, again bade him take up his cross, for it ill became them to listen to such follies. Another half-mile on the way, he asked them to stop and hear him sing the story of White-breasted Deirdre, and how she endured many sorrows, and how the sons of Usna died to serve her. And the young monks were mad to hear him, but when he had ended they grew angry, and beat him for waking forgotten longings in their hearts. So they set the cross upon his back and hurried him to the hill.

When he was come to the top, they took the cross from him, and began to dig a hole for it to stand in, while the beggars gathered round, and talked among themselves. 'I ask a favour before I die,' says Cumhal.

'We will grant you no more delays,' says the abbot.

'I ask no more delays, for I have drawn the sword, and told the truth, and lived my dream, and am content.'

'Would you, then, confess?'

'By sun and moon, not I; I ask but to be let eat the food I carry in my wallet. I carry food in my wallet whenever I go upon a journey, but I do not taste of it unless I am wellnigh starved. I have not eaten now these two days.'

'You may eat, then,' says the abbot, and he turned to help the monks dig the hole.

The gleeman took a loaf and some strips of cold fried bacon out of his wallet and laid them upon the ground. 'I will give a tithe to the poor,' says he, and he cut a tenth part from the loaf and the bacon. 'Who among you is the poorest?' And thereupon was a great clamour, for the beggars began the history of their sorrows and their poverty, and their yellow faces swayed like Gabhra Lough when the floods have filled it with water from the bogs.

He listened for a little, and, says he, 'I am myself the poorest, for I have travelled the bare road, and by the edges of the sea; and the tattered doublet of parti-coloured cloth upon my back and the torn pointed shoes upon my feet have ever irked me, because of the towered city full of noble raiment which was in my heart. And I have been the more alone upon the roads and by the sea because I heard in my heart the rustling of the rose-bordered dress of her who is more subtle than Aengus the Subtle-hearted, and more full of the beauty of laughter than Conan the Bald, and more full of the wisdom of tears than White-breasted Deirdre, and more lovely than a bursting dawn to them that are lost in the darkness. Therefore, I award the tithe to myself; but yet, because I am done with all things, I give it unto you.'

So he flung the bread and the strips of bacon among the beggars, and they fought with many cries until the last scrap was eaten. But meanwhile the monks nailed the gleeman to his cross, and set it upright in the hole, and shovelled the earth into the hole, and trampled it level and hard. So then they went away, but the beggars stayed on, sitting round the cross. But when the sun was sinking, they also got up to go, for the air was getting chilly. And as soon as they had gone a little way, the wolves, who had been showing themselves on the edge of a neighbouring coppice, came nearer, and the birds wheeled closer and closer. 'Stay, outcasts, yet a little while,' the crucified one called in a weak voice to the beggars, 'and keep the beasts and the birds from me.' But the beggars were angry because he had called them outcasts, so they threw stones and mud at him, and one that had a child held it up before his eyes and said that he was its father, and cursed him, and thereupon they left him. Then the wolves gathered at the foot of the cross, and the birds flew lower and lower. And presently the birds lighted all at once upon his head and arms and shoulders, and began to peck at him, and the wolves began to eat his feet. 'Outcasts,' he moaned, have you all turned against the outcast?'

OUT OF THE ROSE

ONE winter evening an old knight in rusted chain armour rode slowly along the woody southern slope of Ben Bulben, watching the sun go down in crimson clouds over the sea. His horse was tired, as after a long journey, and he had upon his helmet the crest of no neighbouring lord or king, but a small rose made of rubies that glimmered every moment to a deeper crimson. His white hair fell in thin curls upon his shoulders, and its disorder added to the melancholy of his face, which was the face of one of those who have come but seldom into the world, and always for its trouble, the dreamers who must do what they dream, the doers who must dream what they do.

After gazing a while towards the sun, he let the reins fall upon the neck of his horse, and, stretching out both arms towards the west, he said, 'O Divine Rose of Intellectual Flame, let the gates of thy peace be opened to me at last!' And suddenly a loud squealing began in the woods some hundreds of yards farther up the mountain-side. He stopped his horse to listen, and heard behind him a sound of feet and of voices. 'They are beating them to make them go into the narrow path by the gorge,' said some one, and in another moment a dozen peasants armed with short spears had come up with the knight, and stood a little apart from him, their blue caps in their hands.

'Where do you go with the spears?' he asked; and

one who seemed the leader answered: 'A troop of wood-thieves came down from the hills a while ago and carried off the pigs belonging to an old man who lives by Glen-Car Lough, and we turned out to go after them. Now that we know they are four times more than we are, we follow to find the way they have taken; and will presently tell our story to De Courcey, and if he will not help us, to Fitzgerald; for De Courcey and Fitzgerald have lately made a peace, and we do not know to whom we belong.'

'But by that time,' said the knight, 'the pigs will have been eaten.'

'A dozen men cannot do more, and it was not reasonable that the whole valley should turn out and risk their lives for two, or for two dozen pigs.'

'Can you tell me,' said the knight, 'if the old man to whom the pigs belong is pious and true of heart?'

'He is as true as another and more pious than any, for he says a prayer to a saint every morning before his breakfast.'

'Then it were well to fight in his cause,' said the knight, 'and if you will fight against the wood-thieves I will take the main brunt of the battle, and you know well that a man in armour is worth many like these wood-thieves, clad in wool and leather.'

And the leader turned to his fellows and asked if they would take the chance; but they seemed anxious to get back to their cabins.

'Are the wood-thieves treacherous and impious?'

'They are treacherous in all their dealings,' said a peasant, 'and no man has known them to pray.'

'Then,' said the knight, 'I will give five crowns for the head of every wood-thief killed by us in the fighting'; and he bid the leader show the way, and they all went on together. After a time they came to where a beaten track wound into the woods, and, taking this, they doubled back upon their previous course, and began to ascend the wooded slope of the mountain. In a little while the path grew very straight and steep, and the knight was forced to dismount and leave his horse tied to a tree-stem. They knew they were on the right track, for they could see the marks of pointed shoes in the soft clay and mingled with them the cloven footprints of the pigs. Presently the path became still more abrupt, and they knew by the ending of the cloven footprints that the thieves were carrying the pigs. Now and then a long mark in the clay showed that a pig had slipped down, and been dragged along for a little way. They had journeyed thus for about twenty minutes, when a confused sound of voices told them that they were coming up with the thieves. And then the voices ceased, and they understood that they had been overheard in their turn. They pressed on rapidly and cautiously, and in about five minutes one of them caught sight of a leather jerkin half hidden by a hazel bush. An arrow struck the knight's chain armour, but glanced off, and then a flight of arrows swept over their heads. They ran and climbed, and climbed and ran towards the thieves, who were now all visible standing up among the bushes with their still quivering bows in their hands: for they had only their spears and they must at once come hand to hand. The knight was in the front and struck down first one and then another of the wood-thieves. The peasants shouted, and, pressing on, drove the wood-thieves before them until they came out on the flat top of the mountain, and there they saw the two pigs quietly grubbing in the short grass, so they ran about them in a circle, and began to move back again towards the narrow path: the old knight coming now the last of all, and striking down thief after thief. The peasants had got no very serious hurts among them, for he had drawn the brunt of the battle upon himself; as could well be seen from the bloody rents in his armour; and when they came to the entrance of the narrow path he told them to drive the pigs down into the valley, while he stood there to guard the way behind them. So in a moment he was alone, and, being weak with loss of blood, might have been ended there and then by the wood-thieves had fear not made them be gone out of sight in a great hurry.

An hour passed, and they did not return; and now the knight could stand on guard no longer, but had to lie down upon the grass. A half-hour more went by, and then a young lad with what appeared to be a number of cock's feathers stuck round his hat came out of the path behind him, and began to move about among the dead thieves, cutting their heads off. Then he laid the heads in a heap before the knight, and said, 'O great knight, I have been bid come and ask you for the crowns you promised for the heads: five crowns a head. They told me to tell you that they have prayed to God and His Mother to give you a long life, but that they are poor peasants, and that they would have the money

before you die. They told me this over and over for
fear I might forget it, and promised to beat me if I did.'

The knight raised himself upon his elbow, and, open-
ing a bag that hung to his belt, counted out the five
crowns for each head. There were thirty heads in all.

'O great knight,' said the lad, 'they have also bid me
take all care of you, and light a fire, and put this oint-
ment upon your wounds.' And he gathered sticks and
leaves together, and, flashing his flint and steel under a
mass of dry leaves, made a very good blaze. Then,
drawing off the coat of mail, he began to anoint the
wounds: but he did it clumsily, like one who does by
rote what he has been told. The knight motioned him
to stop, and said, 'You seem a good lad.'

'I would ask something of you for myself.'

'There are still a few crowns,' said the knight; 'shall
I give them to you?'

'O no,' said the lad. 'They would be no good to me.
There is only one thing that I care about doing, and I
have no need of money to do it. I go from village to
village and from hill to hill, and whenever I come across
a good cock I steal him and take him into the woods,
and I keep him there under a basket until I get another
good cock, and then I set them to fight. The people say
I am an innocent, and do not do me any harm, and
never ask me to do any work but go a message now and
then. It is because I am an innocent that they send me
to get the crowns: any one else would steal them; and
they dare not come back themselves, for now that you
are not with them they are afraid of the wood-thieves.
Did you ever hear how, when the wood-thieves are

christened, the wolves are made their godfathers, and their right arms are not christened at all?'

'If you will not take these crowns, my good lad, I have nothing for you, I fear, unless you would have that old coat of mail which I shall soon need no more.'

'There was something I wanted: yes, I remember now,' said the lad. 'I want you to tell me why you fought like the champions and giants in the stories and for so little a thing. Are you indeed a man like us? Are you not rather an old wizard who lives among these hills, and will not a wind arise presently and crumble you into dust?'

'I will tell you of myself,' replied the knight, 'for now that I am the last of the fellowship, I may tell all and witness for God. Look at the Rose of Rubies on my helmet, and see the symbol of my life and of my hope.' And then he told the lad this story, but with always more frequent pauses; and, while he told it, the lad stuck the cock's feathers in the earth in front of him, and moved them about as though he made them actors in the play.

'I live in a land far from this, and was one of the Knights of Saint John,' said the old man; 'but I was one of those in the Order who always longed for more arduous labours in the service of the truth that can only be understood within the heart. At last there came to us a knight of Palestine, to whom the truth of truths had been revealed by God Himself. He had seen a great Rose of Fire, and a Voice out of the Rose had told him how men would turn from the light of their own hearts, and bow down before outer order and outer fixity, and that then the light would cease, and none escape the curse except the foolish good man who could not think, and the passionate wicked man who would not. Already, the Voice told him, the light of the heart was shining with less lustre, and as it paled, an infection was touching the world with corruption; and none of those who had seen clearly the truth could enter into the Kingdom of God, which is in the Heart of the Rose, if they stayed on willingly in the corrupted world; and so they must prove their anger against the Powers of Corruption by dying in the service of the Rose. While the knight of Palestine was telling us these things the air was filled with fragrance of the Rose. By this we knew that it was the very Voice of God which spoke to us by the knight, and we told him to direct us in all things, and teach us how to obey the Voice. So he bound us with an oath, and gave us signs and words whereby we might know each other even after many years, and he appointed places of meeting, and he sent us out in troops into the world to seek good causes, and die in doing battle for them. At first we thought to die more readily by fasting to death in honour of some saint; but this he told us was evil, for we did it for the sake of death, and thus took out of the hands of God the choice of the time and manner of our death, and by so doing made His power the less. We must choose our service for its excellence, and for this alone, and leave it to God to reward us at His own time and in His own manner. And after this he compelled us to eat always two at a table and watch each other lest we fasted unduly. And the years passed, and one by one my fellows died in the Holy Land, or in warring upon the evil princes of the earth, or in clearing the roads of robbers; and among them died the knight of Palestine, and at last I was alone. I fought in every cause where the few contended against the many, and my hair grew white, and a terrible fear lest I had fallen under the displeasure of God came upon me. But, hearing at last how this western isle was fuller of wars and rapine than any other land, I came hither, and I have found the thing I sought, and, behold! I am filled with a great joy.'

Thereat he began to sing in Latin, and, while he sang, his voice faltered and grew faint. Then his eyes closed, and his lips fell apart, and the lad knew he was dead. 'He has told me a good tale,' said the lad, 'for there was fighting in it, but I did not understand much of it, and it is hard to remember so long a story.'

And, taking the knight's sword, he began to dig a grave in the soft clay. He dug hard, and he had almost done his work when a cock crowed in the valley below. 'Ah,' he said, 'I must have that bird'; and he ran down the narrow path to the valley.

THE WISDOM OF THE KING

THE High Queen of Ireland had died in childbirth, and her child was put to nurse with a woman who lived in a little house within the border of the wood. One night the woman sat rocking the cradle, and meditating upon the beauty of the child, and praying that the gods might grant him wisdom equal to his beauty. There came a knock at the door, and she got up wondering, for the nearest neighbours were in the High King's house a mile away and the night was now late. 'Who is knocking?' she cried, and a thin voice answered, 'Open! for I am a crone of the grey hawk, and I come from the darkness of the great wood.' In terror she drew back the bolt, and a grey-clad woman, of a great age, and of a height more than human, came in and stood by the head of the cradle. The nurse shrank back against the wall, unable to take her eyes from the woman, for she saw by the gleaming of the firelight that the feathers of the grey hawk were upon her head instead of hair. 'Open!' cried another voice, 'for I am a crone of the grey hawk, and I watch over his nest in the darkness of the great wood.' The nurse opened the door again, though her fingers could scarce hold the bolts for trembling, and another grey woman, not less old than the other, and with like feathers instead of hair, came in and stood by the first. In a little, came a third grey woman, and after her a fourth, and then another and another and another, until the hut was full of their immense bodies. They stood silent for a long time, but at last one muttered in a low thin voice: 'Sisters, I knew him far away·by the redness of his heart under his silver skin'; and then another spoke: 'Sisters, I knew him because his heart fluttered like a bird under a net of silver cords'; and then another took up the word: 'Sisters, I knew him because his heart sang like a bird that is happy in a silver cage.' And after that they sang together, those who were nearest rocking the cradle with long wrinkled fingers; and their voices were now tender and caressing, now like the wind blowing in the great wood, and this was their song:—

> Out of sight is out of mind:
> Long have man and woman-kind,
> Heavy of will and light of mood,
> Taken away our wheaten food,
> Taken away our Altar-stone;
> Hail and rain and thunder alone,
> And red hearts we turn to grey,
> Are true till Time gutter away.

When the song had died out, the crone who had first spoken, said: 'We have nothing more to do but to mix a drop of our blood into his blood.' And she scratched her arm with the sharp point of a spindle, which she had made the nurse bring to her, and let a drop of blood, grey as the mist, fall upon the lips of the child; and passed out into the darkness.

When the crones were gone, the nurse came to her courage again, and hurried to the High King's house, and cried out in the midst of the assembly hall that the Sidhe had bent over the child that night; and the king and his poets and men of law went with her to the hut and gathered about the cradle, and were as noisy as magpies, and the child sat up and looked at them.

Two years passed over, and the king died; and the poets and the men of law ruled in the name of the child, but looked to see him become the master himself before long, for no one had seen so wise a child, and everything had been well but for a miracle that began to trouble all men; and all women, who, indeed, talked of it without ceasing. The feathers of the grey hawk had begun to grow in the child's hair, and though his nurse cut them continually, in but a little while they would be more numerous than ever. This had not been a matter of great importance, for miracles were a little thing in those days, but for an ancient law of Ireland that none who had any blemish of body could sit upon the throne; and as a grey hawk is a brute thing of the air, it was not possible to think of one in whose hair its feathers grew as other than marred and blasted; nor could the people separate from their admiration of the wisdom that grew in him a horror as at one of unhuman blood. Yet all were resolved that he should reign, for they had suffered much from foolish kings and their own disorders; and no one had any other fear but that his great wisdom might bid him obey the law, and call some other to reign in his stead.

When the child was seven years old the poets and the men of law were called together by the chief poet, and all these matters weighed and considered. The child had already seen that those about him had hair only, and, though they had told him that they too had had feathers but had lost them because of a sin committed by their forefathers, they knew that he would learn the truth when he began to wander into the country round about. After much consideration they made a new law commanding every one upon pain of death to mingle artificially the feathers of the grey hawk into his hair; and they sent men with nets and slings and bows into the countries round about to gather a sufficiency of feathers. They decreed also that any who told the truth to the child should be put to death.

The years passed, and the child grew from childhood into boyhood and from boyhood into manhood, and became busy with strange and subtle thought, distinctions between things long held the same, resemblance of things long held different. Multitudes came from other lands to see him and to question him, but there were guards set at the frontiers, who compelled all to wear the feathers of the grey hawk in their hair. While they listened to him his words seemed to make all darkness light and filled their hearts like music; but when they returned to their own lands his words seemed far off, and what they could remember too strange and subtle to help them in their lives. A number indeed did live differently afterwards, but their new life was less excellent than the old: some among them had long served a good cause, but when they heard him praise it, they returned to their own lands to find what they had loved less lovable, for he had taught them how little divides the false and true; others, again, who had served no cause, but had sought in peace the welfare of their own households, found their bones softer and less ready for toil, for he had shown them greater purposes; and numbers of the young, when they had heard him upon all these things, remembered certain strange words that made ordinary joys nothing, and sought impossible joys and grew unhappy.

Among those who came to look at him and to listen to him was the daughter of a little king who lived a great way off; and when he saw her he loved, for she was beautiful, with a beauty unlike that of other women; but her heart was like that of other women, and when she thought of the mystery of the hawk feathers she was afraid. Overwhelmed with his greatness, she half accepted, and yet half refused his love, and day by day the king gave her gifts the merchants had carried from India or maybe from China itself; and still she was ever between a smile and a frown; between yielding and withholding. He laid all his wisdom at her feet, and told a multitude of things that even the Sidhe have forgotten, and he thought she understood because her beauty was like wisdom.

There was a tall young man in the house who had yellow hair, and was skilled in wrestling; and one day the king heard his voice among the salley bushes. 'My dear,' it said, 'I hate them for making you weave these dingy feathers into your beautiful hair, and all that the bird of prey upon the throne may sleep easy o' nights'; and then the low, musical voice he loved answered: 'My hair is not beautiful like yours; and now that I have plucked the feathers out of your hair I will put my hands through it, thus, and thus, and thus; for it does not make me afraid.' Then the king remembered many things that he had forgotten without understanding them, chance words of his poets and his men of law, doubts that he had reasoned away; and he called to the lovers in a trembling voice. They came from among the salley bushes and threw themselves at his feet and prayed for pardon. He stooped down and plucked the feathers out of the hair of the woman and turned away without a word. He went to the hall of assembly, and having gathered his poets and his men of law about him, stood upon the dais and spoke in a loud, clear voice: 'Men of law, why did you make me sin against the laws? Men of verse, why did you make me sin against the secrecy of wisdom?—for law was made by man for the welfare of man, but wisdom the gods have made, and no man shall live by its light, for it and the hail and the rain and the thunder follow a way that is deadly to mortal things. Men of law and men of verse, live according to your kind, and call Eochaid of the Hasty Mind to reign over you, for I set out to find my kindred.' He then came down among them, and drew out of the hair of first one and then another the feathers of the grey hawk, and, having scattered them over the rushes upon the floor, passed out, and none dared to follow him, for his eyes gleamed like the eyes of the birds of prey; and no man saw him again or heard his voice.

The Heart of the Spring

THE HEART OF THE SPRING

A very old man, whose face was almost as fleshless as the foot of a bird, sat meditating upon the rocky shore of the flat and hazel-covered isle which fills the widest part of Lough Gill. A russet-faced boy of seventeen years sat by his side, watching the swallows dipping for flies in the still water. The old man was dressed in threadbare blue velvet and the boy wore a frieze coat and had a rosary about his neck. Behind the two, and half hidden by trees, was a little monastery. It had been burned down a long while before by sacrilegious men of the Queen's party, but had been roofed anew with rushes by the boy, that the old man might find shelter in his last days. He had not set his spade, however, into the garden about it, and the lilies and the roses of the monks had spread out until their confused luxuriance met and mingled with the narrowing circle of the fern. Beyond the lilies and the roses the ferns were so deep that a child walking among them would be hidden from sight, even though he stood upon his toes; and beyond the fern rose many hazels and small oak-trees.

'Master,' said the boy, 'this long fasting, and the labour of beckoning after nightfall to the beings who dwell in the waters and among the hazels and oak-trees, is too much for your strength. Rest from all this labour for a little, for your hand this day seemed more heavy upon my shoulder and your feet less steady than I have known them. Men say that you are older than the eagles, and yet you will not seek the rest that belongs to age.' He spoke eagerly, as though his heart were in the words; and the old man answered slowly and deliberately, as though his heart were in distant days and events.

'I will tell you why I have not been able to rest,' he said. 'It is right that you should know, for you have served me faithfully these five years, and even with affection, taking away thereby a little of the doom of loneliness which always falls upon the wise. Now, too, that the end of my labour and the triumph of my hopes is at hand, it is more needful for you to have this knowledge.'

'Master, do not think that I would question you. It is my life to keep the fire alight, and the thatch close that the rain may not come in, and strong, that the wind may not blow it among the trees; and to take down the heavy books from the shelves, and to possess an incurious and reverent heart. God has made out of His abundance a separate wisdom for everything which lives, and to do these things is my wisdom.'

'You are afraid,' said the old man, and his eyes shone with a momentary anger.

'Sometimes at night,' said the boy, 'when you are reading, with a stick of mountain ash in your hand, I look out of the door and see, now a great grey man driving swine among the hazels, and now many little people in red caps who come out of the lake driving little white cows before them. I do not fear these little people so much as the grey man; for, when they come near the house, they milk the cows, and they drink the frothing milk, and begin to dance; and I know there is good in the heart that loves dancing; but I fear them for all that. And I fear the tall white-armed ladies who come out of the air, and move slowly hither and thither, crowning themselves with the roses or with the lilies, and shaking about them their living hair, which moves, for so I have heard them tell the little people, with the motion of their thoughts, now spreading out and now gathering close to their heads. They have mild, beautiful faces, but I am afraid of the Sidhe, and afraid of the art which draws them about us.'

'Why,' said the old man, 'do you fear the ancient gods who made the spears of your father's fathers to be stout in battle, and the little people who came at night from the depth of the lakes and sang among the crickets upon their hearths? And in our evil day they still watch over the loveliness of the earth. But I must tell you why I have fasted and laboured when others would sink into the sleep of age, for without your help once more I shall have fasted and laboured to no good end. When you have done for me this last thing, you may go and build your cottage and till your fields, and take some girl to wife, and forget the ancient gods, for I shall leave behind me in this little house money to make strong the roof-tree of your cottage and to keep cellar and larder full. I have sought through all my life to find the secret of life. I was not happy in my youth, for I knew that it would pass; and I was not happy in my manhood, for I knew that age was coming; and so I gave myself, in youth and manhood and age, to the search for the Great Secret. I longed for a life whose abundance would fill centuries, I scorned the life of fourscore winters. I would be—no, I *will* be!—like the ancient gods of the land.

I read in my youth, in a Hebrew manuscript I found in a Spanish monastery, that there is a moment after the Sun has entered the Ram and before he has passed the Lion, which trembles with the Song of the Immortal Powers, and that whosoever finds this moment and listens to the Song shall become like the Immortal Powers themselves; I came back to Ireland and asked the faery men, and the cow-doctors, if they knew when this moment was; but though all had heard of it, there was none could find the moment upon the hour-glass. So I gave myself to magic, and spent my life in fasting and in labour that I might bring the gods and the Men of Faery to my side; and now at last one of the Men of Faery has told me that the moment is at hand. One, who wore a red cap and whose lips were white with the froth of the new milk, whispered it into my ear. To-morrow, a little before the close of the first hour after dawn, I shall find the moment, and then I will go away to a southern land and build myself a palace of white marble amid orange-trees, and gather the brave and the beautiful about me, and enter into the eternal kingdom of my youth. But, that I may hear the whole Song, I was told by the little fellow with the froth of the new milk on his lips that you must bring great masses of green boughs and pile them about the door and the window of my room; and you must put fresh green rushes upon the floor, and cover the table and the rushes with the roses and the lilies of the monks. You must do this to-night, and in the morning at the end of the first hour after dawn, you must come and find me.'

'Will you be quite young then?' said the boy.

The Heart of the Spring

'I will be as young then as you are, but now I am still old and tired, and you must help me to my chair and to my books.'

When the boy had left the wizard in his room, and had lighted the lamp which, by some contrivance, gave forth a sweet odour as of strange flowers, he went into the wood and began cutting green boughs from the hazels, and great bundles of rushes from the western border of the isle, where the small rocks gave place to gently sloping sand and clay. It was nightfall before he had cut enough for his purpose, and wellnigh midnight before he had carried the last bundle to its place, and gone back for the roses and the lilies. It was one of those warm, beautiful nights when everything seems carved of precious stones. Sleuth Wood away to the south looked as though cut out of green beryl, and the waters that mirrored it shone like pale opal. The roses he was gathering were like glowing rubies, and the lilies had the dull lustre of pearl. Everything had taken upon itself the look of something imperishable, except a glow-worm, whose faint flame burnt on steadily among the shadows, moving slowly hither and thither, the only thing that seemed alive, the only thing that seemed perishable as mortal hope. The boy gathered a great armful of roses and lilies, and thrusting the glow-worm among their pearl and ruby, carried them into the room, where the old man sat in a half-slumber. He laid armful after armful upon the floor and above the table, and then, gently closing the door, threw himself upon his bed of rushes, to dream of a peaceful manhood with a desirable wife and laughing children. At dawn he got up, and went down to the edge of the lake, taking the hour-glass with him. He put some bread and wine into the boat, that his master might not lack food at the outset of his journey, and then sat down to wait the close of the first hour after dawn. Gradually the birds began to sing, and when the last grains of sand were falling, everything suddenly seemed to overflow with their music. It was the most beautiful and living moment of the year; one could listen to the spring's heart beating in it. He got up and went to find his master. The green boughs filled the door, and he had to make a way through them. When he entered the room the sunlight was falling in flickering circles on floor and walls and table, and everything was full of soft green shadows. But the old man sat clasping a mass of roses and lilies in his arms, and with his head sunk upon his breast. On the table, at his left hand, was a leather wallet full of gold and silver pieces, as for a journey, and at his right hand was a long staff. The boy touched him and he did not move. He lifted the hands, but they were quite cold, and they fell heavily.

'It were better for him,' said the lad, 'to have said his prayers and kissed his beads!' He looked at the threadbare blue velvet, and he saw it was covered with the pollen of the flowers, and while he was looking at it a thrush, who had alighted among the boughs that were piled against the window, began to sing.

THE CURSE OF THE FIRES AND OF
THE SHADOWS

ONE summer night, when there was peace, a score of Puritan troopers, under the pious Sir Frederick Hamilton, broke through the door of the Abbey of the White Friars at Sligo. As the door fell with a crash they saw a little knot of friars gathered about the altar, their white habits glimmering in the steady light of the holy candles. All the monks were kneeling except the abbot, who stood upon the altar steps with a great brass crucifix in his hand. 'Shoot them!' cried Sir Frederick Hamilton, but nobody stirred, for all were new converts, and feared the candles and the crucifix. For a little while all were silent, and then five troopers, who were the bodyguard of Sir Frederick Hamilton, lifted their muskets, and shot down five of the friars. The noise and the smoke drove away the mystery of the pale altar lights, and the other troopers took courage and began to strike. In a moment the friars lay about the altar steps, their white habits stained with blood. 'Set fire to the house!' cried Sir Frederick Hamilton, and a trooper carried In a heap of dry straw, and piled it against the western wall, but did not light it, because he was still afraid of crucifix and of candles. Seeing this, the five troopers who were Sir Frederick Hamilton's bodyguard went up to the altar, and taking each a holy candle set the straw in a blaze. The red tongues of fire rushed up towards the roof, and crept along the floor, setting in a blaze the seats and benches, and making the shadows of the troopers dance among the corbels and the memorial tablets.

For a time the altar stood safe and apart in the midst of its white light; the eyes of the troopers turned upon it. The abbot whom they had thought dead had risen to his feet and now stood before it with the crucifix lifted in both hands high above his head. Suddenly he cried with a loud voice, 'Woe unto all who have struck down those who have lived in the Light of the Lord, for they shall wander among shadows and among fires!' And having so cried he fell on his face dead, and the brass crucifix rolled down the steps of the altar. The smoke had now grown very thick, so that it drove the troopers out into the open air. Before them were burning houses. Behind them shone the Abbey windows filled with saints and martyrs, awakened, as from a sacred trance, into an angry and animated life. The eyes of the troopers were dazzled, and for a while could see nothing but the flaming faces of saints and martyrs. Presently, however, they saw a man covered with dust who came running towards them. 'Two messengers,' he cried, 'have been sent by the defeated Irish to raise against you the whole country about Manor Hamilton, and if you do not stop them you will be overpowered in the woods before you reach home again! They ride north-east between Ben Bulben and Cashel-na-Gael.'

Sir Frederick Hamilton called to him the five troopers who had first fired upon the friars and said, 'Mount quickly, and ride through the woods towards the mountain, and get before these men, and kill them.'

In a moment the troopers were gone, and before

many moments they had splashed across the river at what is now called Buckley's Ford, and plunged into the woods. They followed a beaten track that wound along the northern bank of the river. The boughs of the birch and mountain ash mingled above, and hid the cloudy moonlight, leaving the pathway in almost complete darkness. They rode at a rapid trot, now chatting together, now watching some stray weasel or rabbit scuttling away in the darkness. Gradually, as the gloom and silence of the woods oppressed them, they drew closer together, and began to talk rapidly; they were old comrades and knew each other's lives. One was married, and told how glad his wife would be to see him return safe from this harebrained expedition against the White Friars, and to hear how fortune had made amends for rashness. The oldest of the five, whose wife was dead, spoke of a flagon of wine which awaited him upon an upper shelf; while a third, who was the youngest, had a sweetheart watching for his return, and he rode a little way before the others, not talking at all.

Suddenly the young man stopped, and they saw that his horse was trembling. 'I saw something,' he said, 'and yet it may have been but a shadow. It looked like a great worm with a silver crown upon his head.' One of the five put his hand up to his forehead as if about to cross himself, but remembering that he had changed his religion he put it down, and said, 'I am certain it was but a shadow, for there are a great many about us, and of very strange kinds.' Then they rode on in silence. It had been raining in the earlier part of the day, and the drops fell from the branches, wetting their hair and their shoulders. In a little they began to talk again. They had been in many battles against many a rebel together, and now told each other over again the story of their wounds, and half forgot the terrible solitude of the woods.

Suddenly the first two horses neighed, and then stood still, and would go no farther. Before them was a glint of water, and they knew by the rushing sound that it was a river. They dismounted, and after much tugging and coaxing brought the horses to the riverside. In the midst of the water stood a tall old woman with grey hair flowing over a grey dress. She stood up to her knees in the water, and stooped from time to time as though washing. Presently they could see that she was washing something that half floated. The moon cast a flickering light upon it, and they saw that it was the dead body of a man, and, while they were looking at it, the eddy of the river turned the face towards them, and each of the five troopers recognised at the same moment his own face. While they stood dumb and motionless with horror, the woman began to speak, saying slowly and loudly, 'Did you see my son? He has upon his head a crown of silver.' Then the oldest of the troopers, he who had been most often wounded, drew his sword and said, 'I have fought for the truth of my God, and need not fear the shadows of Satan,' and with that rushed into the water. In a moment he returned. The woman had vanished, and though he had thrust his sword into air and water he had found nothing.

The five troopers remounted, and set their horses at

the ford, but all to no purpose. They tried again and again, and went plunging hither and thither, the horses foaming and rearing. 'Let us,' said the old trooper, 'ride back a little into the wood, and strike the river higher up.' They rode in under the boughs, the ground-ivy crackling under the hoofs, and the branches striking against their steel caps. After about twenty minutes' riding they came out again upon the river, and after another ten minutes found a place where it was possible to cross without sinking above the stirrups. The wood upon the other side was very thin, and broke the moonlight into long streams. The wind had arisen, and had begun to drive the clouds rapidly across the face of the moon, so that thin streams of light were dancing among scattered bushes and small fir-trees. The tops of the trees began also to moan, and the sound of it was like the voice of the dead in the wind; and the troopers remembered that the dead in Purgatory are said to be spitted upon the points of the trees and upon the points of the rocks. They turned a little to the south, in the hope that they might strike the beaten path again, but they could find no trace of it.

Meanwhile, the moaning grew louder and louder, and the dancing of the moonlight seemed more and more rapid. Gradually they began to be aware of a sound of distant music. It was the sound of a bagpipe, and they rode towards it with great joy. It came from the bottom of a deep, cuplike hollow. In the midst of the hollow was an old man with a red cap and withered face. He sat beside a fire of sticks, and had a burning torch thrust into the earth at his feet, and played an old bagpipe furiously. His red hair dripped over his face like the iron rust upon a rock. 'Did you see my wife?' he said, looking up a moment; 'she was washing! she was washing!' 'I am afraid of him,' said the young trooper; 'I fear he is not a right man.' 'No,' said the old trooper, 'he is a man like ourselves, for I can see the sun-freckles upon his face. We will compel him to be our guide'; and at that he drew his sword, and the others did the same. They stood in a ring round the piper, and pointed their swords at him, and the old trooper then told him that they must kill two rebels, who had taken the road between Ben Bulben and the great mountain spur that is called Cashel-na-Gael, and that he must get up on the horse before one of them and be their guide, for they had lost their way. The piper pointed to a neighbouring tree, and they saw an old white horse ready bitted, bridled, and saddled. He slung the pipe across his back, and, taking the torch in his hand, got upon the horse, and started off before them, as hard as he could go.

The wood grew thinner now, and the ground began to slope up toward the mountain. The moon had already set, but the stars shone brightly between the clouds. The ground sloped more and more until at last they rode far above the woods upon the wide top of the mountain. The woods lay spread out mile after mile below, and away to the south shot up the red glare of the burning town. The guide drew rein suddenly, and pointing upwards with the hand that did not hold the torch, shrieked out, 'Look; look at the holy candles!' and then plunged forward at a gallop, waving the torch hither and thither. 'Do you hear the hoofs of the messengers?' cried the guide. 'Quick, quick! or they will be gone out of your hands!' and he laughed as with delight of the chase. The troopers thought they could hear far off, and as if below them, rattle of hoofs; but now the ground began to slope more and more, and the speed grew more headlong moment by moment. They tried to pull up, but they could not, for the horses seemed to have gone mad. The guide had thrown the reins on to the neck of the old white horse, and was waving his arms and singing in Gaelic. Suddenly they saw the thin gleam of a river, at an immense distance below, and knew that they were upon the brink of the abyss that is now called Lugnagall, or in English the Steep Place of the Strangers. The six horses sprang forward, and five screams went up into the air, and a moment later five men and horses fell with a dull crash upon the green slopes at the foot of the rocks.

WHERE THERE IS NOTHING, THERE IS GOD

THE little wicker houses at Tullagh, where the Brothers were accustomed to pray, or bend over many handicrafts, when twilight had driven them from the fields, were empty, for the hardness of the winter had brought the brotherhood together in the little wooden house under the shadow of the wooden chapel; and Abbot Malathgeneus, Brother Dove, Brother Bald Fox, Brother Peter, Brother Patrick, Brother Bittern, Brother Fair-Brows, and many too young to have won names in the great battle, sat about the fire with ruddy faces, one mending lines to lay in the river for eels, one fashioning a snare for birds, one mending the broken handle of a spade, one writing in a large book, and one shaping a jewelled box to hold the book; and among the rushes at their feet lay the scholars, who would one day be Brothers, and whose school-house it was, and for the succour of whose tender years the great fire was supposed to leap and flicker. One of these, a child of eight or nine years, called Olioll, lay upon his back looking up through the hole in the roof, through which the smoke went, and watching the stars appearing and disappearing in the smoke with mild eyes, like the eyes of a beast of the field. He turned presently to the Brother who wrote in the big book, and whose duty was to teach the children, and said, 'Brother Dove, to what are the stars fastened?' The Brother, rejoicing to see so much curiosity in the stupidest of his scholars, laid down the pen and said, 'There are nine crystalline spheres, and on the first the Moon is fastened, on the second the planet Mercury, on the third the planet Venus, on the fourth the Sun, on the fifth the planet Mars, on the sixth the planet Jupiter, on the seventh the planet Saturn; these are the wandering stars; and on the eighth are fastened the fixed stars; but the ninth sphere is a sphere of the substance on which the breath of God moved in the beginning.'

'What is beyond that?' said the child.

'There is nothing beyond that; there is God.'

And then the child's eyes strayed to the jewelled box, where one great ruby was gleaming in the light of the fire, and he said, 'Why has Brother Peter put a great ruby on the side of the box?'

'The ruby is a symbol of the love of God.'

'Why is the ruby a symbol of the love of God?'

'Because it is red, like fire, and fire burns up everything, and where there is nothing, there is God.'

The child sank into silence, but presently sat up and said, 'There is somebody outside.'

'No,' replied the Brother. 'It is only the wolves; I have heard them moving about in the snow for some time. They are growing very wild, now that the winter drives them from the mountains. They broke into a fold last night and carried off many sheep, and if we are not careful they will devour everything.'

'No, it is the footstep of a man, for it is heavy; but I can hear the footsteps of the wolves also.'

He had no sooner done speaking than somebody rapped three times, but with no great loudness.

'I will go and open, for he must be very cold.'

'Do not open, for it may be a man-wolf, and he may devour us all.'

But the boy had already drawn back the heavy wooden bolt, and all the faces, most of them a little pale, turned towards the slowly-opening door.

'He has beads and a cross, he cannot be a man-wolf,' said the child, as a man with the snow heavy on his long, ragged beard, and on the matted hair that fell over his shoulders and nearly to his waist, and dropping from the tattered cloak that but half covered his withered brown body, came in and looked from face to face with mild, ecstatic eyes. Standing some way from the fire, and with eyes that had rested at last upon the Abbot Malathgeneus, he cried out, 'O blessed abbot, let me come to the fire and warm myself and dry the snow from my beard and my hair and my cloak; that I may not die of the cold of the mountains and anger the Lord with a wilful martyrdom.'

'Come to the fire,' said the abbot, 'and warm yourself, and eat the food the boy Olioll will bring you. It is sad indeed that any for whom Christ has died should be as poor as you.'

The man sat over the fire, and Olioll took away his now dripping cloak and laid meat and bread and wine before him; but he would eat only of the bread, and he put away the wine, asking for water. When his beard and hair had begun to dry a little and his limbs had ceased to shiver with the cold, he spoke again.

'O blessed abbot, have pity on the poor, have pity on a beggar who has trodden the bare world this many

a year, and give me some labour to do, the hardest
there is, for I am the poorest of God's poor.'

Then the Brothers discussed together what work they
could put him to, and at first to little purpose, for there
was no labour that had not found its labourer in that
busy community; but at last one remembered that
Brother Bald Fox, whose business it was to turn the
great quern in the quern-house, for he was too stupid
for anything else, was getting old for so heavy a labour;
and so the beggar was put to the quern from the
morrow.

The cold passed away, and the spring grew to sum-
mer, and the quern was never idle, nor was it turned
with grudging labour, for when any passed the beggar
was heard singing as he drove the handle round. The
last gloom, too, had passed from that happy commun-
ity, for Olioll, who had always been stupid and unteach-
able, grew clever, and this was the more miraculous
because it had come of a sudden. One day he had
been even duller than usual, and was beaten and told to
know his lesson better on the morrow or be sent into a
lower class among little boys who would make a joke
of him. He had gone out in tears, and when he came
the next day, although his stupidity, born of a mind that
would listen to every wandering sound and brood upon
every wandering light, had so long been the byword of
the school, he knew his lesson so well that he passed to
the head of the class, and from that day was the best of
scholars. At first Brother Dove thought this was an
answer to his own prayers to the Virgin, and took it for
a great proof of the love she bore him; but when many

far more fervid prayers had failed to add a single wheat-sheaf to the harvest, he began to think that the child was trafficking with bards, or Druids, or witches, and re-solved to follow and watch. He had told his thought to the abbot, who bid him come to him the moment he hit the truth; and the next day, which was a Sunday, he stood in the path when the abbot and the Brothers were coming from vespers, with their white habits upon them, and took the abbot by the habit and said: 'The beggar is of the greatest of saints and of the workers of miracle. I followed Olioll but now, and by his slow steps and his bent head I saw that the weariness of his stupidity was over him, and when he came to the little wood by the quern-house I knew by the path broken in the underwood and by the footmarks in the muddy places that he had gone that way many times. I hid behind a bush where the path doubled upon itself at a sloping place, and understood by the tears in his eyes that his stupidity was too old and his wisdom too new to save him from terror of the rod. When he was in the quern-house I went to the window and looked in, and the birds came down and perched upon my head and my shoulders, for they are not timid in that holy place; and a wolf passed by, his right side shaking my habit, his left the leaves of a bush. Olioll opened his book and turned to the page I had told him to learn, and began to cry, and the beggar sat beside him and comforted him until he fell asleep. When his sleep was of the deepest the beggar knelt down and prayed aloud, and said, "O Thou Who dwellest beyond the stars, show forth Thy power as at the beginning, and let knowledge sent from

Thee awaken in his mind, wherein is nothing from the world, that the nine orders of angels may glorify Thy name"; and then a light broke out of the air and wrapped Olioll, and I smelt the breath of roses. I stirred a little in my wonder, and the beggar turned and saw me, and, bending low, said, "O Brother Dove, if I have done wrong, forgive me, and I will do penance. It was my pity moved me"; but I was afraid and I ran away, and did not stop running until I came here.'

Then all the Brothers began talking together, one saying it was such-and-such a saint, and one that it was not he but another; and one that it was none of these, for they were still in their brotherhoods, but that it was such-and-such a one; and the talk was as near to quarrelling as might be in that gentle community, for each would claim so great a saint for his native province. At last the abbot said: 'He is none that you have named, for at Easter I had greeting from all, and each was in his brotherhood; but he is Aengus the Lover of God, and the first of those who have gone to live in the wild places and among the wild beasts. Ten years ago he felt the burden of many labours in a brotherhood under the Hill of Patrick and went into the forest that he might labour only with song to the Lord; but the fame of his holiness brought many thousands to his cell, so that a little pride clung to a soul from which all else had been driven. Nine years ago he dressed himself in rags, and from that day none has seen him, unless, indeed, it be true that he has been seen living among the wolves on the mountains and eating the grass of the fields. Let us go to him and bow down before him; for at last, after long seeking, he has found the nothing that is God; and bid him lead us in the pathway he has trodden.'

They passed in their white habits along the beaten path in the wood, the acolytes swinging their censers before them, and the abbot, with his crozier studded with precious stones, in the midst of the incense; and came before the quern-house and knelt down and began to pray, awaiting the moment when the child would wake, and the Saint cease from his watch and come to look at the sun going down into the unknown darkness, as his way was.

THE OLD MEN OF THE TWILIGHT

AT the place, close to the Dead Man's Point, at the Rosses, where the disused pilot-house looks out to sea through two round windows like eyes, a mud cottage stood in the last century. It also was a watchhouse, for a certain old Michael Bruen, who had been a smuggler, and was still the father and grandfather of smugglers, lived there, and when, after nightfall, a tall French schooner crept over the bay from Roughley, it was his business to hang a horn lantern in the southern window, that the news might travel to Dorren's Island, and thence, by another horn lantern, to the village of the Rosses. But for this glimmering of messages, he had little business with mankind, for he was very old, and had no thought for anything but for the making of his soul, bent double over his Spanish beads. One night he had watched hour after hour, because a gentle and favourable wind was blowing, and *La Mère de Miséricorde* was much overdue. At last he was about to lie down upon his heap of straw, for he knew that she would not dare to round Roughley and come to an anchor after daybreak, when he saw a long line of herons flying slowly from Dorren's Island and towards the pools which lie, half choked with reeds, behind what is called the Second Rosses. He had never before seen herons flying over the sea, for they are shore-keeping birds, and partly because this had startled him out of his drowsiness, and more because the long delay of the schooner had emptied his cupboard, he took down his rusty shot-gun, of which the barrel was tied on with a piece of string, and set out for the pools.

In a little he came upon the herons, of which there were a great number, standing with lifted legs in the shallow water; and crouching down behind a bank of rushes, looked to the priming of his gun, and bent for a moment over his rosary to murmur, 'Holy Saint Patrick, I have a great desire for heron-pie; and if you keep me from missing I will say a rosary to you every night until the pie is eaten.' Then he lay down, and, resting his gun upon a large stone, turned towards a heron which stood upon a bank of smooth grass over a little stream that flowed into the pool; for he feared to take the rheumatism by wading, as he would have to do if he shot one of those which stood in the water. But when he looked along the barrel the heron was gone, and, to his wonder and terror, a man that seemed of an infinitely great age stood in its place. He lowered the gun, and once more the heron stood there with bent head and motionless feathers. He raised the gun, and no sooner did he look along the barrel than the old man was again before him, only to vanish when he lowered the gun for the second time. He laid the gun down, and crossed himself three times, and said a Paternoster and an Ave Maria, and muttered half aloud, 'Some enemy of God is fishing in the blessed water,' and thereupon he aimed very carefully and slowly. He fired, and when the smoke had gone saw an old man, huddled upon the grass, and a long line of herons flying towards the sea. He went round a bend of the pool, and coming to the little stream looked down on a figure wrapped in faded clothes of an ancient pattern and spotted with blood. He shook his head at the sight of so great a wickedness. Suddenly the clothes moved and an arm was stretched upwards towards the rosary which hung about his neck, and long wasted fingers almost touched the cross. He started back, crying, 'Wizard, I will let no wicked thing touch my blessed beads.'

'If you listen to me,' replied a voice so faint that it was like a sigh, 'you will know that I am not a wizard, and you will let me kiss the cross before I die.'

'I will listen to you,' he answered, 'but I will not let you touch my blessed beads,' and sitting on the grass a little way from the dying man, he reloaded his gun and laid it across his knees and composed himself to listen.

'I do not know how many generations ago we, who are now herons, were men of learning; we neither hunted, nor went to battle, nor said prayers, nor sang songs, nor made love. The Druids told us, many a time, of a new Druid Patrick; and most among them were angry with him, while a few thought his doctrine merely their own doctrine set out in new images, and were for giving him welcome; but we yawned when they spoke of him. At last they came crying that he was coming to the king's house, and fell to their dispute, but we would listen to neither party, for we disputed concerning prosody and the relative importance of rhyme and assonance, syllable and accent; nor were we disturbed when they passed our door with sticks of enchantment under their arms, travelling towards the

forest, nor when they returned after nightfall with pale
faces and despairing cries; for the click of our knives
writing our thoughts in Ogham delighted us. The next
day crowds passed going to the king's house, and one
of us, who had laid down his knife to yawn and stretch
himself, heard a voice speaking far off; but our hearts
were deaf, and we carved and disputed and read, and
laughed together. In a little we heard many feet coming
towards the house, and presently two tall figures stood
in the door, the one in white, the other in a crimson
coat; and we knew the Druid Patrick and our king. We
laid down the slender knives and bowed before the
king, but it was not the loud rough voice of our king
that spoke to us, but a voice of rapture: "I preached the
commandments of God," it said, "within the king's
house, and from the centre of the earth to the windows
of Heaven there was a great silence, so that the eagle
floated with unmoving wings, and the fish with un-
moving fins, while the linnets and the wrens and the
sparrows stilled their ever-trembling tongues, and the
clouds were like white marble, and the shrimps in
the far-off sea-pools became still, enduring eternity in
patience, although it was hard. But your slender knives
kept up their clicking, and, all else being silent, the
sound is not to be endured. Because you have lived
where the feet of the angels cannot touch your heads,
nor the hair of the demons sweep your feet-soles, I
shall make you an example for ever and ever; you shall
become grey herons and stand pondering in grey pools
and flit over the world in that hour when it is most full
of sighs; and your deaths shall come by chance and

unforeseen, for you shall not be certain about anything for ever and ever." '

The voice became still, but the voteen bent over his gun with his eyes upon the ground, too stupid to understand what he had heard; and he had remained so, it may be for a long time, had not a tug at his rosary aroused him. The old man of learning had crawled along the grass, and was now trying to draw the cross down low enough for his lips to reach it.

'You must not touch my blessed beads,' cried the voteen, and struck the long withered fingers with the barrel of his gun. He need not have struck him, for the old man fell back upon the grass with a sigh and was quiet. He bent down and began to consider the discoloured clothes, for his fear had grown less when he understood that he had something the man of learning wanted, and now that the blessed beads were safe, his fear had nearly all gone; and surely, he thought, if that cloak be warm and without holes, Saint Patrick would take the enchantment out of it and leave it fit for use. But the old discoloured cloth fell away wherever his fingers touched it, and presently a slight wind blew over the pool and crumbled the old man of learning and all his ancient gear into a little heap of dust, and then made the little heap less and less until there was nothing but the smooth green grass.

PROUD COSTELLO, MACDERMOT'S DAUGHTER, AND THE BITTER TONGUE

COSTELLO had come up from the fields and lay upon the ground before the door of his square tower, resting his head upon his hands and looking at the sunset, and considering the chances of the weather. Though the customs of Elizabeth and James, now going out of fashion in England, had begun to prevail among the gentry, he still wore the great cloak of the native Irish; and the untroubled confidence of his face and his big body had the pride and strength of a simpler age. His eyes wandered from the sunset to where the long white road lost itself over the south-western horizon and to a horseman who toiled slowly up the hill. A few more minutes and the horseman was near enough for his little shapeless body, his long Irish cloak, and the dilapidated bagpipes hanging from his shoulders, and the rough-haired garron under him, to be seen distinctly in the grey dusk. So soon as he had come within earshot, he began crying, 'Is it sleeping you are, Tumaus Costello, when better men break their hearts on the great white roads? Get up out of that, proud Tumaus, for I have news! Get up out of that, you great omadhaun! Shake yourself out of the earth, you great weed of a man!'

Costello had risen to his feet, and as the piper came up to him seized him by the neck of his jacket, lifted him out of his saddle and shook him.

'Let me alone, let me alone,' said the other, but Costello still shook him.

'I have news from MacDermot's daughter Una.' The great fingers were loosened, and the piper fell gasping.

'Why did you not tell me,' said Costello, 'that you came from her? You might have railed your fill.'

'I have come from her, but I will not speak until I am paid for the shaking.'

Costello fumbled at the bag in which he carried his money, and it was some time before it would open, for his hand trembled. 'Here is all the money in my bag,' he said, dropping some French and Spanish money into the hand of the piper, who bit the coins before he would answer.

'That is right, that is a fair price, but I will not speak till I have good protection, for if the MacDermots lay their hands upon me in any boreen after sundown, or in Cool-a-vin by day, I will be left to rot among the nettles of a ditch, or hung where they hung the horse-thieves last Beltaine four years.' And while he spoke he tied the reins of his garron to a bar of rusty iron that was mortared into the wall.

'I will make you my piper and my body-servant,' said Costello, 'and no man dare lay hands upon a man or upon a dog if he belong to Tumaus Costello.'

'And I will only tell my message,' said the other, flinging the saddle on the ground, 'with a noggin of whiskey in my hand, for though I am ragged and empty, my old fathers were well clothed and full, until their house was burnt down and their cattle driven away seven centuries ago by the Dillons, whom I shall yet see on the hob of Hell, and they screeching.'

Costello led him up a narrow winding stone stair into

a rush-strewn chamber, where were none of the comforts which had begun to grow common among the gentry, and pointed to a seat in the great chimney; and when the piper had sat down, filled up a horn noggin and set it on the floor beside him, and a jug beside that, and then turned towards him and said, 'Will MacDermot's daughter come to me, Duallach, son of Daly?'

'MacDermot's daughter will not come to you, for her father has set women to watch her, but I am to tell you that this day week will be the Eve of Saint John and the night of her betrothal to MacNamara of the Lake, and she wants you to be there that, when they tell her to drink to him she loves best, she may drink to you, Tumaus Costello, and let all know where her heart is; and I myself advise you to go with good men about you, for I have seen the horse-thieves with my own eyes.' And then he held the now empty noggin towards Costello, and cried: 'Fill my noggin again, for I wish the day had come when all the water in the world is to shrink into a periwinkle-shell, that I might drink nothing but whiskey.'

Finding that Costello made no reply, but sat in a dream, he burst out: 'Fill my noggin, I tell you, for no Costello is so great in the world that he should not wait upon a Daly, even though the Daly travel the road with his pipes and the Costello have a bare hill, an empty house, a horse, and a handful of cows.'

'Praise the Dalys if you will,' said Costello as he filled the noggin, 'for you have brought me a kind word from my love.'

For the next few days Duallach went here and there

trying to raise a bodyguard, and every man he met had some story of Costello: one told how he killed the wrestler when but a boy by so straining at the belt that went about them both that he broke the big wrestler's back; another how he dragged fierce horses through a ford for a wager; another how when grown to be a man he broke the steel horseshoe in Mayo; but none who would trust himself with a man so passionate and poor in a quarrel with careful and wealthy persons like Mac-Dermot of the Sheep and MacNamara of the Lake.

Then Costello went out himself, and brought in a big half-witted fellow, a farm-labourer who worshipped him for his strength, a fat farmer whose forefathers had served his family, and a couple of lads who looked after his goats and cows; and marshalled them before the fire. They had brought with them their heavy sticks, and Costello gave them an old pistol apiece, and kept them all night drinking and shooting at a white turnip which he pinned against the wall with a skewer. Duallach sat on the bench in the chimney playing 'The Green Bunch of Rushes,' 'The Unchion Stream,' and 'The Princes of Breffny' on his old pipes, and abusing now the appearance of the shooters, now their clumsy shooting, and now Costello because he had no better servants. The labourer, the half-witted fellow, the farmer and the lads were well accustomed to Duallach's abusiveness, but they wondered at the forbearance of Costello, who seldom came either to wake or wedding, and if he had would not have been patient with a scolding piper.

On the next evening they set out for Cool-a-vin, Costello riding a tolerable horse and carrying a sword, the others upon rough-haired ponies, and with their cudgels under their arms. As they rode over the bogs and in the boreens among the hills they could see fire answering fire from hill to hill, from horizon to horizon, and everywhere groups who danced in the red light of the turf. When they came to MacDermot's house they saw before the door an unusually large group of the very poor, dancing about a fire, in the midst of which was a blazing cart-wheel, and from the door and through the loopholes on either side came the light of candles and the sound of many feet dancing a dance of Elizabeth and James.

They tied their horses to bushes, for the number so tied already showed that the stables were full, and shoved their way through a crowd of peasants who stood about the door, and went into the big hall where the dance was. The labourer, the half-witted fellow, the farmer and the two lads mixed with a group of servants who were looking on from an alcove, and Duallach sat with the pipers on their bench, but Costello made his way through the dancers to where MacDermot stood pouring out whiskey, MacNamara at his side.

'Tumaus Costello,' said the old man, 'you have done a good deed to forget what has been, and come to the betrothal of my daughter.'

'I come,' answered Costello, 'because when in the time of Costello De Angalo my ancestors overcame your ancestors and afterwards made peace, a compact was made that a Costello might go with his body-servants and his piper to every feast given by a MacDermot for ever, and a MacDermot with his body-servants and his piper to every feast given by a Costello for ever.'

'If you come with evil thoughts and armed men,' said MacDermot, flushing, 'no matter how good you are with your weapons, it shall go badly with you, for some of my wife's clan have come out of Mayo, and my three brothers and their servants have come down from the Ox Mountains'; and while he spoke he kept his hand inside his coat as though upon the handle of a weapon.

'No,' answered Costello, 'I but come to dance a farewell dance with your daughter.'

MacDermot drew his hand out of his coat and went over to a pale girl who was now standing but a little way off with her mild eyes fixed upon the ground.

'Costello has come to dance a farewell dance, for he knows that you will never see one another again.'

As Costello led her among the dancers her gentle and humble eyes were fixed in love upon his pride and violence. They took their place in the Pavane, that stately dance which, with the Saraband, the Gallead, and the Morris dances, had driven out, among all but the most Irish of the gentry, the quicker rhythms of the verse-interwoven, pantomimic dances of earlier days; and while they danced there came over them the weariness with the world, the melancholy, the pity one for the other, which is the exultation of love. And when a dance ended and the pipers laid down the pipes and lifted the noggins, they stood a little from the others waiting pensively and silently for the dance to begin again and the fire in their hearts to leap up and to wrap them anew; and so they danced Pavane and Saraband and

Gallead and Morris the night long, and many stood still to watch them, and the peasants came about the door and peered in, as though they understood that they would gather their children's children about them long hence, and tell how they had seen Costello dance with MacDermot's daughter Una; and through all the dancing and piping MacNamara went hither and thither talking loudly and making foolish jokes that all might seem well, and old MacDermot grew redder and redder, waiting for the dawn.

At last he saw that the moment to end had come, and, in a pause after a dance, cried out that his daughter would now drink the cup of betrothal; then Una came over to where he was, and the guests stood round in a half-circle, Costello close to the wall, and the piper, the labourer, the farmer, the half-witted man and the two farm lads close behind him. The old man took out of a niche in the wall the silver cup from which her mother and her mother's mother had drunk the toasts of their betrothals, filled it with Spanish wine and handed the cup to his daughter with the customary words, 'Drink to him whom you love the best.'

She held the cup to her lips for a moment, and then said in a clear soft voice, 'I drink to my true love, Tumaus Costello.'

And then the cup rolled over and over on the ground, ringing like a bell, for the old man had struck her in the face and the cup had fallen, and there was a deep silence.

There were many of MacNamara's people among the servants now come out of the alcove, and one of them, a story-teller and poet, who had a plate and chair in MacNamara's kitchen, drew a French knife out of his girdle, but in a moment Costello had struck him to the ground. The click of steel had followed quickly, had not there come a muttering and shouting from the peasants about the door and from those crowding up behind them; for all knew that these were no children of Queen's Irish, but of the wild Irish about Lough Gabhra and Lough Cara, Kellys, Dockerys, Drurys, O'Regans, Mahons, and Lavins, who had left the right arms of their children unchristened that they might give the better blows, and were even said to have named the wolves godfathers to their children.

Costello's knuckles had grown white upon the handle of his sword, but now he drew his hand away, and, followed by those who were with him, went towards the door, the dancers giving way before him, the most angrily and slowly, and with glances at the muttering and shouting peasants, but some gladly and quickly, because the glory of his fame was over him. He passed through the fierce and friendly peasant faces, and came where his horse and the ponies were tied to bushes; and mounted and made his bodyguard mount also and ride into the narrow boreen. When they had gone a little way, Duallach, who rode last, turned towards the house where a little group of MacDermots and MacNamaras stood next to a bigger group of countrymen, and cried, 'MacDermot, you deserve to be as you are this hour, for your hand was always niggardly to piper and fiddler and to poor travelling people.' He had not done before the three old MacDermots from the Ox Mountains had run towards their horses, and old MacDermot himself had caught the bridle of a pony belonging to the Mac-Namaras and was calling to the others to follow him; and many blows and many deaths had been had not the countrymen caught up still blazing sticks from the ashes of the fires and thrown them among the horses so that they broke away from those who held them and scattered through the fields, and before they could be gathered again Costello was far off.

For the next few weeks Costello had no lack of news of Una, for now a woman selling eggs, and now a man or a woman going to the Holy Well, would tell him how his love had fallen ill the day after Saint John's Eve, and how she was a little better or a little worse.

At last a serving-man rode up to Costello, who was helping his two lads to reap a meadow, and gave him a letter, and rode away; and the letter contained these words in English: 'Tumaus Costello, my daughter is very ill. She will die unless you come to her. I therefore command you come to her whose peace you stole by treachery.'

Costello threw down his scythe, and sent one of the lads for Duallach, and himself saddled his horse and Duallach's pony.

When they came to MacDermot's house it was late afternoon, and Lough Gabhra lay down below them, blue and deserted; and though they had seen, when at a distance, dark figures moving about the door, the house appeared not less deserted than the Lough. The door stood half open, and Costello knocked upon it again and again, but there was no answer.

'There is no one here,' said Duallach, 'for Mac-Dermot is too proud to welcome Proud Costello,' and he threw the door open, and they saw a ragged, dirty, very old woman, who sat upon the floor leaning against the wall. Costello knew that it was Bridget Delaney, a deaf and dumb beggar; and she, when she saw him, stood up and made a sign to him to follow, and led him and his companion up a stair and down a long corridor to a closed door. She pushed the door open and went a little way off and sat down as before; Duallach sat upon the ground also, but close to the door, and Costello went and gazed upon Una sleeping upon a bed. He sat upon a chair beside her and waited, and a long time passed and still she slept, and then Duallach motioned to him through the door to wake her, but he hushed his very breath, that she might sleep on. Presently he turned to Duallach and said, 'It is not right that I stay here where there are none of her kindred, for the common people are always ready to blame the beautiful.' And then they went down and stood at the door of the house and waited, but the evening wore on and no one came.

'It was a foolish man that called you Proud Costello,' Duallach said at last; 'had he seen you waiting and waiting where they left none but a beggar to welcome you, it is Humble Costello he would have called you.'

Then Costello mounted and Duallach mounted, but when they had ridden a little way Costello tightened the reins and made his horse stand still. Many minutes passed, and then Duallach cried, 'It is no wonder that you fear to offend MacDermot, for he has many brothers and friends, and though he is old, he is a strong and stirring man, and he is of the Queen's Irish, and the enemies of the Gael are upon his side.'

And Costello answered, flushing and looking towards the house, 'I swear by the Mother of God that I will never return there again if they do not send after me before I pass the ford in the Brown River,' and he rode on, but so very slowly that the sun went down and the bats began to fly over the bogs. When he came to the river he lingered awhile upon the edge, but presently rode out into the middle and stopped his horse in a shallow. Duallach, however, crossed over and waited on a farther bank above a deeper place. After a good while Duallach cried out again, and this time very bitterly, 'It was a fool who begot you and a fool who bore you, and they are fools who say you come of an old and noble stock, for you come of whey-faced beggars who travelled from door to door, bowing to serving-men.'

With bent head, Costello rode through the river and stood beside him, and would have spoken had not hoofs clattered on the farther bank and a horseman splashed towards them. It was a serving-man of MacDermot's, and he said, speaking breathlessly like one who had ridden hard: 'Tumaus Costello, I come to bring you again to MacDermot's house. When you had gone, his daughter Una awoke and called your name, for you had been in her dreams. Bridget Delaney the Dummy saw her lips move, and came where we were hiding in the wood above the house and took MacDermot by the coat and brought him to his daughter. He saw the trouble upon her, and bid me ride his own horse to bring you the quicker.'

Then Costello turned towards the piper Duallach Daly, and taking him about the waist lifted him out of the saddle and threw him against a big stone that was in the river, so that he fell lifeless into a deep place. Then plunging his spurs into the horse, he rode away furiously towards the north-west, along the edge of the river, and did not pause until he came to another and smoother ford, and saw the rising moon mirrored in the water. He paused for a moment irresolute, and then rode into the ford and on over the Ox Mountains, and down towards the sea; his eyes almost continually resting upon the moon. But now his horse, long dark with sweat and breathing hard, for he kept spurring it, fell heavily, throwing him on the roadside. He tried to make it stand up, and failing in this, went on alone towards the moonlight; and came to the sea and saw a schooner lying there at anchor. Now that he could go no farther because of the sea, he found that he was very tired and the night very cold, and went into a shebeen close to the shore and threw himself down upon a bench. The room was full of Spanish and Irish sailors who had just smuggled a cargo of wine, and were waiting a favourable wind to set out again. A Spaniard offered him a drink in bad Gaelic. He drank it and began talking wildly and rapidly.

For some three weeks the wind blew inshore or with too great violence, and the sailors stayed drinking and talking and playing cards, and Costello stayed with them, sleeping upon a bench in the shebeen, and drinking and talking and playing more than any. He soon lost what little money he had, and then his long cloak and his spurs and even his boots. At last a gentle wind blew towards Spain, and the crew rowed out to their schooner, and in a little while the sails had dropped under the horizon. Then Costello turned homeward, his life gaping before him, and walked all day, coming in the early evening to the road that went from near Lough Gabhra to the southern edge of Lough Cay. Here he overtook a crowd of peasants and farmers, who were walking very slowly after two priests and a group of well-dressed persons, certain of whom were carrying a coffin. He stopped an old man and asked whose burying it was and whose people they were, and the old man answered, 'It is the burying of Una, MacDermot's daughter, and we are the MacNamaras and the Mac-Dermots and their following, and you are Tumaus Costello who murdered her.'

Costello went on towards the head of the procession, passing men who looked angrily at him, and only vaguely understood what he had heard. Presently he stopped and asked again whose burying it was, and a man answered, 'We are carrying MacDermot's daughter Una, whom you murdered, to her burying upon Insula Trinitatis,' and the man picked up a stone and threw it at Costello, striking him on the cheek and making the blood flow out over his face. Costello went on, scarcely feeling the blow, and coming to those about the coffin, shouldered his way into the midst of them, and laying his hand upon the coffin, asked in a loud voice, 'Who is in this coffin?'

The three old MacDermots from the Ox Mountains caught up stones and told those about them to do the same; and he was driven from the road, covered with wounds.

When the procession had passed on, Costello began to follow again, and saw from a distance the coffin laid upon a large boat, and those about it get into other boats, and the boats move slowly over the water to Insula Trinitatis; and after a time he saw the boats return and their passengers mingle with the crowd upon the bank, and all scatter by many roads and boreens. It seemed to him that Una was somewhere on the island smiling gently, and when all had gone he swam in the way the boats had been rowed and found the new-made grave beside the ruined Abbey, and threw himself upon it, calling to Una to come to him.

He lay there all that night and through the day after, from time to time calling her to come to him, but when the third night came he had forgotten that her body lay in the earth beneath, but only knew she was somewhere near and would not come to him.

Just before dawn, the hour when the peasants hear his ghostly voice crying out, he called loudly, 'If you do not come to me, Una, I will go and never return,' and before his voice had died away a cold and whirling wind had swept over the island and he saw women of the Sidhe rushing past; and then Una, but no longer smiling, for she passed him swiftly and angrily, and as she passed struck him upon the face, crying, 'Then go and never return.'

Costello got up from the grave, understanding

nothing but that he had made his sweetheart angry and that she wished him to go, and wading out into the lake, began to swim. He swam on, but his limbs seemed too weary to keep him afloat, and when he had gone a little way he sank without a struggle.

The next day a fisherman found him among the reeds upon the lake shore, lying upon the white lake sand, and carried him to his own house. And the peasants lamented over him and sang the keen, and laid him in the Abbey on Insula Trinitatis with only the ruined altar between him and MacDermot's daughter, and planted above them two ash-trees that in after days wove their branches together and mingled their leaves

THE END

STORIES OF RED HANRAHAN

1897

REWRITTEN IN 1907 WITH LADY GREGORY'S HELP

RED HANRAHAN

HANRAHAN, THE HEDGE SCHOOLMASTER, a tall, strong, red-haired young man, came into the barn where some of the men of the village were sitting on Samhain Eve. It had been a dwelling-house, and when the man that owned it had built a better one, he had put the two rooms together, and kept it for a place to store one thing or another. There was a fire on the old hearth, and there were dip candles stuck in bottles, and there was a black quart bottle upon some boards that had been put across two barrels to make a table. Most of the men were sitting beside the fire, and one of them was singing a long wandering song, about a Munster man and a Connacht man that were quarrelling about their two provinces.

Hanrahan went to the man of the house and said, 'I got your message'; but when he had said that, he stopped, for an old mountainy man that had a shirt and trousers of unbleached flannel, and that was sitting by himself near the door, was looking at him, and moving an old pack of cards about in his hands and muttering. 'Don't mind him,' said the man of the house; 'he is only some stranger came in a while ago, and we bade him welcome, it being Samhain night, but I think he is not in his right wits. Listen to him now and you will hear what he is saying.'

They listened then, and they could hear the old man muttering to himself as he turned the cards, 'Spades and Diamonds, Courage and Power; Clubs and Hearts, Knowledge and Pleasure.'

'That is the kind of talk he has been going on with for the last hour,' said the man of the house, and Hanrahan turned his eyes from the old man as if he did not like to be looking at him.

'I got your message,' Hanrahan said then. ' "He is in the barn with his three first cousins from Kilchriest," the messenger said, "and there are some of the neighbours with them." '

'It is my cousin over there is wanting to see you,' said the man of the house, and he called over a young frieze-coated man, who was listening to the song, and said, 'This is Red Hanrahan you have the message for.'

'It is a kind message, indeed,' said the young man, 'for it comes from your sweetheart, Mary Lavelle.'

'How would you get a message from her, and what do you know of her?'

'I don't know her, indeed, but I was in Loughrea yesterday, and a neighbour of hers that had some dealings with me was saying that she bade him send you word, if he met any one from this side in the market, that her mother has died from her, and if you have a mind yet to join with herself, she is willing to keep her word to you.'

'I will go to her indeed,' said Hanrahan.

'And she bade you make no delay, for if she has not a man in the house before the month is out, it is likely the little bit of land will be given to another.'

When Hanrahan heard that, he rose up from the bench he had sat down on. 'I will make no delay indeed,' he said; 'there is a full moon, and if I get as far as

Kilchriest to-night, I will reach to her before the setting of the sun to-morrow.'

When the others heard that, they began to laugh at him for being in such haste to go to his sweetheart, and one asked him if he would leave his school in the old lime-kiln, where he was giving the children such good learning. But he said the children would be glad enough in the morning to find the place empty, and no one to keep them at their task; and as for his school he could set it up again in any place, having as he had his little inkpot hanging from his neck by a chain, and his big Virgil and his primer in the skirt of his coat.

Some of them asked him to drink a glass before he went, and a young man caught hold of his coat, and said he must not leave them without singing the song he had made in praise of Venus and of Mary Lavelle. He drank a glass of whiskey, but he said he would not stop but would set out on his journey.

'There's time enough, Red Hanrahan,' said the man of the house. 'It will be time enough for you to give up sport when you are after your marriage, and it might be a long time before we will see you again.'

'I will not stop,' said Hanrahan; 'my mind would be on the roads all the time, bringing me to the woman that sent for me, and she lonesome and watching till I come.'

Some of the others came about him, pressing him that had been such a pleasant comrade, so full of songs and every kind of trick and fun, not to leave them till the night would be over, but he refused them all, and shook them off, and went to the door. But as he put his foot over the threshold, the strange old man stood up and put his hand that was thin and withered like a bird's claw on Hanrahan's hand, and said: 'It is not Hanrahan, the learned man and the great songmaker, that should go out from a gathering like this, on a Samhain night. And stop here, now,' he said, 'and play a hand with me; and here is an old pack of cards has done its work many a night before this, and old as it is, there has been much of the riches of the world lost and won over it.'

One of the young men said, 'It isn't much of the riches of the world has stopped with yourself, old man,' and he looked at the old man's bare feet, and they all laughed. But Hanrahan did not laugh, but he sat down very quietly, without a word. Then one of them said, 'So you will stop with us after all, Hanrahan'; and the old man said, 'He will stop indeed, did you not hear me asking him?'

They all looked at the old man then as if wondering where he came from. 'It is far I am come,' he said; 'through France I have come, and through Spain, and by Lough Greine of the hidden mouth, and none has refused me anything.' And then he was silent and nobody liked to question him, and they began to play. There were six men at the boards playing, and the others were looking on behind. They played two or three games for nothing, and then the old man took a fourpenny bit, worn very thin and smooth, out from his pocket, and he called to the rest to put something on the game. Then they all put down something on the boards, and little as it was it looked much, from the way it was shoved from one to another, first one man winning it and then his neighbour. And sometimes the luck would go against a man and he would have nothing left, and then one or another would lend him something, and he would pay it again out of his winnings, for neither good nor bad luck stopped long with any one.

And once Hanrahan said as a man would say in a dream, 'It is time for me to be going the road'; but just then a good card came to him, and he played it out, and all the money began to come to him. And once he thought of Mary Lavelle, and he sighed; and that time his luck went from him, and he forgot her again.

But at last the luck went to the old man and it stayed with him, and all they had flowed into him, and he began to laugh little laughs to himself, and to sing over and over to himself, 'Spades and Diamonds, Courage and Power,' and so on, as if it was a verse of a song.

And after a while any one looking at the men, and seeing the way their bodies were rocking to and fro, and the way they kept their eyes on the old man's hands, would think they had drink taken, or that the whole store they had in the world was put on the cards; but that was not so, for the quart bottle had not been disturbed since the game began, and was nearly full yet, and all that was on the game was a few sixpenny bits and shillings, and maybe a handful of coppers.

'You are good men to win and good men to lose,' said the old man; 'you have play in your hearts.' He began then to shuffle the cards and to mix them, very quick and fast, till at last they could not see them to be cards at all, but you would think him to be making rings of fire in the air, as little lads would make them with whirling a lighted stick; and after that it seemed to them that all the room was dark, and they could see nothing but his hands and the cards.

And all in a minute a hare made a leap out from between his hands, and whether it was one of the cards that took that shape, or whether it was made out of nothing in the palms of his hands, nobody knew, but there it was running on the floor of the barn, as quick as any hare that ever lived.

Some looked at the hare, but more kept their eyes on the old man, and while they were looking at him a hound made a leap out between his hands, the same way as the hare did, and after that another hound and another, till there was a whole pack of them following the hare round and round the barn.

The players were all standing up now, with their backs to the boards, shrinking from the hounds, and nearly deafened with the noise of their yelping, but as quick as the hounds were they could not overtake the hare, but it went round, till at the last it seemed as if a blast of wind burst open the barn door, and the hare doubled and made a leap over the boards where the men had been playing, and went out of the door and away through the night, and the hounds over the boards and through the door after it.

Then the old man called out, 'Follow the hounds, follow the hounds, and it is a great hunt you will see to-night,' and he went out after them. But used as the men were to go hunting after hares, and ready as they were for any sport, they were in dread to go out into the night, and it was only Hanrahan that rose up and that said, 'I will follow, I will follow on.'

'You had best stop here, Hanrahan,' the young man that was nearest him said, 'for you might be going into some great danger.' But Hanrahan said, 'I will see fair play, I will see fair play,' and he went stumbling out of the door like a man in a dream, and the door shut after him as he went.

He thought he saw the old man in front of him, but it was only his own shadow that the full moon cast on the road before him, but he could hear the hounds crying after the hare over the wide green fields of Granagh, and he followed them very fast, for there was nothing to stop him; and after a while he came to smaller fields that had little walls of loose stones around them, and he threw the stones down as he crossed them, and did not wait to put them up again; and he passed by the place where the river goes underground at Ballylee, and he could hear the hounds going before him up towards the head of the river. Soon he found it harder to run, for it was uphill he was going, and clouds came over the moon, and it was hard for him to see his way, and once he left the path to take a short-cut, but his foot slipped into a bog-hole and he had to come back to it. And how long he was going he did not know, or what way he went, but at last he was up on the bare mountain, with nothing but the rough heather about him, and he could neither hear the hounds nor any other thing. But their cry began to come to him again, at first far off and then very near, and when it came quite close to him, it went up all of a sudden into the air, and there was the sound of hunting over his head; then it went away northward till he could hear nothing at all. 'That's not fair,' he said, 'that's not fair.' And he could walk no longer, but sat down on the heather where he was, in the heart of Slieve Echtge, for all the strength had gone from him, with the dint of the long journey he had made.

And after a while he took notice that there was a door close to him, and a light coming from it, and he wondered that being so close to him he had not seen it before. And he rose up, and tired as he was he went in at the door, and although it was night-time outside, it was daylight he found within. And presently he met with an old man that had been gathering summer thyme and yellow flag-flowers, and it seemed as if all the sweet smells of the summer were with them. And the old man said, 'It is a long time you have been coming to us, Hanrahan the learned man and the great songmaker.'

And with that he brought him into a very big shining house, and every grand thing Hanrahan had ever heard of, and every colour he had ever seen, was in it. There was a high place at the end of the house, and on it there was sitting in a high chair a woman, the most beautiful the world ever saw, having a long pale face and flowers about it, but she had the tired look of one that had been long waiting. And there were sitting on the step below her chair four grey old women, and the one of them was holding a great cauldron in her lap; and another a great stone on her knees, and heavy as it was it seemed light to her; and another of them had a very long spear that was made of pointed wood; and the last of them had a sword that was without a scabbard.

Hanrahan stood looking at them for a long time, but none of them spoke any word to him or looked at him at all. And he had it in his mind to ask who that woman in the chair was, that was like a queen, and what she was waiting for; but ready as he was with his tongue and afraid of no person, he was in dread now to speak to so beautiful a woman, and in so grand a place. And then he thought to ask what were the four things the four grey old women were holding like great treasures, but he could not think of the right words to bring out.

Then the first of the old women rose up, holding the cauldron between her two hands, and she said, 'Pleasure,' and Hanrahan said no word. Then the second old woman rose up with the stone in her hands, and she said, 'Power'; and the third old woman rose up with a spear in her hand, and she said, 'Courage'; and the last of the old women rose up having the sword in her hands, and she said, 'Knowledge.' And every one, after she had spoken, waited as if for Hanrahan to question her, but he said nothing at all. And then the four old women went out of the door, bringing their four treasures with them, and as they went out one of them said, 'He has no wish for us'; and another said, 'He is weak, he is weak'; and another said, 'He is afraid'; and the last said, 'His wits are gone from him.' And then they all said, 'Echtge, daughter of the Silver Hand, must stay in her sleep. It is a pity, it is a great pity.'

And then the woman that was like a queen gave a very sad sigh, and it seemed to Hanrahan as if the sigh had the sound in it of hidden streams; and if the place he was in had been ten times grander and more shining than it was, he could not have hindered sleep from coming on him; and he staggered like a drunken man and lay down there and then.

When Hanrahan awoke, the sun was shining on his face, but there was white frost on the grass around him, and there was ice on the edge of the stream he was lying by, and that goes running on through Doire-caol and Drim-na-rod. He knew by the shape of the hills and by the shining of Lough Greine in the distance that he was upon one of the hills of Slieve Echtge, but he was not sure how he came there; for all that had happened in the barn had gone from him, and all of his journey but the soreness of his feet and the stiffness in his bones.

It was a year after that, there were men of the village of Cappaghtagle sitting by the fire in a house on the roadside, and Red Hanrahan that was now very thin and worn, and his hair very long and wild, came to the half-door and asked leave to come in and rest himself; and they bid him welcome because it was Samhain night. He sat down with them, and they gave him a glass of whiskey out of a quart bottle; and they saw the little inkpot hanging about his neck, and knew he was a scholar, and asked for stories about the Greeks.

He took the Virgil out of the big pocket of his coat, but the cover was very black and swollen with the wet, and the page when he opened it was very yellow, but that was no great matter, for he looked at it like a man that had never learned to read. Some young man that was there began to laugh at him then, and to ask why did he carry so heavy a book with him when he was not able to read it.

It vexed Hanrahan to hear that, and he put the Virgil back in his pocket and asked if they had a pack of cards among them, for cards were better than books. When they brought out the cards he took them and began to shuffle them, and while he was shuffling them something seemed to come into his mind, and he put his hand to his face like one that is trying to remember, and he said, 'Was I ever here before, or where was I on a night like this?' and then of a sudden he stood up and let the cards fall to the floor, and he said, 'Who was it brought me a message from Mary Lavelle?'

'We never saw you before now, and we never heard of Mary Lavelle,' said the man of the house. 'And who is she,' he said, 'and what is it you are talking about?'

'It was this night a year ago, I was in a barn, and there were men playing cards, and there was money on the table, they were pushing it from one to another here and there—and I got a message, and I was going out of the door to look for my sweetheart that wanted me, Mary Lavelle.' And then Hanrahan called out very loud, 'Where have I been since then? Where was I for the whole year?'

'It is hard to say where you might have been in that time,' said the oldest of the men, 'or what part of the world you may have travelled; and it is like enough you have the dust of many roads on your feet; for there are many go wandering and forgetting like that,' he said, 'when once they have been given the touch.'

'That is true,' said another of the men. 'I knew a woman went wandering like that through the length of seven years; she came back after, and she told her friends she had often been glad enough to eat the food that was put in the pig's trough. And it is best for you to go to the priest now,' he said, 'and let him take off you whatever may have been put upon you.'

'It is to my sweetheart I will go, to Mary Lavelle,' said Hanrahan; 'it is too long I have delayed, how do I know what might have happened her in the length of a year?'

He was going out of the door then, but they all told him it was best for him to stop the night, and to get strength for the journey; and indeed he wanted that, for he was very weak, and when they gave him food he ate it like a man that had never seen food before, and one of them said, 'He is eating as if he had trodden on the hungry grass.' It was in the white light of the morning he set out, and the time seemed long to him till he could get to Mary Lavelle's house. But when he came to it, he found the door broken, and the thatch dropping from the roof, and no living person to be seen. And when he asked the neighbours what had happened her, all they could say was that she had been put out of the house, and had married some labouring man, and they had gone looking for work to London or Liverpool or some big place. And whether she found a worse place or a better he never knew, but anyway he never met with her or with news of her again.

The Twisting of the Rope

THE TWISTING OF THE ROPE

HANRAHAN was walking the roads one time near Kinvara at the fall of day, and he heard the sound of a fiddle from a house a little way off the roadside. He turned up the path to it, for he never had the habit of passing by any place where there was music or dancing or good company, without going in. The man of the house was standing at the door, and when Hanrahan came near he knew him and he said, 'A welcome before you, Hanrahan, you have been lost to us this long time.' But the woman of the house came to the door and she said to her husband, 'I would be as well pleased for Hanrahan not to come in to-night, for he has no good name now among the priests, or with women that mind themselves, and I wouldn't wonder from his walk if he has a drop of drink taken.' But the man said, 'I will never turn away Hanrahan of the poets from my door,' and with that he bade him enter.

There were a good many neighbours gathered in the house, and some of them remembered Hanrahan; but some of the little lads that were in the corners had only heard of him, and they stood up to have a view of him, and one of them said, 'Is not that Hanrahan that had the school, and that was brought away by Them?' But his mother put her hand over his mouth and bade him be quiet, and not be saying things like that. 'For Hanrahan is apt to grow wicked,' she said, 'if he hears talk of that story, or if any one goes questioning him.' One or another called out then, asking him for a song, but the man of the house said it was no time to ask him for a song, before he had rested himself; and he gave him whiskey in a glass, and Hanrahan thanked him and wished him good health and drank it off.

The fiddler was tuning his fiddle for another dance, and the man of the house said to the young men, they would all know what dancing was like when they saw Hanrahan dance, for the like of it had never been seen since he was there before. Hanrahan said he would not dance, he had better use for his feet now, travelling as he was through the four provinces of Ireland. Just as he said that, there came in at the half-door Oona, the daughter of the house, having a few bits of bog-deal from Connemara in her arms for the fire. She threw them on the hearth, and the flame rose up and showed her to be very comely and smiling, and two or three of the young men rose up and asked for a dance. But Hanrahan crossed the floor and brushed the others away, and said it was with him she must dance, after the long road he had travelled before he came to her. And it is likely he said some soft word in her ear, for she said nothing against it, and stood out with him, and there were little blushes in her cheeks. Then other couples stood up, but when the dance was going to begin, Hanrahan chanced to look down, and he took notice of his boots that were worn and broken, and the ragged grey socks showing through them; and he said angrily it was a bad floor, and the music no great thing, and he sat down in the dark place beside the hearth. But if he did, the girl sat down there with him.

The dancing went on, and when that dance was over

another was called for, and no one took much notice of
Oona and Red Hanrahan for a while, in the corner
where they were. But the mother grew to be uneasy,
and she called to Oona to come and help her to set the
table in the inner room. But Oona that had never re-
fused her before said she would come soon, but not
yet, for she was listening to whatever he was saying in
her ear. The mother grew yet more uneasy then, and
she would come nearer them, and let on to be stirring
the fire or sweeping the hearth, and she would listen
for a minute to hear what the poet was saying to her
child. And one time she heard him telling about white-
handed Deirdre, and how she brought the sons of
Usna to their death; and how the blush in her cheeks
was not so red as the blood of kings' sons that was shed
for her, and her sorrows had never gone out of mind;
and he said it was maybe the memory of her that made
the cry of the plover on the bog as sorrowful in the ear
of the poets as the keening of young men for a comrade.
And there would never have been that memory of her,
he said, if it was not for the poets that had put her
beauty in their songs. And the next time she did not
well understand what he was saying, but as far as she
could hear, it had the sound of poetry though it was
not rhymed, and this is what she heard him say: 'The
sun and the moon are the man and the girl, they are my
life and your life, they are travelling and ever travelling
through the skies as if under the one hood. It was God
made them for one another. He made your life and my
life before the beginning of the world, He made them
that they might go through the world, up and down,

227

like the two best dancers that go on with the dance up and down the long floor of the barn, fresh and laughing, when all the rest are tired out and leaning against the wall.'

The old woman went then to where her husband was playing cards, but he would take no notice of her, and then she went to a woman of the neighbours and said, 'Is there no way we can get them from one another?' and without waiting for an answer she said to some young men that were talking together, 'What good are you when you cannot make the best girl in the house come out and dance with you? And go now the whole of you,' she said, 'and see can you bring her away from the poet's talk.' But Oona would not listen to any of them, but only moved her hand as if to send them away. Then they called to Hanrahan and said he had best dance with the girl himself, or let her dance with one of them. When Hanrahan heard what they were saying he said, 'That is so, I will dance with her; there is no man in the house must dance with her but myself.'

He stood up with her then, and led her out by the hand, and some of the young men were vexed, and some began mocking at his ragged coat and his broken boots. But he took no notice, and Oona took no notice, but they looked at one another as if all the world belonged to themselves alone. But another couple that had been sitting together like lovers stood out on the floor at the same time, holding one another's hands and moving their feet to keep time with the music. But Hanrahan turned his back on them as if angry, and in place of dancing he began to sing, and as he sang he held her hand, and his voice grew louder, and the mocking of the young men stopped, and the fiddle stopped, and there was nothing heard but his voice that had in it the sound of the wind. And what he sang was a song he had heard or had made one time in his wanderings on Slieve Echtge, and the words of it as they can be put into English were like this:—

> O Death's old bony finger
> Will never find us there
> In the high hollow townland
> Where love's to give and to spare;
> Where boughs have fruit and blossom
> At all times of the year;
> Where rivers are running over
> With red beer and brown beer.
> An old man plays the bagpipes
> In a golden and silver wood;
> Queens, their eyes blue like the ice,
> Are dancing in a crowd.

And while he was singing it Oona moved nearer to him, and the colour had gone from her cheek, and her eyes were not blue now, but grey with the tears that were in them, and any one that saw her would have thought she was ready to follow him there and then from the west to the east of the world.

But one of the young men called out, 'Where is that country he is singing about? Mind yourself, Oona, it is a long way off, you might be a long time on the road before you would reach to it.' And another said, 'It is not to the Country of the Young you will be going if you go with him, but to Mayo of the bogs.' Oona looked at him then as if she would question him, but he raised her hand in his hand, and called out between singing and shouting, 'It is very near us that country is, it is on every side; it may be on the bare hill behind it is, or it may be in the heart of the wood.' And he said out very loud and clear, 'In the heart of the wood; O, Death will never find us in the heart of the wood. And will you come with me there, Oona?' he said.

But while he was saying this the two old women had gone outside the door, and Oona's mother was crying, and she said, 'He has put an enchantment on Oona. Can we not get the men to put him out of the house?'

'That is a thing you cannot do,' said the other woman, 'for he is a poet of the Gael, and you know well if you would put a poet of the Gael out of the house, he would put a curse on you that would wither the corn in the fields and dry up the milk of the cows, if it had to hang in the air seven years.'

'God help us,' said the mother, 'and why did I ever let him into the house at all, and the wild name he has!'

'It would have been no harm at all to have kept him outside, but there would great harm come upon you if you put him out by force. But listen to the plan I have to get him out of the house by his own doing, without any one putting him from it at all.'

It was not long after that the two women came in again, each of them having a bundle of hay in her apron. Hanrahan was not singing now, but he was talking to Oona very fast and soft, and he was saying, 'The house is narrow, but the world is wide, and there is no true lover that need be afraid of night or morning or sun or stars or shadows of evening, or any earthly thing.'

'Hanrahan,' said the mother then, striking him on the shoulder, 'will you give me a hand here for a minute?' 'Do that, Hanrahan,' said the woman of the neighbours, 'and help us to make this hay into a rope, for you are ready with your hands, and a blast of wind has loosened the thatch on the haystack.'

'I will do that for you,' said he, and he took the little stick in his hands, and the mother began giving out the hay, and he twisting it, but he was hurrying to have done with it, and to be free again. The women went on talking and giving out the hay, and encouraging him, and saying what a good twister of a rope he was, better than their own neighbours or than any one they had ever seen. And Hanrahan saw that Oona was watching him, and he began to twist very quick and with his head high, and to boast of the readiness of his hands, and the learning he had in his head, and the strength in his arms. And as he was boasting, he went backward, twisting the rope always till he came to the door that was open behind him, and without thinking he passed the threshold and was out on the road. And no sooner was he there than the mother made a sudden rush, and threw out the rope after him, and she shut the door and the half-door and put a bolt upon them.

She was well pleased when she had done that, and laughed out loud, and the neighbours laughed and praised her. But they heard him beating at the door, and saying words of cursing outside it, and the mother had but time to stop Oona that had her hand upon the bolt to open it. She made a sign to the fiddler then, and he began a reel, and one of the young men asked no leave but caught hold of Oona and brought her into the thick of the dance. And when it was over and the fiddle had stopped, there was no sound at all of anything outside, but the road was as quiet as before.

As to Hanrahan, when he knew he was shut out and that there was neither shelter nor drink nor a girl's ear for him that night, the anger and the courage went out of him, and he went on to where the waves were beating on the strand.

He sat down on a big stone, and he began swinging his right arm and singing slowly to himself, the way he did always to hearten himself when every other thing failed him. And whether it was that time or another time he made the song that is called to this day 'The Twisting of the Rope', and that begins, 'What was the dead cat that put me in this place,' is not known.

But after he had been singing a while, mist and shadows seemed to gather about him, sometimes coming out of the sea, and sometimes moving upon it. It seemed to him that one of the shadows was the queen-woman he had seen in her sleep at Slieve Echtge; not in her sleep now, but mocking, and calling out to them that were behind her, 'He was weak, he was weak, he had no courage.' And he felt the strands of the rope in his hand yet, and went on twisting it, but it seemed to him as he twisted that it had all the sorrows of the world in it. And then it seemed to him as if the rope had changed in his dream into a great water-worm that came out of the sea, and that twisted itself about him, and held him closer and closer. And then he got free of it, and went on, shaking and unsteady, along the edge of the strand,

and the grey shapes were flying here and there around him. And this is what they were saying: 'It is a pity for him that refuses the call of the daughters of the Sidhe, for he will find no comfort in the love of the women of the earth to the end of life and time, and the cold of the grave is in his heart for ever. It is death he has chosen; let him die, let him die, let him die.'

HANRAHAN AND CATHLEEN, THE DAUGHTER
OF HOULIHAN

IT was travelling northward Hanrahan was one time, giving a hand to a farmer now and again in the hurried time of the year, and telling his stories and making his share of songs at wakes and at weddings.

He chanced one day to overtake on the road to Colooney one Margaret Rooney, a woman he used to know in Munster when he was a young man. She had no good name at that time, and it was the priest routed her out of the place at last. He knew her by her walk and by the colour of her eyes, and by a way she had of putting back the hair off her face with her left hand. She had been wandering about, she said, selling herrings and the like, and now she was going back to Sligo, to the place in the Burrough where she was living with another woman, Mary Gillis, who had much the same story as herself. She would be well pleased, she said, if he would come and stop in the house with them, and be singing his songs to the bocachs and blind men and fiddlers of the Burrough. She remembered him well, she said, and had a wish for him; and as to Mary Gillis, she had some of his songs off by heart, so he need not be afraid of not getting good treatment, and all the bocachs and poor men that heard him would give him a share of their own earnings for his stories and his songs while he was with them, and would carry his name into all the parishes of Ireland.

He was glad enough to go with her, and to find a woman to be listening to the story of his troubles and to be comforting him. It was at the moment of the fall of day when every man may pass as handsome and every woman as comely. She put her arm about him when he told her of the misfortune of the Twisting of the Rope, and in the half-light she looked as well as another.

They kept in talk all the way to the Burrough, and as for Mary Gillis, when she saw him and heard who he was, she went near crying to think of having a man with so great a name in the house.

Hanrahan was well pleased to settle down with them for a while, for he was tired with wandering; and since the day he found the little cabin fallen in, and Mary Lavelle gone from it, and the thatch scattered, he had never asked to have any place of his own; and he had never stopped long enough in any place to see the green leaves come where he had seen the old leaves wither, or to see the wheat harvested where he had seen it sown. It was a good change to him to have shelter from the wet, and a fire in the evening-time, and his share of food put on the table without the asking.

He made a good many of his songs while he was living there, so well cared for and so quiet. The most of them were love songs, but some were songs of repentance, and some were songs about Ireland and her griefs, under one name or another.

Every evening the bocachs and beggars and blind men and fiddlers would gather into the house and listen to his songs and his poems, and his stories about the old time of the Fianna, and they kept them in their memories that were never spoiled with books; and so they brought his name to every wake and wedding and pattern in the whole of Connacht. He was never so well off or made so much of as he was at that time.

One evening of December he was singing a little song that he said he had heard from the green plover of the mountain, about the fair-haired boys that had left Limerick, and that were wandering and going astray in all parts of the world. There were a good many people in the room that night, and two or three little lads that had crept in, and sat on the floor near the fire, and were too busy with the roasting of a potato in the ashes or some such thing to take much notice of him; but they remembered long afterwards, when his name had gone up, the sound of his voice, and what way he had moved his hand, and the look of him as he sat on the edge of the bed, with his shadow falling on the whitewashed wall behind him, and as he moved going up as high as the thatch.

Of a sudden his singing stopped, and his eyes grew misty as if he was looking at some far thing.

Mary Gillis was pouring whiskey into a mug that stood on a table beside him, and she left off pouring and said, 'Is it of leaving us you are thinking?'

Margaret Rooney heard what she said, and did not know why she said it, and she took the words too much in earnest and came over to him, and there was dread in her heart that she was going to lose so good a comrade, and a man that was thought so much of, and that brought so many to her house.

'You would not go away from us, my heart?' she said, catching him by the hand.

Hanrahan and Cathleen

'It is not of that I am thinking,' he said, 'but of Ireland and the weight of grief that is on her.' And he leaned his head against his hand, and began to sing these words, and the sound of his voice was like the wind in a lonely place.

The old brown thorn-trees break in two high over Cummen
    Strand,
Under a bitter black wind that blows from the left hand;
Our courage breaks like an old tree in a black wind and dies,
But we have hidden in our hearts the flame out of the eyes
Of Cathleen, the daughter of Houlihan.

The wind has bundled up the clouds high over Knocknarea,
And thrown the thunder on the stones for all that Maeve can
    say.
Angers that are like noisy clouds have set our hearts abeat;
But we have all bent low and low and kissed the quiet feet
Of Cathleen, the daughter of Houlihan.

The yellow pool has overflowed high up on Clooth-na-Bare,
For the wet winds are blowing out of the clinging air;
Like heavy flooded waters our bodies and our blood;
But purer than a tall candle before the Holy Rood
Is Cathleen, the daughter of Houlihan.

While he was singing, his voice began to break, and tears came rolling down his cheeks, and Margaret Rooney put down her face into her hands and began to cry along with him. Then a blind beggar by the fire shook his rags with a sob, and after that there was no one of them all but cried tears down.

RED HANRAHAN'S CURSE

ONE fine May morning a long time after Hanrahan had left Margaret Rooney's house, he was walking the road near Colooney, and the sound of the birds singing in the bushes that were white with blossom set him singing as he went. It was to his own little place he was going, that was no more than a cabin, but that pleased him well. For he was tired of so many years of wandering from shelter to shelter at all times of the year, and although he was seldom refused a welcome and a share of what was in the house, it seemed to him sometimes that his mind was getting stiff like his joints, and it was not so easy to him as it used to be to make fun and sport through the night, and to set all the boys laughing with his pleasant talk, and to coax the women with his songs. And a while ago, he had turned into a cabin that some poor man had left to go harvesting and had never come to again. And when he had mended the thatch and made a bed in the corner with a few sacks and rushes, and had swept out the floor, he was well content to have a little place for himself, where he could go in and out as he liked, and put his head in his hands through the length of an evening if the fret was on him, and loneliness after the old times. One by one the neighbours began to send their children in to get some learning from him, and with what they brought, a few eggs, or an oaten cake or a couple of sods of turf, he made out a way of living. And if he went for a wild day and night now and again to the Burrough, no one would say a word, knowing him to be a poet, with wandering in his heart.

It was from the Burrough he was coming that May morning, light-hearted enough, and singing some new song that had come to him. But it was not long till a hare ran across his path, and made away into the fields, through the loose stones of the wall. And he knew it was no good sign a hare to have crossed his path, and he remembered the hare that had led him away to Slieve Echtge the time Mary Lavelle was waiting for him, and how he had never known content for any length of time since then. 'And it is likely enough they are putting some bad thing before me now,' he said.

And after he said that, he heard the sound of crying in the field beside him, and he looked over the wall. And there he saw a young girl sitting under a bush of white hawthorn, and crying as if her heart would break. Her face was hidden in her hands, but her soft hair and her white neck and the young look of her put him in mind of Bridget Purcell and Margaret Gillane and Maeve Connolan and Oona Curry and Celia Driscoll, and the rest of the girls he had made songs for and had coaxed the heart from with his flattering tongue.

She looked up, and he saw her to be a girl of the neighbours, a farmer's daughter. 'What is on you, Nora?' he said. 'Nothing you could take from me, Red Hanrahan.' 'If there is any sorrow on you it is I myself should be well able to serve you,' he said then, 'for it is I know the history of the Greeks, and I know well what sorrow is and parting, and the hardship of the world. And if I am not able to save you from trouble,' he said,

'there is many a one I have saved from it with the power
that is in my songs, as it was in the songs of the poets
that were before me from the beginning of the world.
And it is with the rest of the poets I myself will be
sitting and talking in some far place beyond the world,
to the end of life and time,' he said. The girl stopped
her crying, and she said, 'Owen Hanrahan, I often
heard you have had sorrow and persecution, and that
you know all the troubles of the world since the time
you refused your love to the queen-woman in Slieve
Echtge; and that she never left you in quiet since. But
when it is people of this earth that have harmed you, it
is yourself knows well the way to put harm on them
again. And will you do now what I ask you, Owen
Hanrahan?' she said. 'I will do that indeed,' said he.

'It is my father and my mother and my brothers,'
she said, 'that are marrying me to old Paddy Doe, be-
cause he has a farm of a hundred acres under the moun-
tain. And it is what you can do, Hanrahan,' she said,
'put him into a rhyme the same way you put old Peter
Kilmartin in one the time you were young, that sorrow
may be over him rising up and lying down, that will
put him thinking of Coloony churchyard and not of
marriage. And let you make no delay about it, for it is
for to-morrow they have the marriage settled, and I
would sooner see the sun rise on the day of my death
than on that day.'

'I will put him into a song that will bring shame and
sorrow over him; but tell me how many years has he,
for I would put them in the song?'

'O, he has years upon years. He is as old as you

yourself, Red Hanrahan.' 'As old as myself,' said Hanrahan, and his voice was as if broken; 'as old as myself; there are twenty years and more between us! It is a bad day indeed for Owen Hanrahan when a young girl with the blossom of May in her cheeks thinks him to be an old man. And my grief!' he said, 'you have put a thorn in my heart.'

He turned from her then and went down the road till he came to a stone, and he sat down on it, for it seemed as if all the weight of the years had come on him in the minute. And he remembered it was not many days ago that a woman in some house had said, 'It is not Red Hanrahan you are now but Yellow Hanrahan, for your hair is turned to the colour of a wisp of tow.' And another woman he had asked for a drink had not given him new milk but sour; and sometimes the girls would be whispering and laughing with young ignorant men while he himself was in the middle of giving out his poems or his talk. And he thought of the stiffness of his joints when he first rose of a morning, and the pain of his knees after making a journey, and it seemed to him as if he was come to be a very old man, with cold in the shoulders and speckled shins and his wind breaking and he himself withering away. And with those thoughts there came on him a great anger against old age and all it brought with it. And just then he looked up and saw a great spotted eagle sailing slowly towards Ballygawley, and he cried out, 'You, too, eagle of Ballygawley, are old, and your wings are full of gaps, and I will put you and your ancient comrades, the Pike of Dargan Lake and the Yew of the

Steep Place of the Strangers into my rhyme, that there may be a curse on you for ever.'

There was a bush beside him to the left, flowering like the rest, and a little gust of wind blew the white blossoms over his coat. 'May blossoms,' he said, gathering them up in the hollow of his hand, 'you never know age because you die away in your beauty, and I will put you into my rhyme and give you my blessing.'

He rose up then and plucked a little branch from the bush, and carried it in his hand. But it is old and broken he looked going home that day with the stoop in his shoulders and the darkness in his face.

When he got to his cabin there was no one there, and he went and lay down on the bed for a while as he was used to do when he wanted to make a poem or a praise or a curse. And it was not long he was in making it this time, for the power of the curse-making bards was upon him. And when he had made it he searched his mind how he could send it out over the whole countryside.

Some of the scholars began coming in then, to see if there would be any school that day, and Hanrahan rose up and sat on the bench by the hearth, and they all stood around him.

They thought he would bring out the Virgil or the Mass-book or the primer, but instead of that he held up the little branch of hawthorn he had in his hand yet. 'Children,' he said, 'this is a new lesson I have for you to-day.

'You yourselves and the beautiful people of the world are like this blossom, and old age is the wind that comes and blows the blossom away. And I have made a curse upon old age and upon the old men, and listen now while I give it out to you.' And this is what he said:—

The poet, Owen Hanrahan, under a bush of may,
Calls down a curse on his own head because it withers grey;
Then on the speckled eagle-cock of Ballygawley Hill
Because it is the oldest thing that knows of cark and ill;
And on the yew that has been green from the times out of mind
By the Steep Place of the Strangers and the Gap of the Wind;
And on the great grey pike that broods in Castle Dargan Lake,
Having in his long body a many a hook and ache;
Then curses he old Paddy Bruen of the Well of Bride
Because no hair is on his head and drowsiness inside.
Then Paddy's neighbour, Peter Hart, and Michael Gill, his
        friend,
Because their wandering histories are never at an end.
And then old Shemus Cullinan, shepherd of the Green Lands,
Because he holds two crutches between his crooked hands;
Then calls a curse from the dark North upon old Paddy Doe,
Who plans to lay his withering head upon a breast of snow,
Who plans to wreck a singing voice and break a merry heart;
He bids a curse hang over him till breath and body part,
But he calls down a blessing on the blossom of the may
Because it comes in beauty, and in beauty blows away.

He said it over to the children verse by verse till all of them could say a part of it, and some that were the quickest could say the whole of it.

'That will do for to-day,' he said then. 'And what you have to do now is to go out and sing that song for a while, to the tune of "The Green Bunch of Rushes," to every one you meet, and to the old men themselves.'

'I will do that,' said one of the little lads; 'I know old

Paddy Doe well. Last Saint John's Eve we dropped a mouse down his chimney, but this is better than a mouse.'

'I will go into the town of Sligo and sing it in the street,' said another of the boys. 'Do that,' said Hanrahan, 'and go into the Burrough and tell it to Margaret Rooney and Mary Gillis, and bid them sing it, and to make the beggars and the bocachs sing it wherever they go.' The children ran out then, full of pride and of mischief, calling out the song as they ran, and Hanrahan knew there was no danger it would not be heard.

He was sitting outside the door the next morning, looking at his scholars as they came by in twos and threes. They were nearly all come, and he was considering the place of the sun in the heavens to know whether it was time to begin, when he heard a sound that was like the buzzing of a swarm of bees in the air, or the rushing of a hidden river in time of flood. Then he saw a crowd coming up to the cabin from the road, and he took notice that all the crowd was made up of old men, and that the leaders of it were Paddy Bruen, Michael Gill and Paddy Doe, and there was not one in the crowd but had in his hand an ash stick or a black-thorn. As soon as they caught sight of him, the sticks began to wave hither and thither like branches in a storm, and the old feet to run.

He waited no longer, but made off up the hill behind the cabin till he was out of their sight.

After a while he came back round the hill, where he was hidden by the furze growing along a ditch. And when he came in sight of his cabin he saw that all the old men had gathered around it, and one of them was just at that time thrusting a rake with a wisp of lighted straw on it into the thatch.

'My grief!' he said. 'I have set Old Age and Time and Weariness and Sickness against me, and I must go wandering again. And, O Blessed Queen of Heaven,' he said, 'protect me from the Eagle of Ballygawley, the Yew Tree of the Steep Place of the Strangers, the Pike of Castle Dargan Lake, and from the lighted wisps of their kindred, the Old Men!'

HANRAHAN'S VISION

IT was in the month of June Hanrahan was on the road near Sligo, but he did not go into the town, but turned towards Ben Bulben; for there were thoughts of the old times coming upon him, and he had no mind to meet with common men. And as he walked he was singing to himself a song that had come to him one time in his dreams:—

O Death's old bony finger
Will never find us there
In the high hollow townland
Where love's to give and to spare;
Where boughs have fruit and blossom
At all times of the year;
Where rivers are running over
With red beer and brown beer.
An old man plays the bagpipes
In a golden and silver wood;
Queens, their eyes blue like the ice,
Are dancing in a crowd.

The little fox he murmured,
'O what of the world's bane?'
The sun was laughing sweetly,
The moon plucked at my rein,
But the little red fox murmured,
'O do not pluck at his rein,
He is riding to the townland
That is the world's bane.'

When their hearts are so high
That they would come to blows,
They unhook their heavy swords
From golden and silver boughs;

Hanrahan's Vision

But all that are killed in battle
Awaken to life again.
It is lucky that their story
Is not known among men,
For O the strong farmers
That would let the spade lie,
Their hearts would be like a cup
That somebody had drunk dry.

Michael will unhook his trumpet
From a bough overhead,
And blow a little noise
When the supper has been spread.
Gabriel will come from the water
With a fish-tail, and talk
Of wonders that have happened
On wet roads where men walk,
And lift up an old horn
Of hammered silver, and drink
Till he has fallen asleep
Upon the starry brink.

Hanrahan had begun to climb the mountain then,
and he gave over singing, for it was a long climb for
him, and every now and again he had to sit down and
to rest for a while. And one time he was resting he took
notice of a wild brier bush, with blossoms on it, that
was growing beside a rath, and it brought to mind the
wild roses he used to bring to Mary Lavelle, and to no
woman after her. And he tore off a little branch of the
bush, that had buds on it and open blossoms, and he
went on with his song:—

The little fox he murmured,
'O what of the world's bane?'

> The sun was laughing sweetly,
> The moon plucked at my rein;
> But the little red fox murmured,
> 'O do not pluck at his rein,
> He is riding to the townland
> That is the world's bane.'

And he went on climbing the hill, and left the rath, and there came to his mind some of the old poems that told of lovers, good and bad, and of some that were awakened from the sleep of the grave itself by the strength of one another's love, and brought away to a life in some shadowy place, where they are waiting for the Judgment and banished from the face of God.

And at last, at the fall of day, he came to the Steep Place of the Strangers, and there he laid himself down along a ridge of rocks and looked into the valley, that was full of grey mist spreading from mountain to mountain.

And it seemed to him as he looked that the mist changed to shapes of shadowy men and women, and his heart began to beat with the fear and the joy of the sight. And his hands, that were always restless, began to pluck off the leaves of the roses on the little branch, and he watched them as they went floating down into the valley in a little fluttering troop.

Suddenly he heard a faint music, a music that had more laughter in it and more crying than all the music of this world. And his heart rose when he heard that, and he began to laugh out loud, for he knew that music was made by some who had a beauty and a greatness beyond the people of this world. And it seemed to him

that the little soft rose-leaves as they went fluttering
down into the valley began to change their shape till
they looked like a troop of men and women far off in
the mist, with the colour of the roses on them. And
then that colour changed to many colours, and what
he saw was a long line of tall beautiful young men, and
of queen-women, that were not going from him but
coming towards him and past him, and their faces were
full of tenderness for all their proud looks, and were
very pale and worn, as if they were seeking and ever
seeking for high sorrowful things. And shadowy arms
were stretched out of the mist as if to take hold of them,
but could not touch them, for the quiet that was about
them could not be broken. And before them and be-
yond them, but at a distance as if in reverence, there
were other shapes, sinking and rising and coming and
going, and Hanrahan knew them by their whirling
flight to be the Sidhe, the ancient defeated gods; and
the shadowy arms did not rise to take hold of the Sidhe,
who are of those that can neither sin nor obey. And
they all lessened then in the distance, and they seemed
to be going towards the white door that is in the side
of the mountain.

The mist spread out before him now like a deserted
sea washing the mountains with long grey waves, but
while he was looking at it, it began to fill again with a
flowing broken witless life that was a part of itself, and
arms and pale heads covered with tossing hair appeared
in the greyness. It rose higher and higher till it was
level with the edge of the steep rock, and then the
shapes seemed all but solid, and that new procession

half lost in mist passed very slowly with uneven steps, and in the midst of each shadow there was something shining in the starlight. They came nearer and nearer, and Hanrahan saw that they also were lovers, and that they had heart-shaped mirrors instead of hearts, and they were looking and ever looking on their own faces in one another's mirrors. They passed on, sinking downward as they passed, and other shapes rose in their place, and these did not keep side by side, but followed after one another, holding out wild beckoning arms, and he saw that those who were followed were women, and as to their heads they were beyond all beauty, but as to their bodies they were but shadows without life, and their long hair was moving and trembling about them, as if it lived with some terrible life of its own. And then the mist rose of a sudden and hid them, and then a light gust of wind blew them away towards the north-east, and covered Hanrahan at the same time with a white wing of cloud.

He stood up trembling and was going to turn away from the valley, when he saw two dark and half-hidden forms standing as if in the air just beyond the rock, and one of them that had the sorrowful eyes of a beggar said to him in a woman's voice, 'Speak to me, for no one in this world or any other world has spoken to me for seven hundred years.'

'Tell me who are those that have passed by,' said Hanrahan.

'Those that passed first,' the woman said, 'are the lovers that had the greatest name in the old times, Blanaid and Deirdre and Grania and their dear comrades, and a great many that are not so well known but are as well loved. And because it was not only the blossom of youth they were looking for in one another, but the beauty that is as lasting as the night and the stars; the night and the stars hold them for ever from the warring and the perishing, in spite of the death and bitterness their love brought into the world. And those that came next,' she said, 'and that still breathe the sweet air and have the mirrors in their hearts, are not put in songs by the poets, because they sought only to triumph one over the other, and so to prove their strength and beauty, and out of this they made a kind of love. And as to the women with shadow-bodies, they desired neither to triumph nor to love but only to be loved, and there is no blood in their hearts or in their bodies until it flows through them from a kiss, and their life is but for a moment. All these are unhappy, but I am the unhappiest of all, for I am Dervorgilla, and this is Diarmuid, and it was our sin brought the Norman into Ireland. And the curses of all the generations are upon us, and none are punished as we are punished. It was but the blossom of the man and of the woman we loved in one another, and so when we died there was no lasting unbreakable quiet about us, and the bitterness of the battles we brought into Ireland turned to our own punishment. We go wandering together for ever, but Diarmuid that was my lover sees me always as a body that has been a long time in the ground, and I know that is the way he sees me. Ask me more, ask me more, for all the years have left their wisdom in my heart, and no one has listened to me for seven hundred years.'

A great terror had fallen upon Hanrahan, and lifting his arms above his head he screamed out loud three times, and the cattle in the valley lifted their heads and lowed, and the birds in the wood at the edge of the mountain awaked out of their sleep and fluttered through the trembling leaves. But a little below the edge of the rock, the troop of rose-leaves still fluttered in the air, for the gateway of Eternity had opened and shut again in one beat of the heart.

The Death of Hanrahan

THE DEATH OF HANRAHAN

HANRAHAN, that was never long in one place, was back again among the villages that are at the foot of Slieve Echtge, Illeton and Scalp and Ballylee, stopping sometimes in one house and sometimes in another, and finding a welcome in every place for the sake of the old times and of his poetry and his learning. There was some silver and some copper money in the little leather bag under his coat, but it was seldom he needed to take anything from it, for it was little he used, and there was not one of the people that would have taken payment from him. His hand had grown heavy on the blackthorn he leaned on, and his cheeks were hollow and worn, but so far as food went, potatoes and milk and a bit of oaten cake, he had what he wanted of it; and it is not on the edge of so wild and boggy a place as Echtge a mug of spirits would be wanting, with the taste of the turf-smoke on it. He would wander about the big wood at Kinadife, or he would sit through many hours of the day among the rushes about Lake Belshragh, listening to the streams from the hills, or watching the shadows in the brown bog pools; sitting so quiet as not to startle the deer that came down from the heather to the grass and the tilled fields at the fall of night. As the days went by it seemed as if he was beginning to belong to some world out of sight and misty, that has for its mearing the colours that are beyond all other colours and the silences that are beyond all silences of this world. And sometimes he would hear coming and going in the wood music that when it stopped went from his memory like a dream; and once in the stillness of midday he heard a sound like the clashing of many swords, that went on for a long time without any break. And at the fall of night and at moonrise the lake would grow to be like a gateway of silver and shining stones, and there would come from its silence the faint sound of keening and of frightened laughter broken by the wind, and many pale beckoning hands.

He was sitting looking into the water one evening in harvest time, thinking of all the secrets that were shut into the lakes and the mountains, when he heard a cry coming from the south, very faint at first, but getting louder and clearer as the shadow of the rushes grew longer, till he could hear the words: 'I am beautiful, I am beautiful. The birds in the air, the moths under the leaves, the flies over the water look at me, for they never saw any one so beautiful as myself. I am young, I am young: look upon me, mountains; look upon me, perishing woods, for my body will be shining like the white waters when you have been hurried away. You and the whole race of men, and the race of the beasts, and the race of the fish, and the winged race, are dropping like a candle that is nearly burned out. But I laugh aloud because I am in my youth.' The voice would break off from time to time, as if tired, and then it would begin again, calling out always the same words, 'I am beautiful, I am beautiful.' Presently the bushes at the edge of the little lake trembled for a moment, and a very old woman forced her way among them, and passed by Hanrahan, walking with very slow steps. Her face was of the colour of earth, and more wrinkled than the face of any old hag that was ever seen, and her grey hair was hanging in wisps, and the rags she was wearing did not hide her dark skin that was roughened by all weathers. She passed by him with her eyes wide open, and her head high, and her arms hanging straight beside her, and she went into the shadow of the hills towards the west.

A sort of dread came over Hanrahan when he saw her, for he knew her to be one Winny Byrne of the Cross-Roads, that went begging from place to place crying always the same cry, and he had often heard that she had once such wisdom that all the women of the neighbours used to go looking for advice from her, and that she had a voice so beautiful that men and women would come from every part to hear her sing at a wake or a wedding; and that the Others, the great Sidhe, had stolen her wits one Samhain night many years ago, when she had fallen asleep on the edge of a rath and had seen in her dreams the servants of Echtge of the hills.

And as she vanished away up the hillside, it seemed as if her cry, 'I am beautiful, I am beautiful,' was coming from among the stars in the heavens.

There was a cold wind creeping among the rushes, and Hanrahan began to shiver, and he rose up to go to some house where there would be a fire on the hearth. But instead of turning down the hill as he was used, he went on up the hill, along the little track that was maybe a road and maybe the dry bed of a stream. It was the same way Winny had gone, and it led to the little cabin where she stopped when she stopped in any place at all. He walked very slowly up the hill as if he had a great load on his back, and at last he saw a light a little to the left, and he thought it likely it was from Winny's house it was shining, and he turned from the path to go to it. But clouds had come over the sky, and he could not well see his way, and after he had gone a few steps his foot slipped and he fell into a bog drain, and though he dragged himself out of it, holding on to the roots of the heather, the fall had given him a great shake, and he felt better fit to lie down than to go travelling. But he had always great courage, and he made his way on, step by step, till at last he came to Winny's cabin, that had no window, but the light was shining from the door. He thought to go into it and to rest for a while, but when he came to the door he did not see Winny inside it, but what he saw was four old grey-haired women playing cards, but Winny herself was not among them. Hanrahan sat down on a heap of turf beside the door, for he was tired out and out, and had no wish for talking or for card-playing, and his bones and his joints aching the way they were. He could hear the four women talking as they played, and calling out their hands. And it seemed to him that they were saying, like the strange man in the barn long ago, 'Spades and Diamonds, Courage and Power. Clubs and Hearts, Knowledge and Pleasure.' And he went on saying those words over and over to himself; and whether or not he was in his dreams, the pain that was in his shoulder never left him. And after a while the four women in the cabin began to quarrel, and each one to say the other had not played fair, and their voices grew from loud to louder, and their screams and their curses, till at last the whole air was filled with the noise of them around and above the house, and Hanrahan, hearing it between sleep and waking, said, 'That is the sound of the fighting between the friends and the ill-wishers of a man that is near his death. And I wonder,' he said, 'who is the man in this lonely place that is near his death.'

It seemed as if he had been asleep a long time, and he opened his eyes, and the face he saw over him was the old wrinkled face of Winny of the Cross-Roads. She was looking hard at him, as if to make sure he was not dead, and she wiped away the blood that had grown dry on his face with a wet cloth, and after a while she partly helped him and partly lifted him into the cabin, and laid him down on what served her for a bed. She gave him a couple of potatoes from a pot on the fire, and, what served him better, a mug of spring water. He slept a little now and again, and sometimes he heard her singing to herself as she moved about the house, and so the night wore away. When the sky began to brighten with the dawn he felt for the bag where his little store of money was, and held it out to her, and she took out a bit of copper and a bit of silver money, but she let it drop again as if it was nothing to her, maybe because it was not money she was used to beg for, but food and rags; or maybe because the rising of the dawn was filling her with pride and a new belief in her own great beauty. She went out and cut a few armfuls of heather, and brought it in and heaped it over Hanrahan, saying something about the cold of the morning, and while she did that he took notice of the wrinkles in her face, and the greyness of her hair, and the broken teeth that were black and full of gaps. And when he was well covered with the heather she went out of the door and away down the side of the mountain, and he could hear the cry, 'I am beautiful, I am beautiful,' getting less and less as she went, till at last it died away altogether.

Hanrahan lay there through the length of the day, in his pains and his weakness, and when the shadows of the evening were falling he heard her voice again coming up the hillside, and she came in and boiled the potatoes and shared them with him the same way as before. And one day after another passed like that, and the weight of his flesh was heavy about him. But little by little as he grew weaker he knew there were some greater than himself in the room with him, and that the house began to be filled with them; and it seemed to him they had all power in their hands, and that they might with one touch of the hand break down the wall the hardness of pain had built about him, and take him into their own world. And sometimes he could hear voices, very faint and joyful, crying from the rafters or out of the flame on the hearth, and other times the whole house was filled with music that went through it like a wind. And after a while his weakness left no place for pain, and there grew up about him a great silence like the silence in the heart of a lake, and there came through it, like the flame of a rushlight, the faint joyful voices ever and always.

One morning he heard music somewhere outside the door, and as the day passed it grew louder and louder until it drowned the faint joyful voices, and even Winny's cry upon the hillside at the fall of evening. About midnight and in a moment, the walls seemed to melt away and to leave his bed floating on a pale misty light that shone on every side as far as the eye could see; and after the first blinding of his eyes he saw that it was full of great shadowy figures rushing here and there.

At the same time the music came very clearly to him, and he knew that it was but the continual clashing of swords.

'I am after my death,' he said, 'and in the very heart of the music of Heaven. O Cherubim and Seraphim, receive my soul!'

At his cry the light where it was nearest to him filled with sparks of yet brighter light, and he saw that these were the points of swords turned towards his heart; and then a sudden flame, bright and burning like God's love or God's hate, swept over the light and went out and he was in darkness. At first he could see nothing, for all was as dark as if there was black bog earth about him, but all of a sudden the fire blazed up as if a wisp of straw had been thrown upon it. And as he looked at it, the light was shining on the big pot that was hanging from a hook, and on the flat stone where Winny used to bake a cake now and again, and on the long rusty knife she used to be cutting the roots of the heather with, and on the long blackthorn stick he had brought into the house himself. And when he saw those four things, some memory came into Hanrahan's mind, and strength came back to him, and he rose sitting up in the bed, and he said very loud and clear, 'The Cauldron, the Stone, the

Sword, the Spear. What are they? Who do they belong to? And I have asked the question this time.'

And then he fell back again, weak, and the breath going from him.

Winny Byrne, that had been tending the fire, came over then, having her eyes fixed on the bed; and the faint laughing voices began crying out again, and a pale light, grey like a wave, came creeping over the room, and he did not know from what secret world it came. He saw Winny's withered face and her withered arms that were grey like crumbled earth, and weak as he was he shrank back farther towards the wall. And then there came out of the mud-stiffened rags arms as white and as shadowy as the foam on a river, and they were put about his body, and a voice that he could hear well but that seemed to come from a long way off said to him in a whisper, 'You will go looking for me no more upon the breasts of women.'

'Who are you?' he said then.

'I am one of the lasting people, of the lasting unwearied Voïces, that make my dwelling in the broken and the dying, and those that have lost their wits; and I came looking for you, and you are mine until the whole world is burned out like a candle that is spent. And look up now,' she said, 'for the wisps that are for our wedding are lighted.'

He saw then that the house was crowded with pale shadowy hands, and that every hand was holding what was sometimes like a wisp lighted for a marriage, and sometimes like a tall white candle for the dead.

When the sun rose on the morning of the morrow

The Death of Hanrahan

Winny of the Cross-Roads rose up from where she was sitting beside the body, and began her begging from townland to townland, singing the same song as she walked: 'I am beautiful, I am beautiful. The birds in the air, the moths under the leaves, the flies over the water look at me. I am young: look upon me, mountains; look upon me, perishing woods, for my body will be shining like the white waters when you have been hurried away. You and the whole race of men, and the race of the beasts, and the race of the fish, and the winged race, are dropping like a candle that is nearly burned out. But I laugh aloud, because I am in my youth.'

She did not come back that night or any night to the cabin, and it was not till the end of two days that the turf-cutters going to the bog found the body of Red Owen Hanrahan, and gathered men to wake him and women to keen him, and gave him a burying worthy of so great a poet.

THE END

ROSA ALCHEMICA

THE TABLES OF THE LAW

AND

THE ADORATION OF THE MAGI
1897

'O, blessed and happy he who, knowing the mysteries of the gods, sanctifies his life, and purifies his soul, celebrating orgies in the mountains with holy purifications.'—EURIPIDES

TO
A. E.

ROSA ALCHEMICA

I

It is now more than ten years since I met, for the last time, Michael Robartes, and for the first time and the last time his friends and fellow-students; and witnessed his and their tragic end, and passed through strange experiences, which have changed me so that my writings have grown less popular and less intelligible, and may compel me to take refuge in the habit of Saint Dominic. I had just published *Rosa Alchemica*, a little work on the Alchemists, somewhat in the manner of Sir Thomas Browne, and had received many letters from believers in the arcane sciences, upbraiding what they called my timidity, for they could not believe so evident sympathy but the sympathy of the artist, which is half pity, for everything which has moved men's hearts in any age. I had discovered, early in my researches, that their doctrine was no merely chemical fantasy, but a philosophy they applied to the world, to the elements and to man himself; and that they sought to fashion gold out of common metals merely as part of a universal transmutation of all things into some divine and imperishable substance; and this enabled me to make my little book a fanciful reverie over the transmutation of life into art, and a cry of measureless desire for a world made wholly of essences.

I was sitting dreaming of what I had written, in my house in one of the old parts of Dublin; a house my ancestors had made almost famous through their part in the politics of the city and their friendships with the famous men of their generations; and was feeling an unwonted happiness at having at last accomplished a long-cherished design, and changed my rooms into an expression of this favourite doctrine. The portraits, of more historical than artistic interest, had gone; and tapestry, full of the blue and bronze of peacocks, fell over the doors, and shut out all history and activity untouched with beauty and peace; and now when I looked at my Crivelli and pondered on the rose in the hand of the Virgin, wherein the form was so delicate and precise that it seemed more like a thought than a flower, or my Francesca, so full of ghostly astonishment, I knew a Christian's ecstasy without his slavery to rule and custom. When I pondered over the antique bronze gods and goddesses, which I had mortgaged my house to buy, I had all a pagan's delight in various beauty and without his terror at sleepless destiny and his labour with many sacrifices; and I had but to go to my bookshelf, where every book was bound in leather, stamped with intricate ornament, and of a carefully chosen colour: Shakespeare in the orange of the glory of the world, Dante in the dull red of his anger, Milton in the blue-grey of his formal calm; to know what I would of human passions without their bitterness and without satiety. I had gathered about me all gods because I believed in none, and experienced every pleasure because I gave myself to none, but held myself apart, individual, indissoluble, a mirror of polished steel. I looked in the triumph of this imagination at the birds of Hera, glittering in the light of the fire as though of Byzantine mosaic; and to my mind, for which symbolism was a necessity, they seemed the doorkeepers of my world, shutting out all that was not of as affluent a beauty as their own; and for a moment I thought, as I had thought in so many other moments, that it was possible to rob life of every bitterness except the bitterness of death; and then a thought which had followed this thought, time after time, filled me with a passionate sorrow. All those forms: that Madonna with her brooding purity, those delighted ghostly faces under the morning light, those bronze divinities with their passionless dignity, those wild shapes rushing from despair to despair, belonged to a divine world wherein I had no part; and every experience, however profound, every perception, however exquisite, would bring me the bitter dream of a limitless energy I could never know, and even in my most perfect moment I would be two selves, the one watching with heavy eyes the other's moment of content. I had heaped about me the gold born in the crucibles of others; but the supreme dream of the alchemist, the transmutation of the weary heart into a weariless spirit, was as far from me as, I doubted not, it had been from him also. I turned to my last purchase, a set of alchemical apparatus which, the dealer in the Rue Le Peletier had assured me, once belonged to Raymond Lully, and as I joined the alembic to the athanor and laid the *lavacrum maris* at their side, I understood the alchemical doctrine, that all beings, divided from the great deep where spirits wander, one and yet a multitude, are weary; and sympathised, in the pride of my connoisseurship, with the consuminy thirst for destruction which made the alchemist veil under his symbols of lions and dragons, of eagles and ravens, of dew and of nitre, a search for an essence which would dissolve all mortal things. I repeated to myself the ninth key of Basilius Valentinus, in which he compares the fire of the Last Day to the fire of the alchemist, and the world to the alchemist's furnace, and would have us know that all must be dissolved before the divine substance, material gold or immaterial ecstasy, awake. I had dissolved indeed the mortal world and lived amid immortal essences, but had obtained no miraculous ecstasy. As I thought of these things, I drew aside the curtains and looked out into the darkness, and it seemed to my troubled fancy that all those little points of light filling the sky were the furnaces of innumerable divine alchemists, who labour continually, turning lead into gold, weariness into ecstasy, bodies into souls, the darkness into God; and at their perfect labour my mortality grew heavy, and I cried out, as so many dreamers and men of letters in our age have cried, for the birth of that elaborate spiritual beauty which could alone uplift souls weighted with so many dreams.

II

My reverie was broken by a loud knocking at the door, and I wondered the more at this because I had no visitors, and had bid my servants do all things silently, lest they broke the dream of an all but secret life. Feeling a little curious, I resolved to go to the door myself, and, taking one of the silver candlesticks from the mantelpiece, began to descend the stairs. The servants appeared to be out, for though the sound poured through every corner and crevice of the house there was no stir in the lower rooms. I remembered that because my needs were so few, my part in life so little, they had begun to come and go as they would, often leaving me alone for hours. The emptiness and silence of a world from which I had driven everything but dreams suddenly overwhelmed me, and I shuddered as I drew the bolt. I found before me Michael Robartes, whom I had not seen for years, and whose wild red hair, fierce eyes, sensitive, tremulous lips and rough clothes, made him look now, just as they used to do fifteen years before, something between a debauchee, a saint, and a peasant. He had recently come to Ireland, he said, and wished to see me on a matter of importance: indeed, the only matter of importance for him and for me. His voice brought up before me our student years in Paris, and, remembering the magnetic power he had once possessed over me, a little fear mingled with much annoyance at this irrelevant intrusion, as I led the way up the wide staircase, where Swift had passed joking and railing, and Curran telling stories and quoting Greek, in simpler days, before men's minds, subtilised and complicated by the romantic movement in art and literature, began to tremble on the verge of some unimagined revelation. I felt that my hand shook, and saw that the light of the candle wavered more than it need have upon the gods and nymphs set upon the wall by some Italian plasterer of the eighteenth century, making them look like the first

beings slowly shaping in the formless and void dark-
ness. When the door had closed, and the peacock curtain
fell between us and the world, I felt, in a way I could
not understand, that some singular and unexpected thing
was about to happen. I went over to the mantelpiece,
and finding that a little chainless bronze censer, set,
upon the outside, with pieces of painted china by
Orazio Fontana, which I had filled with antique amu-
lets, had fallen upon its side and poured out its con-
tents, I began to gather the amulets into the bowl,
partly to collect my thoughts and partly with that
habitual reverence which seemed to me the due of
things so long connected with secret hopes and fears.
'I see,' said Michael Robartes, 'that you are still fond of
incense, and I can show you an incense more precious
than any you have ever seen,' and as he spoke he took
the censer out of my hand and put the amulets in a little
heap between the athanor and the alembic. I sat down,
and he sat down at the side of the fire, and sat there for
a while looking into the fire, and holding the censer in
his hand. 'I have come to ask you something,' he said,
'and the incense will fill the room, and our thoughts,
with its sweet odour while we are talking. I got it from
an old man in Syria, who said it was made from flowers,
of one kind with the flowers that laid their heavy
purple petals upon the hands and upon the hair and
upon the feet of Christ in the Garden of Gethsemane,
and folded Him in their heavy breath, until He cried
against the cross and His destiny.' He shook some dust
into the censer out of a small silk bag, and set the censer
upon the floor and lit the dust, which sent up a blue

stream of smoke, that spread out over the ceiling, and flowed downwards again until it was like Milton's banyan tree. It filled me, as incense often does, with a faint sleepiness, so that I started when he said, 'I have come to ask you that question which I asked you in Paris, and which you left Paris rather than answer.'

He had turned his eyes towards me, and I saw them glitter in the firelight, through the incense cloud, as I replied: 'You mean, will I become an initiate of your Order of the Alchemical Rose? I would not consent in Paris, when I was full of unsatisfied desire, and now that I have at last fashioned my life according to my desire, am I likely to consent?'

'You have changed greatly since then,' he answered. 'I have read your books, and now I see you among all these images, and I understand you better than you do yourself, for I have been with many and many dreamers at the same crossways. You have shut away the world and gathered the gods about you, and if you do not throw yourself at their feet, you will be always full of lassitude, and of wavering purpose, for a man must forget he is miserable in the bustle and noise of the multitude in this world and in time; or seek a mystical union with the multitude who govern this world and time.' And then he murmured something I could not hear, and as though to some one I could not see.

For a moment the room appeared to darken, as it used to do when he was about to perform some singular experiment, and in the darkness the peacocks upon the doors seemed to glow with a more intense colour. I cast off the illusion, which was, I believed, merely caused by memory, and by the twilight of incense, for I would not acknowledge that he could overcome my now mature intellect; and I said, 'Even if I grant that I need a spiritual belief and some form of worship, why should I go to Eleusis and not to Calvary?' He leaned forward and began speaking with a slightly rhythmical intonation, and as he spoke I had to struggle again with the shadow, as of some older night than the night of the sun, which began to dim the light of the candles and to blot out the little gleams upon the corner of picture-frames and on the bronze divinities, and to turn the blue of the incense to a heavy purple; while it left the peacocks to glimmer and glow as though each separate colour were a living spirit. I had fallen into a profound dream-like reverie in which I heard him speaking as at a distance. 'And yet there is no one who communes with only one god,' he was saying, 'and the more a man lives in imagination and in a refined understanding, the more gods does he meet with and talk with, and the more does he come under the power of Roland, who sounded in the Valley of Roncesvalles the last trumpet of the body's will and pleasure; and of Hamlet, who saw them perishing away, and sighed; and of Faust, who looked for them up and down the world and could not find them; and under the power of all those countless divinities who have taken upon themselves spiritual bodies in the minds of the modern poets and romance-writers, and under the power of the old divinities, who since the Renaissance have won everything of their ancient worship except the sacrifice of birds and fishes, the fragrance of garlands and the smoke of incense. The many think humanity made these divinities, and that it can unmake them again; but we who have seen them pass in rattling harness, and in soft robes, and heard them speak with articulate voices while we lay in death-like trance, know that they are always making and unmaking humanity, which is indeed but the trembling of their lips.'

He had stood up and begun to walk to and fro, and had become in my waking dream a shuttle weaving an immense purple web whose folds had begun to fill the room. The room seemed to have become inexplicably silent, as though all but the web and the weaving were at an end in the world. 'They have come to us; they have come to us,' the voice began again; 'all that have ever been in your reverie, all that you have met with in books. There is Lear, his head still wet with the thunderstorm, and he laughs because you thought yourself an existence who are but a shadow, and him a shadow who is an eternal god; and there is Beatrice, with her lips half parted in a smile, as though all the stars were about to pass away in a sigh of love; and there is the mother of the God of humility, He who has cast so great a spell over men that they have tried to unpeople their hearts that He might reign alone, but she holds in her hand the rose whose every petal is a god; and there, O, swiftly she comes! is Aphrodite under a twilight falling from the wings of numberless sparrows, and about her feet are the grey and white doves.' In the midst of my dream I saw him hold out his left arm and pass his right hand over it as though he stroked the wings of doves. I made a violent effort which seemed almost to tear me in two, and said with forced determination, 'You would sweep me away into an indefinite world which fills me with terror; and yet a man is a great man just in so far as he can make his mind reflect everything with indifferent precision like a mirror.' I seemed to be perfectly master of myself, and went on, but more rapidly, 'I command you to leave me at once, for your ideas and fantasies are but the illusions that creep like maggots into civilisations when they begin to decline, and into minds when they begin to decay.' I had grown suddenly angry, and seizing the alembic from the table, was about to rise and strike him with it, when the peacocks on the door behind him appeared to grow immense; and then the alembic fell from my fingers and I was drowned in a tide of green and blue and bronze feathers, and as I struggled hopelessly I heard a distant voice saying, 'Our master Avicenna has written that all life proceeds out of corruption.' The glittering feathers had now covered me completely, and I knew that I had struggled for hundreds of years, and was conquered at last. I was sinking into the depth when the green and blue and bronze that seemed to fill the world became a sea of flame and swept me away, and as I was swirled along I heard a voice over my head cry, 'The mirror is broken in two pieces,' and another voice answer, 'The mirror is broken in four pieces,' and a more distant voice cry with an exultant cry, 'The mirror is broken into numberless pieces'; and then a multitude of pale hands were reaching towards me, and strange gentle faces bending above me, and half-wailing and half-caressing voices uttering words that were forgotten the moment they were spoken. I was being lifted out of the tide of flame, and felt my memories, my hopes, my thoughts, my will, everything I held to be myself, melting away; then I seemed to rise through numberless companies of beings who were, I understood, in some way more certain than thought, each wrapped in his eternal moment, in the perfect lifting of an arm, in a little circlet of rhythmical words, in dreaming with dim eyes and half-closed eyelids. And then I passed beyond these forms, which were so beautiful they had almost ceased to be, and, having endured strange moods, melancholy, as it seemed, with the weight of many worlds, I passed into that Death which is Beauty herself, and into that Loneliness which all the multitudes desire without ceasing. All things that had ever lived seemed to come and dwell in my heart, and I in theirs; and I had never again known mortality or tears, had I not suddenly fallen from the certainty of vision into the uncertainty of dream, and become a drop of molten gold falling with immense rapidity, through a night elaborate with stars, and all about me a melancholy exultant wailing. I fell and fell and fell, and then the wailing was but the wailing of the wind in the chimney, and I awoke to find myself leaning upon the table and supporting my head with my hands. I saw the alembic swaying from side to side in the distant corner it had rolled to, and Michael Robartes watching me and waiting. 'I will go wherever you will,' I said, 'and do whatever you bid me, for I have been with eternal things.' 'I knew,' he replied, 'you must needs answer as you have answered, when I heard the storm begin. You must come to a great distance, for we were

commanded to build our temple between the pure mul-
titude by the waves and the impure multitude of men.'

III

I did not speak as we drove through the deserted
streets, for my mind was curiously empty of familiar
thoughts and experiences; it seemed to have been
plucked out of the definite world and cast naked upon a
shoreless sea. There were moments when the vision
appeared on the point of returning, and I would half
remember, with an ecstasy of joy or sorrow, crimes and
heroisms, fortunes and misfortunes; or begin to con-
template, with a sudden leaping of the heart, hopes and
terrors, desires and ambitions, alien to my orderly and
careful life; and then I would awake shuddering at the
thought that some great imponderable being had swept
through my mind. It was indeed days before this feeling
passed perfectly away, and even now, when I have
sought refuge in the only definite faith, I feel a great
tolerance for those people with incoherent personal-
ities, who gather in the chapels and meeting-places of
certain obscure sects, because I also have felt fixed
habits and principles dissolving before a power, which
was *hysterica passio* or sheer madness, if you will, but
was so powerful in its melancholy exultation that I
tremble lest it wake again and drive me from my new-
found peace.

When we came in the grey light to the great half-
empty terminus, it seemed to me I was so changed that
I was no more, as man is, a moment shuddering at eter-

nity, but eternity weeping and laughing over a moment; and when we had started and Michael Robartes had fallen asleep, as he soon did, his sleeping face, in which there was no sign of all that had so shaken me and that now kept me wakeful, was to my excited mind more like a mask than a face. The fancy possessed me that the man behind it had dissolved away like salt in water, and that it laughed and sighed, appealed and denounced at the bidding of beings greater or less than man. 'This is not Michael Robartes at all: Michael Robartes is dead; dead for ten, for twenty years perhaps,' I kept repeating to myself. I fell at last into a feverish sleep, waking up from time to time when we rushed past some little town, its slated roofs shining with wet, or still lake gleaming in the cold morning light. I had been too preoccupied to ask where we were going, or to notice what tickets Michael Robartes had taken, but I knew now from the direction of the sun that we were going westward; and presently I knew also, by the way in which the trees had grown into the semblance of tattered beggars flying with bent heads towards the east, that we were approaching the western coast. Then immediately I saw the sea between the low hills upon the left, its dull grey broken into white patches and lines.

When we left the train we had still, I found, some way to go, and set out, buttoning our coats about us, for the wind was bitter and violent. Michael Robartes was silent, seeming anxious to leave me to my thoughts; and as we walked between the sea and the rocky side of a great promontory, I realised with a new perfection what a shock had been given to all my habits of thought

279

and of feeling, if indeed some mysterious change had not taken place in the substance of my mind, for the grey waves, plumed with scudding foam, had grown part of a teeming, fantastic inner life; and when Michael Robartes pointed to a square ancient-looking house, with a much smaller and newer building under its lee, set out on the very end of a dilapidated and almost deserted pier, and said it was the Temple of the Alchemical Rose, I was possessed with the fantasy that the sea, which kept covering it with showers of white foam, was claiming it as part of some indefinite and passionate life, which had begun to war upon our orderly and careful days, and was about to plunge the world into a night as obscure as that which followed the downfall of the classical world. One part of my mind mocked this fantastic terror, but the other, the part that still lay half plunged in vision, listened to the clash of unknown armies, and shuddered at unimaginable fanaticisms, that hung in those grey leaping waves.

We had gone but a few paces along the pier when we came upon an old man, who was evidently a watchman, for he sat in an overset barrel, close to a place where masons had been lately working upon a break in the pier, and had in front of him a fire such as one sees slung under tinkers' carts. I saw that he was also a voteen, as the peasants say, for there was a rosary hanging from a nail on the rim of the barrel, and as I saw I shuddered, and I did not know why I shuddered. We had passed him a few yards when I heard him cry in Gaelic, 'Idolaters, idolaters, go down to Hell with your witches and your devils; go down to Hell that the herrings may come again into the bay'; and for some moments I could hear him half screaming and half muttering behind us. 'Are you not afraid,' I said, 'that these wild fishing people may do some desperate thing against you?'

'I and mine,' he answered, 'are long past human hurt or help, being incorporate with immortal spirits, and when we die it shall be the consummation of the supreme work. A time will come for these people also, and they will sacrifice a mullet to Artemis, or some other fish to some new divinity, unless indeed their own divinities set up once more their temples of grey stone. Their reign has never ceased, but only waned in power a little, for the Sidhe still pass in every wind, and dance and play at hurley, but they cannot build their temples again till there have been martyrdoms and victories, and perhaps even that long-foretold battle in the Valley of the Black Pig.'

Keeping close to the wall that went about the pier on the seaward side, to escape the driving foam and the wind, which threatened every moment to lift us off our feet, we made our way in silence to the door of the square building. Michael Robartes opened it with a key, on which I saw the rust of many salt winds, and led me along a bare passage and up an uncarpeted stair to a little room surrounded with bookshelves. A meal would be brought, but only of fruit, for I must submit to a tempered fast before the ceremony, he explained, and with it a book on the doctrine and method of the Order, over which I was to spend what remained of the winter daylight. He then left me, promising to return an hour before the ceremony. I began searching among the bookshelves, and found one of the most exhaustive alchemical libraries I have ever seen. There were the works of Morienus, who hid his immortal body under a shirt of hair-cloth; of Avicenna, who was a drunkard and yet controlled numberless legions of spirits; of Alfarabi, who put so many spirits into his lute that he could make men laugh, or weep, or fall in deadly trance as he would; of Lully, who transformed himself into the likeness of a red cock; of Flamel, who with his wife Pernella achieved the elixir many hundreds of years ago, and is fabled to live still in Arabia among the Dervishes; and of many of less fame. There were very few mystics but alchemical mystics, and because, I had little doubt, of the devotion to one god of the greater number and of the limited sense of beauty, which Robartes would hold an inevitable consequence; but I did notice a complete set of facsimiles of the prophetical writings of William Blake, and probably because of the multitudes that thronged his illumination and were 'like the gay fishes on the wave when the moon sucks up the dew.' I noted also many poets and prose writers of every age, but only those who were a little weary of life, as indeed the greatest have been everywhere, and who cast their imagination to us, as a something they needed no longer now that they were going up in their fiery chariots.

Presently I heard a tap at the door, and a woman came in and laid a little fruit upon the table. I judged that she had once been handsome, but her cheeks were hollowed by what I would have held, had I seen her anywhere else, an excitement of the flesh and a thirst for pleasure, instead of which it doubtless was an excitement of the imagination and a thirst for beauty. I asked her some question concerning the ceremony, but getting no answer except a shake of the head, saw that I must await initiation in silence. When I had eaten, she came again, and having laid a curiously wrought bronze box on the table, lighted the candles, and took away the plates and the remnants. So soon as I was alone, I turned to the box, and found that the peacocks of Hera spread out their tails over the sides and lid, against a background on which were wrought great stars, as though to affirm that the heavens were a part of their glory. In the box was a book bound in vellum, and having upon the vellum and in very delicate colours, and in gold, the Alchemical Rose with many spears thrusting against it, but in vain, as was shown by the shattered points of those nearest to the petals. The book was written upon vellum, and in beautiful clear letters, interspersed with symbolical pictures and illuminations, after the manner of the *Splendor Solis*.

The first chapter described how six students, of Celtic descent, gave themselves separately to the study of alchemy, and solved, one the mystery of the Pelican, another the mystery of the Green Dragon, another the mystery of the Eagle, another that of Salt and Mercury. What seemed a succession of accidents, but was, the book declared, the contrivance of preternatural powers, brought them together in the garden of an inn in the South of France, and while they talked together the thought came to them that alchemy was the gradual distillation of the contents of the soul, until they were ready to put off the mortal and put on the immortal. An owl passed, rustling among the vine-leaves overhead, and then an old woman came, leaning upon a stick, and, sitting close to them, took up the thought where they had dropped it. Having expounded the whole principle of spiritual alchemy, and bid them found the Order of the Alchemical Rose, she passed from among them, and when they would have followed was nowhere to be seen. They formed themselves into an Order, holding their goods and making their researches in common, and, as they became perfect in the alchemical doctrine, apparitions came and went among them, and taught them more and more marvellous mysteries. The book then went on to expound so much of these as the neophyte was permitted to know, dealing at the outset and at considerable length with the independent reality of our thoughts, which was, it declared, the doctrine from which all true doctrines rose. If you imagine, it said, the semblance of a living being, it is at once possessed by a wandering soul, and goes hither and thither working good or evil, until the moment of its death has come; and gave many examples, received, it said, from many gods. Eros had taught them how to fashion forms in which a divine soul could dwell and whisper what it would into sleeping minds; and Ate, forms from which demonic beings could pour madness, or unquiet dreams, into sleeping blood; and Hermes, that if you powerfully imagined a hound at your bedside it would keep watch there until you woke, and drive away all but the mightiest demons, but that if your imagination was weakly, the hound would be weakly also, and the demons prevail, and the hound soon die; and Aphrodite, that if you made, by a strong imagining, a dove crowned with silver and bade it flutter over your head, its soft cooing would make sweet dreams of immortal love gather and brood over mortal sleep; and all divinities alike had revealed with many warnings and lamentations that all minds are continually giving birth to such beings, and sending them forth to work health or disease, joy or madness. If you would give forms to the evil powers, it went on, you were to make them ugly, thrusting out a lip with the thirsts of life, or breaking the proportions of a body with the burdens of life; but the divine powers would only appear in beautiful shapes, which are but, as it were, shapes trembling out of existence, folding up into a timeless ecstasy, drifting with half-shut eyes into a sleepy stillness. The bodiless souls who descended into these forms were what men called the moods; and worked all great changes in the world; for just as the magician or the artist could call them when he would, so they could call out of the mind of the magician or the artist, or if they were demons, out of the mind of the mad or the ignoble, what shape they would, and through its voice and its gestures pour themselves out upon the world. In this way all great events were accomplished; a mood, a divinity, or a demon, first descending like a faint sigh into men's minds and then changing their thoughts and their actions until hair that was yellow had grown black, or hair that was black had grown yellow, and empires moved their border, as though they were but drifts of leaves. The rest of the book contained symbols of form, and sound, and colour, and their attribution to divinities and demons, so that the initiate might fashion a shape for any divinity or any demon, and be as powerful as Avicenna among those who live under the roots of tears and of laughter.

IV

A couple of hours after sunset Michael Robartes returned and told me that I would have to learn the steps of an exceedingly antique dance, because before my initiation could be perfected I had to join three times in a magical dance, for rhythm was the wheel of Eternity, on which alone the transient and accidental could be broken, and the spirit set free. I found that the steps, which were simple enough, resembled certain antique Greek dances, and having been a good dancer in my youth and the master of many curious Gaelic steps, I soon had them in my memory. He then robed me and himself in a costume which suggested by its shape both Greece and Egypt, but by its crimson colour a more passionate life than theirs; and having put into my hands a little chainless censer of bronze, wrought into the likeness of a rose, by some modern craftsman, he told me to open a small door opposite to the door by which I had entered. I put my hand to the handle, but the moment I did so the fumes of the incense, helped perhaps by his mysterious glamour, made me fall again into a dream, in which I seemed to be a mask, lying on the counter of a little Eastern shop. Many persons, with eyes so bright and still that I knew them for more than

human, came in and tried me on their faces, but at last
flung me into a corner laughing; but all this passed in
a moment, for when I awoke my hand was still upon
the handle. I opened the door, and found myself in a
marvellous passage, along whose sides were many di-
vinities wrought in a mosaic, not less beautiful than the
mosaic in the Baptistery at Ravenna, but of a less severe
beauty; the predominant colour of each divinity, which
was surely a symbolic colour, being repeated in the
lamps that hung from the ceiling, a curiously scented
lamp before every divinity. I passed on, marvelling ex-
ceedingly how these enthusiasts could have created all
this beauty in so remote a place, and half persuaded to
believe in a material alchemy, by the sight of so much
hidden wealth; the censer filling the air, as I passed,
with smoke of ever-changing colour.

I stopped before a door, on whose bronze panels
were wrought great waves in whose shadow were faint
suggestions of terrible faces. Those beyond it seemed
to have heard our steps, for a voice cried, 'Is the work
of the Incorruptible Fire at an end?' and immediately
Michael Robartes answered, 'The perfect gold has come
from the athanor.' The door swung open, and we were
in a great circular room, and among men and women
who were dancing slowly in crimson robes. Upon the
ceiling was an immense rose wrought in mosaic; and
about the walls, also in mosaic, was a battle of gods and
angels, the gods glimmering like rubies and sapphires,
and the angels of the one greyness, because, as Michael
Robartes whispered, they had renounced their divinity,
and turned from the unfolding of their separate hearts,

out of love for a God of humility and sorrow. Pillars supported the roof and made a kind of circular cloister, each pillar being a column of confused shapes, divinities, it seemed, of the wind, who, in a whirling dance of more than human vehemence, rose playing upon pipes and cymbals; and from among these shapes were thrust out hands, and in these hands were censers. I was bid place my censer also in a hand and take my place and dance, and as I turned from the pillars towards the dancers, I saw that the floor was of a green stone, and that a pale Christ on a pale cross was wrought in the midst. I asked Robartes the meaning of this, and was told that they desired 'to trouble His unity with their multitudinous feet.' The dance wound in and out, tracing upon the floor the shapes of petals that copied the petals in the rose overhead, and to the sound of hidden instruments which were perhaps of an antique pattern, for I have never heard the like; and every moment the dance was more passionate, until all the winds of the world seemed to have awakened under our feet. After a little I had grown weary, and stood under a pillar watching the coming and going of those flame-like figures; until gradually I sank into a half-dream, from which I was awakened by seeing the petals of the great rose, which had no longer the look of mosaic, falling slowly through the incense-heavy air, and, as they fell, shaping into the likeness of living beings of an extraordinary beauty. Still faint and cloud-like, they began to dance, and as they danced took a more and more definite shape, so that I was able to distinguish beautiful Grecian faces and august Egyptian faces, and now and

again to name a divinity by the staff in his hand or by a
bird fluttering over his head; and soon every mortal
foot danced by the white foot of an immortal; and in
the troubled eyes that looked into untroubled shadowy
eyes, I saw the brightness of uttermost desire as though
they had found at length, after unreckonable wander-
ing, the lost love of their youth. Sometimes, but only
for a moment, I saw a faint solitary figure with a veiled
face, and carrying a faint torch, flit among the dancers,
but like a dream within a dream, like a shadow of a
shadow, and I knew by an understanding born from a
deeper fountain than thought, that it was Eros himself,
and that his face was veiled because no man or woman
from the beginning of the world has ever known what
Love is, or looked into his eyes, for Eros alone of divin-
ities is altogether a spirit, and hides in passions not of
his essence if he would commune with a mortal heart.
So that if a man love nobly he knows Love through in-
finite pity, unspeakable trust, unending sympathy; and
if ignobly through vehement jealousy, sudden hatred,
and unappeasable desire; but unveiled Love he never
knows. While I thought these things, a voice cried to
me from the crimson figures, 'Into the dance! there is
none that can be spared out of the dance; into the dance!
into the dance! that the gods may make them bodies
out of the substance of our hearts'; and before I could
answer, a mysterious wave of passion, that seemed like
the soul of the dance moving within our souls, took
hold of me, and I was swept, neither consenting nor
refusing, into the midst. I was dancing with an im-
mortal august woman, who had black lilies in her hair,

and her dreamy gesture seemed laden with a wisdom more profound than the darkness that is between star and star, and with a love like the love that breathed upon the waters; and as we danced on and on, the incense drifted over us and round us, covering us away as in the heart of the world, and ages seemed to pass, and tempests to awake and perish in the folds of our robes and in her heavy hair.

Suddenly I remembered that her eyelids had never quivered, and that her lilies had not dropped a black petal, nor shaken from their places, and understood with a great horror that I danced with one who was more or less than human, and who was drinking up my soul as an ox drinks up a wayside pool; and I fell, and darkness passed over me.

V

I awoke suddenly as though something had awakened me, and saw that I was lying on a roughly painted floor, and that on the ceiling, which was at no great distance, was a roughly painted rose, and about me on the walls half-finished paintings. The pillars and the censers had gone; and near me a score of sleepers lay wrapped in disordered robes, their upturned faces looking to my imagination like hollow masks; and a chill dawn was shining down upon them from a long window I had not noticed before; and outside the sea roared. I saw Michael Robartes lying at a little distance and beside him an overset bowl of wrought bronze which looked as though it had once held incense. As I sat thus, I heard a sudden tumult of angry men's and women's voices mix with the roaring of the sea; and leaping to my feet, I went quickly to Michael Robartes, and tried to shake him out of his sleep. I then seized him by the shoulder and tried to lift him, but he fell backwards, and sighed faintly; and the voices became louder and angrier; and there was a sound of heavy blows upon the door, which opened on to the pier. Suddenly I heard a sound of rending wood, and I knew it had begun to give, and I ran to the door of the room. I pushed it open and came out upon a passage whose bare boards clattered under my feet, and found in the passage another door which led into an empty kitchen; and as I passed through the door I heard two crashes in quick succession, and knew by the sudden noise of feet and the shouts that the door which opened on to the pier had fallen inwards. I ran from the kitchen and out into a small yard, and from this down some steps which descended the seaward and sloping side of the pier, and from the steps clambered along the water's edge, with the angry voices ringing in my ears. This part of the pier had been but lately refaced with blocks of granite, so that it was almost clear of seaweed; but when I came to the old part, I found it so slippery with green weed that I had to climb up on to the roadway. I looked towards the Temple of the Alchemical Rose, where the fishermen and the women were still shouting, but somewhat more faintly, and saw that there was no one about the door or upon the pier; but as I looked, a little crowd hurried out of the door and began gathering large stones from where they were heaped up in readiness for the next time a storm shattered the pier, when they would be laid under blocks of granite. While I stood watching the crowd, an old man, who was, I think, the voteen, pointed to me, and screamed out something, and the crowd whitened, for all the faces had turned towards me. I ran, and it was well for me that pullers of the oar are poorer men with their feet than with their arms and their bodies; and yet while I ran I scarcely heard the following feet or the angry voices, for many voices of exultation and lamentation, which were forgotten as a dream is forgotten the moment they were heard, seemed to be ringing in the air over my head.

There are moments even now when I seem to hear those voices of exultation and lamentation, and when the indefinite world, which has but half lost its mastery over my heart and my intellect, seems about to claim a perfect mastery; but I carry the rosary about my neck, and when I hear, or seem to hear them, I press it to my heart and say, 'He whose name is Legion is at our doors deceiving our intellects with subtlety and flattering our hearts with beauty, and we have no trust but in Thee'; and then the war that rages within me at other times is still, and I am at peace.

THE TABLES OF THE LAW

I

'WILL you permit me, Aherne,' I said, 'to ask you a question, which I have wanted to ask you for years, and have not asked because we have grown nearly strangers? Why did you refuse the biretta, and almost at the last moment? When you and I lived together, you cared neither for wine, women, nor money, and had thoughts for nothing but theology and mysticism.' I had watched through dinner for a moment to put my question, and ventured now, because he had thrown off a little of the reserve and indifference which, ever since his last return from Italy, had taken the place of our once close friendship. He had just questioned me, too, about certain private and almost sacred things, and my frankness had earned, I thought, a like frankness from him.

When I began to speak he was lifting a glass of that wine which he could choose so well and valued so little; and while I spoke, he set it slowly and meditatively upon the table and held it there, its deep red light dyeing his long delicate fingers. The impression of his face and form, as they were then, is still vivid with me, and is inseparable from another and fanciful impression: the impression of a man holding a flame in his naked hand. He was to me, at that moment, the supreme type of our race, which, when it has risen above, or is sunken below, the formalisms of half-education and the rationalisms of conventional affirmation and denial, turns away, unless my hopes for the world and for the Church have made me blind, from practicable desires and intuitions towards desires so unbounded that no human vessel can contain them, intuitions so immaterial that their sudden and far-off fire leaves heavy darkness about hand and foot. He had the nature, which is half monk, half soldier of fortune, and must needs turn action into dreaming, and dreaming into action; and for such there is no order, no finality, no contentment in this world. When he and I had been students in Paris, we had belonged to a little group which devoted itself to speculations about alchemy and mysticism. More orthodox in most of his beliefs than Michael Robartes, he had surpassed him in a fanciful hatred of all life, and this hatred had found expression in the curious paradox—half borrowed from some fanatical monk, half invented by himself—that the beautiful arts were sent into the world to overthrow nations, and finally life herself, by sowing everywhere unlimited desires, like torches thrown into a burning city. This idea was not at the time, I believe, more than a paradox, a plume of the pride of youth; and it was only after his return to Ireland that he endured the fermentation of belief which is coming upon our people with the reawakening of their imaginative life.

Presently he stood up, saying, 'Come, and I will show you why; you at any rate will understand,' and taking candles from the table, he lit the way into the long paved passage that led to his private chapel. We passed between the portraits of the Jesuits and priests —some of no little fame—his family had given to the

Church; and engravings and photographs of pictures that had especially moved him; and the few paintings his small fortune, eked out by an almost penurious abstinence from the things most men desire, had enabled him to buy in his travels. The photographs and engravings were from the masterpieces of many schools; but in all the beauty, whether it was a beauty of religion, of love, or of some fantastical vision of mountain and wood, was the beauty achieved by temperaments which seek always an absolute emotion, and which have their most continual, though not most perfect, expression in the legends and vigils and music of the Celtic peoples. The certitude of a fierce or gracious fervour in the enraptured faces of the angels of Francesca, and in the august faces of the sibyls of Michaelangelo; and the incertitude, as of souls trembling between the excitement of the spirit and the excitement of the flesh, in wavering faces from frescoes in the churches of Siena, and in the faces like thin flames, imagined by the modern symbolists and Pre-Raphaelites, had often made that long, grey, dim, empty, echoing passage become to my eyes a vestibule of eternity.

Almost every detail of the chapel, which we entered by a narrow Gothic door, whose threshold had been worn smooth by the secret worshippers of the penal times, was vivid in my memory; for it was in this chapel that I had first, and when but a boy, been moved by the mediaevalism which is now, I think, the governing influence in my life. The only thing that seemed new was a square bronze box which stood upon the altar before the six unlighted candles and the ebony crucifix, and was like those made in ancient times of more precious substances to hold the sacred books. Aherne made me sit down on an oak bench, and having bowed very low before the crucifix, took the bronze box from the altar, and sat down beside me with the box upon his knees.

'You will perhaps have forgotten,' he said, 'most of what you have read about Joachim of Flora, for he is little more than a name to even the well-read. He was an abbot in Cortale in the twelfth century, and is best known for his prophecy, in a book called *Expositio in Apocalypsin*, that the Kingdom of the Father was past, the Kingdom of the Son passing, the Kingdom of the Spirit yet to come. The Kingdom of the Spirit was to be a complete triumph of the Spirit, the *spiritualis intelligentia* he called it, over the dead letter. He had many followers among the more extreme Franciscans, and these were accused of possessing a secret book of his called the *Liber inducens in Evangelium aeternum*. Again and again groups of visionaries were accused of possessing this terrible book, in which the freedom of the Renaissance lay hidden, until at last Pope Alexander IV. had it found and cast into the flames. I have here the greatest treasure the world contains. I have a copy of that book; and see what great artists have made the robes in which it is wrapped. This bronze box was made by Benvenuto Cellini, who covered it with gods and demons, whose eyes are closed to signify an absorption in the inner light.' He lifted the lid and took out a book bound in leather, covered with filigree work of tarnished silver. 'And this cover was bound by one of the binders that bound for Canevari; while Giulio Clovio, an artist of the later Renaissance, whose work is soft and gentle, took out the beginning page of every chapter of the old copy, and set in its place a page surmounted by an elaborate letter and a miniature of some one of the great whose example was cited in the chapter; and wherever the writing left a little space elsewhere, he put some delicate emblem or intricate pattern.'

I took the book in my hands and began turning over the gilded, many-coloured pages, holding it close to the candle to discover the texture of the paper.

'Where did you get this amazing book?' I said. 'If genuine, and I cannot judge by this light, you have discovered one of the most precious things in the world.'

'It is certainly genuine,' he replied. 'When the original was destroyed, one copy alone remained, and was in the hands of a lute-player of Florence, and from him it passed to his son, and so from generation to generation until it came to the lute-player who was father to Benvenuto Cellini, and from him it passed to Giulio Clovio, and from Giulio Clovio to a Roman engraver; and then from generation to generation, the story of its wandering passing on with it, until it came into the possession of the family of Aretino, and so Giulio Aretino, an artist and worker in metals, and student of the cabbalistic reveries of Pico della Mirandola. He spent many nights with me at Rome, discussing philosophy; and at last I won his confidence so perfectly that he showed me this, his greatest treasure; and, finding how much I valued it, and feeling that he himself was growing old and beyond the help of its teaching, he sold it to me for no great sum, considering its great preciousness.'

'What is the doctrine?' I said. 'Some mediaeval straw-splitting about the nature of the Trinity, which is only useful to-day to show how many things are unimportant to us, which once shook the world?'

'I could never make you understand,' he said with a sigh, 'that nothing is unimportant in belief, but even you will admit that this book goes to the heart. Do you see the tables on which the commandments were written in Latin?' I looked to the end of the room, opposite to the altar, and saw that the two marble tablets were gone, and that two large empty tablets of ivory, like large copies of the little tablets we set over our desks, had taken their place. 'It has swept the commandments of the Father away,' he went on, 'and displaced the commandments of the Son by the commandments of the Holy Spirit. The first book is called *Fractura Tabularum*. In the first chapter it mentions the names of the great artists who made them graven things and the likeness of many things, and adored them and served them; and the second the names of the great wits who took the name of the Lord their God in vain; and that long third chapter, set with the emblems of sanctified faces, and having wings upon its borders, is the praise of breakers of the seventh day and wasters of the six days, who yet lived comely and pleasant days. Those two chapters tell of men and women who railed upon their parents, remembering that their god was older than the god of their parents; and that which has the sword of Michael for an emblem commends the kings that wrought secret murder and so won for their people a peace that was *amore somnoque gravata et vestibus versicoloribus*, "heavy with love and sleep and many-coloured raiment"; and that with the pale star at the closing has the lives of the noble youths who loved the wives of others and were transformed into memories, which have transformed many poorer hearts into sweet flames; and that with the winged head is the history of the robbers who lived upon the sea or in the desert, lives which it compares to the twittering of the string of a bow, *nervi stridentis instar*; and those two last, that are fire and gold, and devoted to the satirists who bore false witness against their neighbours and yet illustrated eternal wrath, and to those that have coveted more than other men wealth and women, and have thereby and therefore mastered and magnified great empires.

'The second book, which is called *Straminis Deflagratio*, recounts the conversations Joachim of Flora held in his monastery at Cortale, and afterwards in his monastery in the mountains of La Sila, with travellers and pilgrims, upon the laws of many countries; how chastity was a virtue and robbery a little thing in such a land, and robbery a crime and unchastity a little thing in such a land; and of the persons who had flung themselves upon these laws and become *decussa veste Dei sidera*, stars shaken out of the raiment of God.

'The third book, which is the close, is called *Lex Secreta*, and describes the true inspiration of action, the only Eternal Evangel; and ends with a vision, which he saw among the mountains of La Sila, of his disciples sitting throned in the blue deep of the air, and laughing aloud, with a laughter that was like the rustling of the wings of Time: *Coelis in coeruleis ridentes sedebant discipuli mei super thronos: talis erat risus, qualis temporis pennati susurrus.'*

'I know little of Joachim of Flora,' I said, 'except that Dante set him in Paradise among the great doctors. If he held a heresy so singular, I cannot understand how no rumours of it came to the ears of Dante; and Dante made no peace with the enemies of the Church.'

'Joachim of Flora acknowledged openly the authority of the Church, and even asked that all his published writings, and those to be published by his desire after his death, should be submitted to the censorship of the Pope. He considered that those whose work was to live and not to reveal were children and that the Pope was their father; but he taught in secret that certain others, and in always increasing numbers, were elected, not to live, but to reveal that hidden substance of God which is colour and music and softness and a sweet odour; and that these have no father but the Holy Spirit. Just as poets and painters and musicians labour at their works, building them with lawless and lawful things alike, so long as they embody the beauty that is beyond the grave, these children of the Holy Spirit labour at their moments with eyes upon the shining substance on which Time has heaped the refuse of creation; for the world only exists to be a tale in the ears of coming generations; and terror and content, birth and death, love and hatred, and the fruit of the Tree, are but instruments for that supreme art which is to win

300

us from life and gather us into eternity like doves into their dove-cots.

'I shall go away in a little while and travel into many lands, that I may know all accidents and destinies, and when I return, will write my secret law upon those ivory tablets, just as poets and romance-writers have written the principles of their art in prefaces; and will gather pupils about me that they may discover their law in the study of my law, and the Kingdom of the Holy Spirit be more widely and firmly established.'

He was pacing up and down, and I listened to the fervour of his words and watched the excitement of his gestures with not a little concern. I had been accustomed to welcome the most singular speculations, and had always found them as harmless as the Persian cat, who half closes her meditative eyes and stretches out her long claws, before my fire. But now I would battle in the interests of orthodoxy, even of the commonplace; and yet could find nothing better to say than: 'It is not necessary to judge every one by the law, for we have also Christ's commandment of love.'

He turned and said, looking at me with shining eyes:

'Jonathan Swift made a soul for the gentlemen of this city by hating his neighbour as himself.'

'At any rate, you cannot deny that to teach so dangerous a doctrine is to accept a terrible responsibility.'

'Leonardo da Vinci,' he replied, 'has this noble sentence: "The hope and desire of returning home to one's former state is like the moth's desire for the light; and the man who with constant longing awaits each new month and new year, deeming that the things he longs for are ever too late in coming, does not perceive that he is longing for his own destruction." How then can the pathway which will lead us into the heart of God be other than dangerous? Why should you, who are no materialist, cherish the continuity and order of the world as those do who have only the world? You do not value the writers who will express nothing unless their reason understands how it will make what is called the right more easy; why, then, will you deny a like freedom to the supreme art, the art which is the foundation of all arts? Yes, I shall send out of this chapel saints, lovers, rebels, and prophets: souls that will surround themselves with peace, as with a nest made with grass; and others over whom I shall weep. The dust shall fall for many years over this little box; and then I shall open it; and the tumults which are, perhaps, the flames of the Last Day shall come from under the lid.'

I did not reason with him that night, because his excitement was great and I feared to make him angry; and when I called at his house a few days later, he was gone and his house was locked up and empty. I have deeply regretted my failure both to combat his heresy and to test the genuineness of his strange book. Since my conversion I have indeed done penance for an error which I was only able to measure after some years.

II

I was walking along one of the Dublin quays, on the side nearest the river, about ten years after our conversation, stopping from time to time to turn over the works upon an old bookstall, and thinking, curiously enough, of the terrible destiny of Michael Robartes, and his brotherhood, when I saw a tall and bent man walking slowly along the other side of the quay. I recognised, with a start, in a lifeless mask with dim eyes, the once resolute and delicate face of Owen Aherne. I crossed the quay quickly, but had not gone many yards before he turned away, as though he had seen me, and hurried down a side street; I followed, but only to lose him among the intricate streets on the north side of the river. During the next few weeks I inquired of everybody who had once known him, but he had made himself known to nobody; and I knocked, without result, at the door of his old house; and had nearly persuaded myself that I was mistaken, when I saw him again in a narrow street behind the Four Courts, and followed him to the door of his house.

I laid my hand on his arm; he turned quite without surprise; and indeed it is possible that to him, whose inner life had soaked up the outer life, a parting of years was a parting from forenoon to afternoon. He stood holding the door half open, as though he would keep me from entering; and would perhaps have parted from me without further words had I not said: 'Owen Aherne, you trusted me once, will you not trust me again, and tell me what has come of the ideas we discussed in this house ten years ago?—but perhaps you have already forgotten them.'

'You have a right to hear,' he said, 'for since I have told you the ideas, I should tell you the extreme danger they contain, or rather the boundless wickedness they contain; but when you have heard this we must part, and part for ever, because I am lost, and must be hidden!'

I followed him through the paved passage, and saw that its corners were choked with dust and cobwebs; and that the pictures were grey with dust and shrouded with cobwebs; and that the dust and cobwebs which covered the ruby and sapphire of the saints on the window had made it very dim. He pointed to where the ivory tablets glimmered faintly in the dimness, and I saw that they were covered with small writing, and went up to them and began to read the writing. It was in Latin, and was an elaborate casuistry, illustrated with many examples, but whether from his own life or from the lives of others I do not know. I had read but a few sentences when I imagined that a faint perfume had begun to fill the room, and turning round asked Owen Aherne if he were lighting the incense.

'No,' he replied, and pointed where the thurible lay rusty and empty on one of the benches; as he spoke the faint perfume seemed to vanish, and I was persuaded I had imagined it.

'Has the philosophy of the *Liber inducens in Evangelium aeternum* made you very unhappy?' I said.

'At first I was full of happiness,' he replied, 'for I felt a divine ecstasy, an immortal fire in every passion, in every hope, in every desire, in every dream; and I saw, in the shadows under leaves, in the hollow waters, in the eyes of men and women, its image, as in a mirror; and it was as though I was about to touch the Heart of

God. Then all changed and I was full of misery; and in my misery it was revealed to me that man can only come to that Heart through the sense of separation from it which we call sin, and I understood that I could not sin, because I had discovered the law of my being, and could only express or fail to express my being, and I understood that God has made a simple and an arbitrary law that we may sin and repent!'

He had sat down on one of the wooden benches and now became silent, his bowed head and hanging arms and listless body having more of dejection than any image I have met with in life or in any art. I went and stood leaning against the altar, and watched him, not knowing what I should say; and I noticed his black closely-buttoned coat, his short hair, and shaven head, which preserved a memory of his priestly ambition, and understood how Catholicism had seized him in the midst of the vertigo he called philosophy; and I noticed his lightless eyes and his earth-coloured complexion, and understood how she had failed to do more than hold him on the margin: and I was full of an anguish of pity.

'It may be,' he went on, 'that the angels who have hearts of the Divine Ecstasy, and bodies of the Divine Intellect, need nothing but a thirst for the immortal element, in hope, in desire, in dreams; but we whose hearts perish every moment, and whose bodies melt away like a sigh, must bow and obey!'

I went nearer to him and said, 'Prayer and repentance will make you like other men.'

'No, no,' he said, 'I am not among those for whom Christ died, and this is why I must be hidden. I have a leprosy that even eternity cannot cure. I have seen the whole, and how can I come again to believe that a part is the whole? I have lost my soul because I have looked out of the eyes of the angels.'

Suddenly I saw, or imagined that I saw, the room darken, and faint figures robed in purple, and lifting faint torches with arms that gleamed like silver, bending above Owen Aherne; and I saw, or imagined that I saw, drops, as of burning gum, fall from the torches, and a heavy purple smoke, as of incense, come pouring from the flames and sweeping about us. Owen Aherne, more happy than I who have been half initiated into the Order of the Alchemical Rose, or protected perhaps by his great piety, had sunk again into dejection and listlessness, and saw none of these things; but my knees shook under me, for the purple-robed figures were less faint every moment, and now I could hear the hissing of the gum in the torches. They did not appear to see me, for their eyes were upon Owen Aherne; now and again I could hear them sigh as though with sorrow for his sorrow, and presently I heard words which I could not understand except that they were words of sorrow, and sweet as though immortal was talking to immortal. Then one of them waved her torch, and all the torches waved, and for a moment it was as though some great bird made of flames had fluttered its plumage, and a voice cried as from far up in the air, 'He has charged even his angels with folly, and they also bow and obey; but let your heart mingle with our hearts, which are wrought of Divine Ecstasy, and your body with our bodies, which are wrought of Divine Intellect.' And at

306

that cry I understood that the Order of the Alchemical Rose was not of this earth, and that it was still seeking over this earth for whatever souls it could gather within its glittering net; and when all the faces turned towards me, and I saw the mild eyes and the unshaken eyelids, I was full of terror, and thought they were about to fling their torches upon me, so that all I held dear, all that bound me to spiritual and social order, would be burnt up, and my soul left naked and shivering among the winds that blow from beyond this world and from beyond the stars; and then a voice cried, 'Why do you fly from our torches that were made out of the trees under which Christ wept in the Garden of Gethsemane? Why do you fly from our torches that were made out of sweet wood, after it had perished from the world?'

It was not until the door of the house had closed behind my flight, and the noise of the street was breaking on my ears, that I came back to myself and to a little of my courage; and I have never dared to pass the house of Owen Aherne from that day, even though I believe him to have been driven into some distant country by the spirits whose name is legion, and whose throne is in the indefinite abyss, and whom he obeys and cannot see.

THE ADORATION OF THE MAGI

I WAS sitting reading late into the night a little after my last meeting with Aherne, when I heard a light knocking on my front door; and found upon the doorstep three very old men with stout sticks in their hands, who said they had been told I would be up and about, and that they were to tell me important things. I brought them into my study, and when the peacock curtains had closed behind us, I set their chairs for them close to the fire, for I saw that the frost was on their great-coats of frieze and upon the long beards that flowed almost to their waists. They took off their great-coats, and leaned over the fire warming their hands, and I saw that their clothes had much of the country of our time, but a little also, as it seemed to me, of the town life of a more courtly time. When they had warmed themselves—and they warmed themselves, I thought, less because of the cold of the night than because of a pleasure in warmth for the sake of warmth—they turned towards me, so that the light of the lamp fell full upon their weather-beaten faces, and told the story I am about to tell. Now one talked and now another, and they often interrupted one another, with a desire, like that of countrymen, when they tell a story, to leave no detail untold. When they had finished they made me take notes of whatever conversation they had quoted, so that I might have the exact words, and got up to go, and when I asked them where they were going, and what they were doing, and by what names I should call them, they would tell me nothing, except that they had been commanded to travel over Ireland continually, and upon foot and at night, that they might live close to the stones and the trees and at the hours when the Immortals are awake.

I have let some years go by before writing out this story, for I am always in dread of the illusions which come of that inquietude of the veil of the Temple, which M. Mallarmé considers a characteristic of our times; and only write it now because I have grown to believe that there is no dangerous idea which does not become less dangerous when written out in sincere and careful English.

The three old men were three brothers, who had lived in one of the western islands from their early manhood, and had cared all their lives for nothing except for those classical writers and old Gaelic writers who expounded an heroic and simple life. Night after night in winter, Gaelic story-tellers would chant old poems to them over the poteen; and night after night in summer, when the Gaelic story-tellers were at work in the fields or away at the fishing, they would read to one another Virgil and Homer, for they would not enjoy in solitude, but as the ancients enjoyed. At last a man, who told them he was Michael Robartes, came to them in a fishing-boat, like Saint Brendan drawn by some vision and called by some voice; and told them of the coming again of the gods and the ancient things; and their hearts, which had never endured the body and pressure of our time, but only of distant times, found nothing unlikely in anything he told them, but accepted all simply and were happy. Years passed, and one day, when the oldest of the old men, who had travelled in his youth and thought sometimes of other lands, looked out on the grey waters, on which the people see the dim outline of the Islands of the Young—the Happy Islands where the Gaelic heroes live the lives of Homer's Phaeacians—a voice came out of the air over the waters and told him of the death of Michael Robartes. While they were still mourning, the next oldest of the old men fell asleep whilst he was reading out the Fifth Eclogue of Virgil, and a strange voice spoke through him, and bid them set out for Paris, where a dying woman would give them secret names and thereby so transform the world that another Leda would open her knees to the swan, another Achilles beleaguer Troy.

They left their island, and were at first troubled at all they saw in the world, and came to Paris, and there the youngest met a person in a dream, who told him they were to wander about at hazard until those who had been guiding their footsteps had brought them to a street and a house, whose likeness was shown him in the dream. They wandered hither and thither for many days, until one morning they came into some narrow and shabby streets, on the south of the Seine, where women with pale faces and untidy hair looked at them out of the windows; and just as they were about to turn back because Wisdom could not have alighted in so foolish a neighbourhood, they came to the street and the house of the dream. The oldest of the old men, who still remembered some of the modern languages he had known in his youth, went up to the door and knocked, and when he had knocked, the next in age to him said it was not a good house, and could not be the house they were looking for, and urged him to ask for somebody who could not be there and go away. The door was opened by an old over-dressed woman, who said, 'O, you are her three kinsmen from Ireland. She has been expecting you all day.' The old men looked at one another and followed her upstairs, passing doors from which pale and untidy women thrust out their heads, and into a room where a beautiful woman lay asleep, another woman sitting by her.

The old woman said, 'Yes, they have come at last; now she will be able to die in peace,' and went out.

'We have been deceived by devils,' said one of the old men, 'for the Immortals would not speak through a woman like this.'

'Yes,' said another, 'we have been deceived by devils, and we must go away quickly.'

'Yes,' said the third, 'we have been deceived by devils, but let us kneel down for a little, for we are by the death-bed of one that has been beautiful.' They knelt down, and the woman sitting by the bed whispered, and as though overcome with fear, and with lowered head, 'At the moment when you knocked she was suddenly convulsed and cried out as I have heard a woman in childbirth and fell backward as though in a swoon.' Then they watched for a little the face upon the pillow and wondered at its look, as of unquenchable desire, and at the porcelain-like refinement of the vessel in which so malevolent a flame had burned.

Suddenly the second oldest of them crowed like a cock, till the room seemed to shake with the crowing.

The woman in the bed still slept on in her death-like sleep, but the woman who sat by her head crossed herself and grew pale, and the youngest of the old men cried out, 'A devil has gone into him, and we must begone or it will go into us also.' Before they could rise from their knees, a resonant chanting voice came from the lips that had crowed and said:—

'I am not a devil, but I am Hermes the Shepherd of the Dead, I run upon the errands of the gods, and you have heard my sign. The woman who lies there has given birth, and that which she bore has the likeness of a unicorn and is most unlike man of all living things, being cold, hard and virginal. It seemed to be born dancing; and was gone from the room wellnigh upon the instant, for it is of the nature of the unicorn to understand the shortness of life. She does not know it has gone, for she fell into a stupor while it danced, but bend down your ears that you may learn the names that it must obey.' Neither of the other two old men spoke, but doubtless looked at the speaker with perplexity, for the voice began again: 'When the Immortals would overthrow the things that are to-day and bring the things that were yesterday, they have no one to help them, but one whom the things that are to-day have cast out. Bow down and very low, for they have chosen this woman in whose heart all follies have gathered, and in whose body all desires have awakened; this woman who has been driven out of Time and has lain upon the bosom of Eternity.'

The voice ended with a sigh, and immediately the old man awoke out of sleep, and said, 'Has a voice spoken through me, as it did when I fell asleep over my Virgil, or have I only been asleep?'

The oldest of them said, 'A voice has spoken through you. Where has your soul been while the voice was speaking through you?'

'I do not know where my soul has been, but I dreamed I was under the roof of a manger, and I looked down and I saw an ox and an ass; and I saw a red cock perching on the hay-rack; and a woman hugging a child; and three old men in chain armour kneeling with their heads bowed very low in front of the woman and the child. While I was looking the cock crowed and a man with wings on his heels swept up through the air, and as he passed me, cried out, "Foolish old men, you had once all the wisdom of the stars." I do not understand my dream or what it would have us do, but you who have heard the voice out of the wisdom of my sleep know what we have to do.'

Then the oldest of the old men told him they were to take the parchments they had brought with them out of their pockets and spread them on the ground. When they had spread them on the ground, they took out of their pockets their pens, made of three feathers which had fallen from the wing of the old eagle that is believed to have talked of wisdom with Saint Patrick.

'He meant, I think,' said the youngest, as he put their ink-bottles by the side of the rolls of parchment, 'that when people are good the world likes them and takes possession of them, and so eternity comes through people who are not good or who have been forgotten. Perhaps Christianity was good and the world liked it, so now it is going away and the Immortals are beginning to awake.'

'What you say has no wisdom,' said the oldest, 'because if there are many Immortals, there cannot be only one Immortal.'

'Yet it seems,' said the youngest, 'that the names we are to take down are the names of one, so it must be that he can take many forms.'

Then the woman on the bed moved as in a dream, and held out her arms as though to clasp the being that had left her, and murmured names of endearment, and yet strange names, 'Harsh sweetness,' 'Dear bitterness,' 'O solitude,' 'O terror,' and after lay still for a while. Then her voice changed, and she, no longer afraid and happy but seeming like any dying woman, murmured a name so faintly that the woman who sat by the bed bent down and put her ear close to her mouth.

The oldest of the old men said in French, 'There must have been yet one name which she had not given us, for she murmured a name while the spirit was going out of the body,' and the woman said, 'She was merely murmuring over the name of a symbolist painter she was fond of. He used to go to something he called the Black Mass, and it was he who taught her to see visions and to hear voices.'

This is all the old men told me, and when I think of their speech and of their silence, of their coming and of their going, I am almost persuaded that had I followed them out of the house, I would have found no footsteps on the snow. They may, for all I or any man can say, have been themselves Immortals: immortal demons, come to put an untrue story into my mind for some purpose I do not understand. Whatever they were, I have turned into a pathway which will lead me from them and from the Order of the Alchemical Rose. I no longer live an elaborate and haughty life, but seek to lose myself among the prayers and the sorrows of the multitude. I pray best in poor chapels, where frieze coats brush against me as I kneel, and when I pray against the demons I repeat a prayer which was made I know not how many centuries ago to help some poor Gaelic man or woman who had suffered with a suffering like mine:—

> *Seacht b-páidreacha fó seacht*
> *Chuir Muire faoi n-a Mac,*
> *Chuir Brighid faoi n-a brat,*
> *Chuir Dia faoi n-a neart,*
> *Eidir sinn 'san Sluagh Sidhe,*
> *Eidir sinn 'san Sluagh Gaoith.*

> Seven paters seven times,
> Send Mary by her Son,
> Send Bridget by her mantle,
> Send God by His strength,
> Between us and the faery host,
> Between us and the demons of the air.

THE END

PER AMICA SILENTIA LUNAE
1917

PROLOGUE

MY DEAR 'MAURICE'—You will remember that
afternoon in Calvados last summer when your
black Persian 'Minnaloushe,' who had walked behind
us for a good mile, heard a wing flutter in a bramble-
bush? For a long time we called him endearing names
in vain. He seemed resolute to spend his night among
the brambles. He had interrupted a conversation, often
interrupted before, upon certain thoughts so long habi-
tual that I may be permitted to call them my convic-
tions. When I came back to London my mind ran again
and again to those conversations and I could not rest
till I had written out in this little book all that I had said
or would have said. Read it some day when 'Minna-
loushe' is asleep.

W. B. YEATS

May 11, 1917

EGO DOMINUS TUUS

Hic

ON THE GREY SAND beside the shallow stream
  Under your old wind-beaten tower, where still
A lamp burns on beside the open book
That Michael Robartes left, you walk in the moon,
And, though you have passed the best of life, still trace,
Enthralled by the unconquerable delusion,
Magical shapes.

Ille

By the help of an image
I call to my own opposite, summon all
That I have handled least, least looked upon.

Hic

And I would find myself and not an image.

Ille

That is our modern hope, and by its light
We have lit upon the gentle, sensitive mind
And lost the old nonchalance of the hand;
Whether we have chosen chisel, pen or brush,
We are but critics, or but half create,
Timid, entangled, empty and abashed,
Lacking the countenance of our friends.

Hic

And yet

The chief imagination of Christendom,

Dante Alighieri, so utterly found himself
That he has made that hollow face of his
More plain to the mind's eye than any face
But that of Christ.

ILLE

         And did he find himself
Or was the hunger that had made it hollow
A hunger for the apple on the bough
Most out of reach? and is that spectral image
The man that Lapo and that Guido knew?
I think he fashioned from his opposite
An image that might have been a stony face
Staring upon a Bedouin's horse-hair roof
From doored and windowed cliff, or half upturned
Among the coarse grass and the camel-dung.
He set his chisel to the hardest stone.
Being mocked by Guido for his lecherous life,
Derided and deriding, driven out
To climb that stair and eat that bitter bread,
He found the unpersuadable justice, he found
The most exalted lady loved by a man.

HIC

Yet surely there are men who have made their art
Out of no tragic war, lovers of life,
Impulsive men that look for happiness
And sing when they have found it.

ILLE

            No, not sing,
For those that love the world serve it in action,

Ego Dominus Tuus

Grow rich, popular and full of influence,
And should they paint or write, still it is action:
The struggle of the fly in marmalade.
The rhetorician would deceive his neighbours,
The sentimentalist himself; while art
Is but a vision of reality.
What portion in the world can the artist have
Who has awakened from the common dream
But dissipation and despair?

Hic

                    And yet
No one denies to Keats love of the world;
Remember his deliberate happiness.

Ille

His art is happy, but who knows his mind?
I see a schoolboy when I think of him,
With face and nose pressed to a sweet-shop window,
For certainly he sank into his grave
His senses and his heart unsatisfied,
And made—being poor, ailing and ignorant,
Shut out from all the luxury of the world,
The coarse-bred son of a livery-stable keeper—
Luxuriant song.

Hic

                    Why should you leave the lamp
Burning alone beside an open book,
And trace these characters upon the sands?
A style is found by sedentary toil
And by the imitation of great masters.

Per Amica Silentia Lunae

ILLE

Because I seek an image, not a book.
Those men that in their writings are most wise
Own nothing but their blind, stupefied hearts.
I call to the mysterious one who yet
Shall walk the wet sands by the edge of the stream
And look most like me, being indeed my double,
And prove of all imaginable things
The most unlike, being my anti-self,
And, standing by these characters, disclose
All that I seek; and whisper it as though
He were afraid the birds, who cry aloud
Their momentary cries before it is dawn,
Would carry it away to blasphemous men.

December 1915

Anima Hominis

ANIMA HOMINIS

I

WHEN I COME HOME after meeting men who are strange to me, and sometimes even after talking to women, I go over all I have said in gloom and disappointment. Perhaps I have overstated everything from a desire to vex or startle, from hostility that is but fear; or all my natural thoughts have been drowned by an undisciplined sympathy. My fellow-diners have hardly seemed of mixed humanity, and how should I keep my head among images of good and evil, crude allegories?

But when I shut my door and light the candle, I invite a marmorean Muse, an art where no thought or emotion has come to mind because another man has thought or felt something different, for now there must be no reaction, action only, and the world must move my heart but to the heart's discovery of itself, and I begin to dream of eyelids that do not quiver before the bayonet: all my thoughts have ease and joy, I am all virtue and confidence. When I come to put in rhyme what I have found, it will be a hard toil, but for a moment I believe I have found myself and not my anti-self. It is only the shrinking from toil, perhaps, that convinces me that I have been no more myself than is the cat the medicinal grass it is eating in the garden.

How could I have mistaken for myself an heroic condition that from early boyhood has made me superstitious? That which comes as complete, as minutely organised, as are those elaborate, brightly lighted buildings and sceneries appearing in a moment, as I lie between sleeping and waking, must come from above me and beyond me. At times I remember that place in Dante where he sees in his chamber the 'Lord of Terrible Aspect,' and how, seeming 'to rejoice inwardly that it was a marvel to see, speaking, he said many things among the which I could understand but few, and of these this: ego dominus tuus'; or should the conditions come, not, as it were, in a gesture—as the image of a man—but in some fine landscape, it is of Boehme, maybe, that I think, and of that country where we 'eternally solace ourselves in the excellent beautiful flourishing of all manner of flowers and forms, both trees and plants, and all kinds of fruit.'

II

When I consider the minds of my friends, among artists and emotional writers, I discover a like contrast. I have sometimes told one close friend that her only fault is a habit of harsh judgment with those who have not her sympathy, and she has written comedies where the wickedest people seem but bold children. She does not know why she has created that world where no one is ever judged, a high celebration of indulgence, but to me it seems that her ideal of beauty is the compensating dream of a nature wearied out by over-much judgment. I know a famous actress who, in private life, is like the captain of some buccaneer ship holding his crew to good behaviour at the mouth of a blunderbuss, and upon the stage she excels in the representation of women who stir to pity and to desire because they need our protection, and is most adorable as one of those young queens imagined by Maeterlinck who have so little will, so little self, that they are like shadows sighing at the edge of the world. When I last saw her in her own house she lived in a torrent of words and movements, she could not listen, and all about her upon the walls were women drawn by Burne-Jones in his latest period. She had invited me in the hope that I would defend those women, who were always listening, and are as necessary to her as a contemplative Buddha to a Japanese Samurai, against a French critic who would persuade her to take into her heart in their stead a Post-Impressionist picture of a fat, flushed woman lying naked upon a Turkey carpet.

There are indeed certain men whose art is less an opposing virtue than a compensation for some accident of health or circumstance. During the riots over the first production of *The Playboy of the Western World*, Synge was confused, without clear thought, and was soon ill —indeed the strain of that week may perhaps have hastened his death—and he was, as is usual with gentle and silent men, scrupulously accurate in all his statements. In his art he made, to delight his own and his mind's eye voluble daredevils who 'go romancing through a romping lifetime . . . to the dawning of the Judgment Day.' At other moments this man, condemned to the life of a monk by bad health, takes an amused pleasure in 'great queens . . . making themselves matches from the start to the end.' Indeed, in all his imagination he delights in fine physical life, in life when the moon pulls up the tide. The last act of *Deirdre of the Sorrows*, where his art is at its noblest, was written upon his death-bed. He was not sure of any world to come, he was leaving his betrothed and his unwritten play—'O, what a waste of time,' he said to me; he hated to die, and in the last speeches of Deirdre and in the middle act he accepted death and dismissed life with a gracious gesture. He gave to Deirdre the emotion that seemed to him most desirable, most difficult, most fitting, and maybe saw in those delighted seven years, now dwindling from her, the fulfilment of his own life.

III

When I think of any great poetical writer of the past (a realist is a historian and obscures the cleavage by the record of his eyes), I comprehend, if I know the lineaments of his life, that the work is the man's flight from his entire horoscope, his blind struggle in the network of the stars. William Morris, a happy, busy, most irascible man, described dim colour and pensive emotion, following, beyond any man of his time, an indolent Muse; while Savage Landor topped us all in calm nobility when the pen was in his hand, as in the daily violence of his passion when he had laid it down. He had in his *Imaginary Conversations* reminded us, as it were, that the Venus de Milo is a stone, and yet he wrote when the copies did not come from the printer as soon as he expected: 'I have . . . had the resolution to tear in pieces all my sketches and projects and to forswear all future undertakings. I have tried to sleep away my time and pass two-thirds of the twenty-four hours in bed. I may speak of myself as a dead man.' I imagine Keats to have been born with that thirst for luxury common to many at the outsetting of the Romantic Movement, and not able, like wealthy Beckford, to slake it with beautiful and strange objects. It drove him to imaginary delights; ignorant, poor, and in poor health, and not perfectly well-bred, he knew himself driven from tangible luxury; meeting Shelley, he was resentful and suspicious because he, as Leigh Hunt recalls, 'being a little too sensitive on the score of his origin, felt inclined to see in every man of birth his natural enemy.'

IV

Some thirty years ago I read a prose allegory by Simeon Solomon, long out of print and unprocurable, and remember or seem to remember a sentence, 'a hollow image of fulfilled desire.' All happy art seems to me that hollow image, but when its lineaments express also the poverty or the exasperation that set its maker to the work, we call it tragic art. Keats but gave us his dream of luxury; but while reading Dante we never long escape the conflict, partly because the verses are at moments a mirror of his history, and yet more because that history is so clear and simple that it has the quality of art. I am no Dante scholar, and I but read him in Shadwell or in Dante Rossetti, but I am always persuaded that he celebrated the most pure lady poet ever sung and the Divine Justice, not merely because death

took that lady and Florence banished her singer, but
because he had to struggle in his own heart with his un-
just anger and his lust; while, unlike those of the great
poets who are at peace with the world and at war with
themselves, he fought a double war. 'Always,' says
Boccaccio, 'both in youth and maturity he found room
among his virtues for lechery'; or as Matthew Arnold
preferred to change the phrase, 'his conduct was ex-
ceeding irregular.' Guido Cavalcanti, as Rossetti trans-
lates him, finds 'too much baseness' in his friend:—

> And still thy speech of me, heartfelt and kind,
> Hath made me treasure up thy poetry;
> But now I dare not, for thy abject life,
> Make manifest that I approve thy rhymes.

And when Dante meets Beatrice in Eden, does she
not reproach him because, when she had taken her pre-
sence away, he followed, in spite of warning dreams, false
images, and now, to save him in his own despite, she
has 'visited . . . the Portals of the Dead,' and chosen
Virgil for his courier? While Gino da Pistoia complains
that in his *Commedia* his 'lovely heresies . . . beat the
right down and let the wrong go free':—

> Therefore his vain decrees, wherein he lied,
> Must be like empty nutshells flung aside;
> Yet through the rash false witness set to grow,
> French and Italian vengeance on such pride
> May fall like Antony on Cicero.

Dante himself sings to Giovanni Guirino 'at the
approach of death':—

> The King, by whose rich grave his servants be
> With plenty beyond measure set to dwell,

330

Anima Hominis

Ordains that I my bitter wrath dispel,
And lift mine eyes to the great Consistory.

V

We make out of the quarrel with others, rhetoric, but of the quarrel with ourselves, poetry. Unlike the rhetoricians, who get a confident voice from remembering the crowd they have won or may win, we sing amid our uncertainty; and, smitten even in the presence of the most high beauty by the knowledge of our solitude, our rhythm shudders. I think, too, that no fine poet, no matter how disordered his life, has ever, even in his mere life, had pleasure for his end. Johnson and Dowson, friends of my youth, were dissipated men, the one a drunkard, the other a drunkard and mad about women, and yet they had the gravity of men who had found life out and were awakening from the dream; and both, one in life and art and one in art and less in life, had a continual preoccupation with religion. Nor has any poet I have read of or heard of or met with been a sentimentalist. The other self, the anti-self or the antithetical self, as one may choose to name it, comes but to those who are no longer deceived, whose passion is reality. The sentimentalists are practical men who believe in money, in position, in a marriage bell, and whose understanding of happiness is to be so busy whether at work or at play that all is forgotten but the momentary aim. They find their pleasure in a cup that is filled from Lethe's wharf, and for the awakening, for the vision, for the revelation of reality, tradition offers us a different word—ecstasy.

An old artist wrote to me of his wanderings by the quays of New York, and how he found there a woman nursing a sick child, and drew her story from her. She spoke, too, of other children who had died: a long tragic story. 'I wanted to paint her,' he wrote; 'if I denied myself any of the pain I could not believe in my own ecstasy.' We must not make a false faith by hiding from our thoughts the causes of doubt, for faith is the highest achievement of the human intellect, the only gift man can make to God, and therefore it must be offered in sincerity. Neither must we create, by hiding ugliness, a false beauty as our offering to the world. He only can create the greatest imaginable beauty who has endured all imaginable pangs, for only when we have seen and foreseen what we dread shall we be rewarded by that dazzling, unforeseen, wing-footed wanderer. We could not find him if he were not in some sense of our being, and yet of our being but as water with fire, a noise with silence. He is of all things not impossible the most difficult, for that only which comes easily can never be a portion of our being; 'soon got, soon gone,' as the proverb says. I shall find the dark grow luminous, the void fruitful when I understand I have nothing, that the ringers in the tower have appointed for the hymen of the soul a passing bell.

The last knowledge has often come most quickly to turbulent men, and for a season brought new turbulence. When life puts away her conjuring tricks one by one, those that deceive us longest may well be the wine-cup and the sensual kiss, for our Chambers of Commerce and of Commons have not the divine architecture of the body, nor has their frenzy been ripened by the sun. The poet, because he may not stand within the sacred house but lives amid the whirlwinds that beset its threshold, may find his pardon.

VI

I think the Christian saint and hero, instead of being merely dissatisfied, make deliberate sacrifice. I remember reading once an autobiography of a man who had made a daring journey in disguise to Russian exiles in Siberia, and his telling how, very timid as a child, he schooled himself by wandering at night through dangerous streets. Saint and hero cannot be content to pass at moments to that hollow image and after become their heterogeneous selves, but would always, if they could, resemble the antithetical self. There is a shadow of type on type, for in all great poetical styles there is saint or hero, but when it is all over Dante can return to his chambering and Shakespeare to his 'pottle-pot.' They sought no impossible perfection but when they handled paper or parchment. So too will saint or hero, because he works in his own flesh and blood and not in paper or parchment, have more deliberate understanding of that other flesh and blood.

Some years ago I began to believe that our culture, with its doctrine of sincerity and self-realisation, made us gentle and passive, and that the Middle Ages and the Renaissance were right to found theirs upon the imitation of Christ or of some classic hero. Saint Francis and Caesar Borgia made themselves overmastering, creative persons by turning from the mirror to meditation upon a mask. When I had this thought I could see nothing else in life. I could not write the play I had planned, for all became allegorical, and though I tore up hundreds of pages in my endeavour to escape from allegory, my imagination became sterile for nearly five years and I only escaped at last when I had mocked in a comedy my own thought. I was always thinking of the element of imitation in style and in life, and of the life beyond heroic imitation. I find in an old diary: 'I think all happiness depends on the energy to assume the mask of some other life, on a re-birth as something not one's self, something created in a moment and perpetually renewed; in playing a game like that of a child where one loses the infinite pain of self-realisation, in a grotesque or solemn painted face put on that one may hide from the terror of judgment. . . . Perhaps all the sins and energies of the world are but the world's flight from an infinite blinding beam'; and again at an earlier date: 'If we cannot imagine ourselves as different from what we are, and try to assume that second self, we cannot impose a discipline upon ourselves though we may accept one from others. Active virtue, as distinguished from the passive acceptance of a code, is therefore theatrical, consciously dramatic, the wearing of a mask. . . . Wordsworth, great poet though he be, is so often flat and heavy partly because his moral sense, being a discipline he had not created, a mere obedience, has no theatrical element. This increases his popularity with the better kind of journalists and politicians who have written books.'

334

Anima Hominis

VII

I thought the hero found hanging upon some oak of Dodona an ancient mask, where perhaps there lingered something of Egypt, and that he changed it to his fancy, touching it a little here and there, gilding the eyebrows or putting a gilt line where the cheek-bone comes; that when at last he looked out of its eyes he knew another's breath came and went within his breath upon the carven lips, and that his eyes were upon the instant fixed upon a visionary world: how else could the god have come to us in the forest? The good, unlearned books say that He who keeps the distant stars within His fold comes without intermediary, but Plutarch's precepts and the experience of old women in Soho, ministering their witchcraft to servant-girls at a shilling apiece, will have it that a strange living man may win for Daimon[1] an illustrious dead man; but now I add another thought: the Daimon comes not as like to like but seeking its own opposite, for man and Daimon feed the hunger in one another's hearts. Because the ghost is simple, the man heterogeneous and confused, they are but knit together when the man has found a mask whose lineaments permit the expression of all the man most lacks, and it may be dreads, and of that only.

The more insatiable in all desire, the more resolute to refuse deception or an easy victory, the more close

[1] I could not distinguish at the time between the permanent Daimon and the impermanent, who may be 'an illustrious dead man,' though I knew the distinction was there. I shall deal with the matter in *A Vision*.   *February* 1924.

will be the bond, the more violent and definite the antipathy.

VIII

I think that all religious men have believed that there is a hand not ours in the events of life, and that, as somebody says in *Wilhelm Meister*, accident is destiny; and I think it was Heraclitus who said: the Daimon is our destiny. When I think of life as a struggle with the Daimon who would ever set us to the hardest work among those not impossible, I understand why there is a deep enmity between a man and his destiny, and why a man loves nothing but his destiny. In an Anglo-Saxon poem a certain man is called, as though to call him something that summed up all heroism, 'Doom eager.' I am persuaded that the Daimon delivers and deceives us, and that he wove that netting from the stars and threw the net from his shoulder. Then my imagination runs from Daimon to sweetheart, and I divine an analogy that evades the intellect. I remember that Greek antiquity has bid us look for the principal stars, that govern enemy and sweetheart alike, among those that are about to set, in the Seventh House as the astrologers say; and that it may be 'sexual love,' which is 'founded upon spiritual hate,' is an image of the warfare of man and Daimon; and I even wonder if there may not be some secret communion, some whispering in the dark between Daimon and sweetheart. I remember how often women when in love grow superstitious, and believe that they can bring their lovers good luck; and I remember an old Irish story of three young men who went seeking for help in battle into the house of the gods at Slieve-na-mon. 'You must first be married,' some god told them, 'because a man's good or evil luck comes to him through a woman.'

I sometimes fence for half an hour at the day's end, and when I close my eyes upon the pillow I see a foil playing before me, the button to my face. We meet always in the deep of the mind, whatever our work, wherever our reverie carries us, that other Will.

IX

The poet finds and makes his mask in disappointment, the hero in defeat. The desire that is satisfied is not a great desire, nor has the shoulder used all its might that an unbreakable gate has never strained. The saint alone is not deceived, neither thrusting with his shoulder nor holding out unsatisfied hands. He would climb without wandering to the antithetical self of the world, the Indian narrowing his thought in meditation or driving it ·away in contemplation, the Christian copying Christ, the antithetical self of the classic world. For a hero loves the world till it breaks him, and the poet till it has broken faith; but while the world was yet debonair, the saint has turned away, and because he renounced experience itself, he will wear his mask as he finds it. The poet or the hero, no matter upon what bark they found their mask, so teeming their fancy, somewhat change its lineaments, but the saint, whose life is but a round of customary duty, needs nothing the whole world does not need, and day by day he scourges in his body the Roman and Christian conquerors: Alexander and Caesar are famished in his cell. His nativity is neither in disappointment nor in defeat, but in a temptation like that of Christ in the Wilderness, a contemplation in a single instant perpetually renewed of the Kingdoms of the World; all—because all renounced—continually present showing their empty thrones. Edwin Ellis, remembering that Christ also measured the sacrifice, imagined himself in a fine poem as meeting at Golgotha the phantom of 'Christ the Less,' the Christ who might have lived a prosperous life without the knowledge of sin, and who now wanders 'companionless, a weary spectre day and night.'

> I saw him go and cried to him,
> 'Eli, thou hast forsaken me.'
> The nails were burning through each limb,
> He fled to find felicity.

And yet is the saint spared—despite his martyr's crown and his vigil of desire—defeat, disappointed love, and the sorrow of parting.

> O Night, that didst lead thus,
> O Night, more lovely than the dawn of light,
> O Night, that broughtest us
> Lover to lover's sight,
> Lover with loved in marriage of delight!

> Upon my flowery breast,
> Wholly for him, and save himself for none,
> There did I give sweet rest

338

To my beloved one;
The fanning of the cedars breathed thereon.

When the first morning air
Blew from the tower, and waved his locks aside,
His hand, with gentle care,
Did wound me in the side,
And in my body all my senses died.

All things I then forgot,
My cheek on him who for my coming came;
All ceased and I was not,
Leaving my cares and shame
Among the lilies, and forgetting them.[1]

X

It is not permitted to a man who takes up pen or chisel, to seek originality, for passion is his only business, and he cannot but mould or sing after a new fashion because no disaster is like another. He is like those phantom lovers in the Japanese play who, compelled to wander side by side and never mingle, cry: 'We neither wake nor sleep and, passing our nights in a sorrow which is in the end a vision, what are these scenes of spring to us?' If when we have found a mask we fancy that it will not match our mood till we have touched with gold the cheek, we do it turtively, and only where the oaks of Dodona cast their deepest shadow, for could he see our handiwork the Daimon would fling himself out, being our enemy.

[1] Translated by Arthur Symons from 'San Juan de la Cruz'.

XI

Many years ago I saw, between sleeping and waking, a woman of incredible beauty shooting an arrow into the sky, and from the moment when I made my first guess at her meaning I have thought much of the difference between the winding movement of Nature and the straight line, which is called in Balzac's *Séraphita* the 'Mark of Man,' but is better described as the mark of saint or sage. I think that we who are poets and artists, not being permitted to shoot beyond the tangible, must go from desire to weariness and so to desire again, and live but for the moment when vision comes to our weariness like terrible lightning, in the humility of the brutes. I do not doubt those heaving circles, those winding arcs, whether in one man's life or in that of an age, are mathematical, and that some in the world, or beyond the world, have foreknown the event and pricked upon the calendar the life-span of a Christ, a Buddha, a Napoleon: that every movement, in feeling or in thought, prepares in the dark by its own increasing clarity and confidence its own executioner. We seek reality with the slow toil of our weakness and are smitten from the boundless and the unforeseen. Only when we are saint or sage, and renounce experience itself, can we, in imagery of the Christian Cabbala, leave the sudden lightning and the path of the serpent and become the bowman who aims his arrow at the centre of the sun.

XII

The doctors of medicine have discovered that certain dreams of the night, for I do not grant them all, are the day's unfulfilled desire, and that our terror of desires condemned by the conscience has distorted and disturbed our dreams. They have only studied the breaking into dream of elements that have remained unsatisfied without purifying discouragement. We can satisfy in life a few of our passions and each passion but a little, and our characters indeed but differ because no two men bargain alike. The bargain, the compromise, is always threatened, and when it is broken we become mad or hysterical or are in some way deluded; and so when a starved or banished passion shows in a dream we, before awaking, break the logic that had given it the capacity of action and throw it into chaos again. But the passions, when we know that they cannot find fulfilment, become vision; and a vision, whether we wake or sleep, prolongs its power by rhythm and pattern, the wheel where the world is butterfly. We need no protection, but it does, for if we become interested in ourselves, in our own lives, we pass out of the vision. Whether it is we or the vision that create the pattern, who set the wheel turning, it is hard to say, but certainly we have a hundred ways of keeping it near us: we select our images from past times, we turn from our own age and try to feel Chaucer nearer than the daily paper. It compels us to cover all it cannot incorporate, and would carry us when it comes in sleep to that moment when even sleep closes her eyes and dreams begin to dream; and we are taken up into a clear light and are forgetful even of our own names and actions and yet in perfect possession of ourselves murmur like Faust, 'Stay, moment,' and murmur in vain.

XIII

A poet, when he is growing old, will ask himself if he cannot keep his mask and his vision without new bitterness, new disappointment. Could he if he would, knowing how frail his vigour from youth up, copy Landor who lived loving and hating, ridiculous and unconquered, into extreme old age, all lost but the favour of his Muses?

> The Mother of the Muses, we are taught,
> Is Memory; she has left me; they remain,
> And shake my shoulder, urging me to sing.

Surely, he may think, now that I have found vision and mask I need not suffer any longer. He will buy perhaps some small old house, where, like Ariosto, he can dig his garden, and think that in the return of birds and leaves, or moon and sun, and in the evening flight of the rooks he may discover rhythm and pattern like those in sleep and so never awake out of vision. Then he will remember Wordsworth withering into eighty years, honoured and empty-witted, and climb to some waste room and find, forgotten there by youth, some bitter crust.

February 25, 1917

Animi Mundi

ANIMA MUNDI

I

I HAVE ALWAYS SOUGHT to bring my mind close to the mind of Indian and Japanese poets, old women in Connacht, mediums in Soho, lay brothers whom I imagine dreaming in some mediaeval monastery the dreams of their village, learned authors who refer all to antiquity; to immerse it in the general mind where that mind is scarce separable from what we have begun to call 'the subconscious'; to liberate it from all that comes of councils and committees, from the world as it is seen from universities or from populous towns; and that I might so believe I have murmured evocations and frequented mediums, delighted in all that displayed great problems through sensuous images or exciting phrases, accepting from abstract schools but a few technical words that are so old they seem but broken architraves fallen amid bramble and grass, and have put myself to school where all things are seen: *A Tenedo tacitae per amica silentia lunae.* At one time I thought to prove my conclusions by quoting from diaries where I have recorded certain strange events the moment they happened, but now I have changed my mind   I will but say, like the Arab boy that became Vizier: 'O brother, I have taken stock in the desert sand and of the sayings of antiquity.'

There is a letter of Goethe's, though I cannot remember where, that explains evocation, though he was but thinking of literature. He described some friend who had complained of literary sterility as too intelligent. One must allow the images to form with all their associations before one criticises. 'If one is critical too soon,' he wrote, 'they will not form at all.' If you suspend the critical faculty, I have discovered, either as the result of training, or, if you have the gift, by passing into a slight trance, images pass rapidly before you. If you can suspend also desire, and let them form at their own will, your absorption becomes more complete and they are more clear in colour, more precise in articulation, and you and they begin to move in the midst of what seems a powerful light. But the images pass before you linked by certain associations, and indeed in the first instance you have called them up by their association with traditional forms and sounds. You have discovered how, if you can but suspend will and intellect, to bring up from the 'subconscious' anything you already possess a fragment of. Those who follow the old rule keep their bodies still and their minds awake and clear, dreading especially any confusion between the images of the mind and the objects of sense; they seek to become, as it were, polished mirrors.

I had no natural gift for this clear quiet, as I soon discovered, for my mind is abnormally restless; and I was seldom delighted by that sudden luminous definition of form which makes one understand almost in spite of oneself that one is not merely imagining. I therefore invented a new process. I had found that after evocation my sleep became at moments full of light and form, all that I had failed to find while awake; and I elaborated a symbolism of natural objects that I might give myself dreams during sleep, or rather visions, for they had none of the confusion of dreams, by laying upon my pillow or beside my bed certain flowers or leaves. Even to-day, after twenty years, the exaltations and the messages that came to me from bits of hawthorn or some other plant seem, of all moments of my life, the happiest and the wisest. After a time, perhaps because the novelty wearing off, the symbol lost its power, or because my work at the Irish Theatre became too exciting, my sleep lost its responsiveness. I had fellow-scholars, and now it was I and now they who made some discovery. Before the mind's eye, whether in sleep or waking, came images that one was to discover presently in some book one had never read, and after looking in vain for explanation to the current theory of forgotten personal memory, I came to believe in a Great Memory passing on from generation to generation. But that was not enough, for these images showed intention and choice. They had a relation to what one knew and yet were an extension of one's knowledge. If no mind was there, why should I suddenly come upon salt and antimony, upon the liquefaction of the gold, as they were understood by the alchemists, or upon some detail of cabbalistic symbolism verified at last by a learned scholar from his never-published manuscripts, and who can have put together so ingeniously, working by some law of association and yet with clear intention and personal application, certain mythological images? They had shown themselves to several minds, a fragment at a time, and had only shown their meaning when the puzzle picture had been put together. The thought was again and again before me that this study had created a contact or mingling with minds who had followed a like study in some other age, and that these minds still saw and thought and chose. Our daily thought was certainly but the line of foam at the shallow edge of a vast luminous sea; Henry More's *Anima Mundi*, Wordsworth's 'immortal sea which brought us hither', and near whose edge the children sport, and in that sea there were some who swam or sailed, explorers who perhaps knew all its shores.

III

I had always to compel myself to fix the imagination upon the minds behind the personifications, and yet the personifications were themselves living and vivid. The minds that swayed these seemingly fluid images had doubtless form, and those images themselves seemed, as it were, mirrored in a living substance whose form is but change of form. From tradition and perception, one thought of one's own life as symbolised by earth, the place of heterogeneous things, the images as mirrored in water, and the images themselves one could divine but as air; and beyond it all there were, I felt confident, certain aims and governing loves, the fire that makes all simple. Yet the images themselves were fourfold, and one judged their meaning in part from the predominance of one out of the four elements, or that of the fifth element, the veil hiding another four, a bird born out of the fire.

IV

We longed to know something—even if it were but the family and Christian names—of those minds that we could divine, and that yet remained always, as it seemed, impersonal. The sense of contact came perhaps but two or three times with clearness and certainty, but it left, among all to whom it came, some trace, a sudden silence, as it were, in the midst of thought or perhaps at moments of crisis a faint voice. Were our masters right when they declared so solidly that we should be content to know these presences that seemed friendly and near but as 'the phantom' in Coleridge's poem, and to think of them perhaps as having, as Saint Thomas says, entered upon the eternal possession of themselves in one single moment?

> All look and likeness caught from earth,
> All accident of kin and birth,
> Had passed away. There was no trace
> Of aught on that illumined face,
> Upraised beneath the rifted stone,
> But of one spirit all her own;
> She, she herself and only she,
> Shone through her body visibly.

V

One night I heard a voice that said: 'The love of God for every human soul is infinite, for every human soul

347

is unique; no other can satisfy the same need in God.'
Our masters had not denied that personality outlives
the body or even that its rougher shape may cling to us
a while after death, but only that we should seek it in
those who are dead. Yet when I went among the country-
people, I found that they sought and found the old
fragilities, infirmities, physiognomies that living stirred
affection. The Spiddal knowledgeable man, who had
his knowledge from his sister's ghost, noticed every
Hallow-e'en, when he met her at the end of the garden,
that her hair was greyer. Had she perhaps to exhaust her
allotted years in the neighbourhood of her home, hav-
ing died before her time? Because no authority seemed
greater than that of this knowledge running backward
to the beginning of the world, I began that study of
spiritism so despised by Stanislas de Gaeta, the one
eloquent learned scholar who has written of magic in
our generation.

VI

I know much that I could never have known had I not
learnt to consider in the after life what, there as here, is
rough and disjointed; nor have I found that the mediums
in Connacht and Soho have anything I cannot find
some light on in Henry More, who was called during
his life the holiest man now walking upon the earth.

All souls have a vehicle or body, and when one has
said that with More and the Platonists one has escaped
from the abstract schools who seek always the power of
some Church or institution, and found oneself with great
poetry, and superstition which is but popular poetry, in

a pleasant, dangerous world. Beauty is indeed but bodily life in some ideal condition. The vehicle of the human soul is what used to be called the animal spirits, and Henry More quotes from Hippocrates this sentence: 'The mind of man is . . . not nourished from meats and drinks from the belly, but by a clear luminous substance that redounds by separation from the blood.' These animal spirits fill up all parts of the body and make up the body of air, as certain writers of the seventeenth century have called it.[1] The soul has a plastic power, and can after death, or during life, should the vehicle leave the body for a while, mould it to any shape it will by an act of imagination, though the more unlike to the habitual that shape is, the greater the effort. To living and dead alike, the purity and abundance of the animal spirits are a chief power. The soul can mould from these an apparition clothed as if in life, and make it visible by showing it to our mind's eye, or by building into its substance certain particles drawn from the body of a medium till it is as visible and tangible as any other object. To help that building the ancients offered sheaves of corn, fragrant gum, and the odour of fruit and flowers, and the blood of victims. The half-materialised

---

[1] This passage, I think, correctly represents the thought of Henry More, but it would, I now believe, have corresponded better with facts if I had described this 'clear luminous substance' as a sense-material envelope, moulded upon 'the body of air,' or true 'vehicle'; and if I had confined to it the words 'animal spirits.' It must, however, be looked upon as surviving, for a time, the death of the physical body. The spirits do not get from it the material from which their forms are made, but their forms take light from it as one candle takes light from another.   1924.

vehicle slowly exudes from the skin in dull luminous drops or condenses from a luminous cloud, the light fading as weight and density increase. The witch, going beyond the medium, offered to the slowly animating phantom certain drops of her blood. The vehicle once separate from the living man or woman may be moulded by the souls of others as readily as by its own soul, and even, it seems, by the souls of the living. It becomes a part for a while of that stream of images which I have compared to reflections upon water. But how does it follow that souls who never have handled the modelling tool or the brush make perfect images? Those material-isations who imprint their powerful faces upon paraffin wax, leave there sculpture that would have taken a good artist, making and imagining, many hours. How did it follow that an ignorant woman could, as Henry More believed, project her vehicle in so good a likeness of a hare that horse and hound and huntsman followed with the bugle blowing? Is not the problem the same as of those finely articulated scenes and patterns that come out of the dark, seemingly completed in the winking of an eye, as we are lying half asleep, and of all those elab-orate images that drift in moments of inspiration or evocation before the mind's eye? Our animal spirits or vehicles are but, as it were, a condensation of the vehicle of *Anima Mundi*, and give substance to its images in the faint materialisation of our common thought, or more grossly when a ghost is our visitor. It should be no great feat, once those images have dipped into our vehicle, to take their portraits in the photographic camera. Henry More will have it that a hen scared by a hawk when the cock is treading hatches out a hawk-headed chicken (I am no stickler for the fact), because before the soul of the unborn bird could give the shape 'the deeply impassioned fancy of the mother' called from the general cistern of form a competing image. 'The soul of the world,' he runs on, 'interposes and insinuates into all generations of things while the matter is fluid and yielding, which would induce a man to believe that she may not stand idle in the transformation of the vehicle of the daemons, but assist the fancies and desires, and so help to clothe them and to utter them according to their own pleasures; or it may be sometimes against their wills as the unwieldiness of the mother's fancy forces upon her a monstrous birth.' Though images appear to flow and drift, it may be that we but change in our relation to them, now losing, now finding with the shifting of our minds; and certainly Henry More speaks by the book, in claiming that those images may be hard to the right touch as 'pillars of crystal' and as solidly coloured as our own to the right eyes. Shelley, a good Platonist, seems in his earliest work to set this general soul in the place of God, an opinion, one may find from More's friend Cudworth, now affirmed, now combated by classic authority; but More would steady us with a definition. The general soul as apart from its vehicle is 'a substance incorporeal but without sense and animadversion pervading the whole matter of the universe and exercising a plastic power therein, according to the sundry predispositions and occasions, in the parts it works upon, raising such phenomena in the world, by directing the parts of the matter and their motion, as cannot be resolved into mere mechanical powers.' I must assume that 'sense and animadversion,' perception and direction, are always faculties of the individual soul, and that, as Blake said, 'God only acts or is in existing beings or men.'

VII

The old theological conception of the individual soul as bodiless or abstract led to what Henry More calls 'contradictory debate' as to how many angels 'could dance booted and spurred upon the point of a needle,' and made it possible for rationalist physiology to persuade us that our thought has no corporeal existence but in the molecules of the brain. Shelley was of opinion that the 'thoughts which are called real or external objects' differed but in regularity of occurrence from 'hallucinations, dreams and ideas of madmen,' and noticed that he had dreamed, therefore lessening the difference, 'three several times between intervals of two or more years the same precise dream.' If all our mental images no less than apparitions (and I see no reason to distinguish) are forms existing in the general vehicle of *Anima Mundi*, and mirrored in our particular vehicle, many crooked things are made straight. I am persuaded that a logical process, or a series of related images, has body and period, and I think of *Anima Mundi* as a great pool or garden where it moves through its allotted growth like a great water-plant or fragrantly branches in the air. Indeed as Spenser's Garden of Adonis:—

Anima Mundi

There is the first seminary
Of all things that are born to live and die
According to their kynds.

The soul by changes of 'vital congruity,' More says,
draws to it a certain thought, and this thought draws by
its association the sequence of many thoughts, endow-
ing them with a life in the vehicle meted out according
to the intensity of the first perception. A seed is set
growing, and this growth may go on apart from the
power, apart even from the knowledge of the soul. If I
wish to 'transfer' a thought I may think, let us say, of
Cinderella's slipper, and my subject may see an old
woman coming out of a chimney; or going to sleep I
may wish to wake at seven o'clock and, though I never
think of it again, I shall wake upon the instant. The
thought has completed itself, certain acts of logic, turns,
and knots in the stem have been accomplished out of
sight and out of reach, as it were. We are always starting
these parasitic vegetables and letting them coil beyond
our knowledge, and may become like that lady in Bal-
zac who, after a life of sanctity, plans upon her death-
bed to fly with her renounced lover. After death a
dream, a desire she had perhaps ceased to believe in,
perhaps ceased almost to remember, must have recurred
again and again with its anguish and its happiness.
We can only refuse to start the wandering sequence
or, if start it does, hold it in the intellectual light where
time gallops, and so keep it from slipping down into
the sluggish vehicle. The toil of the living is to free
themselves from an endless sequence of objects, and
that of the dead to free themselves from an endless

sequence of thoughts. One sequence begets another, and these have power because of all those things we do, not for their own sake but for an imagined good.

VIII

Spiritism, whether of folk-lore or of the séance-room, the visions of Swedenborg, and the speculation of the Platonists and Japanese plays, will have it that we may see at certain roads and in certain houses old murders acted over again, and in certain fields dead huntsmen riding with horse and hound, or ancient armies fighting above bones or ashes. We carry to *Anima Mundi* our memory, and that memory is for a time our external world; and all passionate moments recur again and again, for passion desires its own recurrence more than any event, and whatever there is of corresponding complacency or remorse is our beginning of judgment; nor do we remember only the events of life, for thoughts bred of longing and of fear, all those parasitic vegetables that have slipped through our fingers, come again like a rope's end to smite us upon the face; and as Cornelius Agrippa writes: 'We may dream ourselves to be consumed in flame and persecuted by daemons,' and certain spirits have complained that they would be hard put to it to arouse those who died, believing they could not awake till a trumpet shrilled. A ghost in a Japanese play is set afire by a fantastic scruple, and though a Buddhist priest explains that the fire would go out of itself if the ghost but ceased to believe in it, it cannot cease to believe. Cornelius Agrippa called such dreaming souls hobgoblins, and when Hamlet refused the bare bodkin because of what dreams may come, it was from no mere literary fancy. The soul can indeed, it appears, change these objects built about us by the memory, as it may change its shape; but the greater the change, the greater the effort and the sooner the return to the habitual images. Doubtless in either case the effort is often beyond its power. Years ago I was present when a woman consulted Madame Blavatsky for a friend who saw her newly-dead husband nightly as a decaying corpse and smelt the odour of the grave. 'When he was dying,' said Madame Blavatsky, 'he thought the grave the end, and now that he is dead cannot throw off that imagination.' A Brahmin once told an actress friend of mine that he disliked acting, because if a man died playing Hamlet, he would be Hamlet in eternity. Yet after a time the soul partly frees itself and becomes 'the shape-changer' of the legends, and can cast, like the mediaeval magician, what illusions it would. There is an Irish countryman in one of Lady Gregory's books who had eaten with a stranger on the road, and some while later vomited, to discover he had but eaten chopped-up grass. One thinks, too, of the spirits that show themselves in the images of wild creatures.

IX

The dead, as the passionate necessity wears out, come into a measure of freedom and may turn the impulse of events, started while living, in some new direction, but they cannot originate except through the living. Then gradually they perceive, although they are still but living in their memories, harmonies, symbols, and patterns, as though all were being refashioned by an artist, and they are moved by emotions, sweet for no imagined good but in themselves, like those of children dancing in a ring; and I do not doubt that they make love in that union which Swedenborg has said is of the whole body and seems from far off an incandescence. Hitherto shade has communicated with shade in moments of common memory that recur like the figures of a dance in terror or in joy, but now they run together like to like, and their covens and fleets have rhythm and pattern. This running together and running of all to a centre, and yet without loss of identity, has been prepared for by their exploration of their moral life, of its beneficiaries and its victims, and even of all its untrodden paths, and all their thoughts have moulded the vehicle and become event and circumstance.

X

There are two realities, the terrestrial and the condition of fire.[1] All power is from the terrestrial condition, for there all opposites meet and there only is the extreme of choice possible, full freedom. And there the

[1] When writing this essay I did not see how complete must be the antithesis between man and Daimon. The repose of man is the choice of the Daimon, and the repose of the Daimon the choice of man; and what I have called man's terrestrial state the Daimon's condition of fire. I might have seen this, as it all follows from the words written by the beggar in *The Hour-Glass* upon the walls of Babylon.   1924.

heterogeneous is, and evil, for evil is the strain one upon another of opposites; but in the condition of fire is all music and all rest. Between is the condition of air where images have but a borrowed life, that of memory or that reflected upon them when they symbolise colours and intensities of fire: the place of shades who are 'in the whirl of those who are fading,' and who cry like those amorous shades in the Japanese play:—

> That we may acquire power
> Even in our faint substance,
> We will show forth even now,
> And though it be but in a dream,
> Our form of repentance.

After so many rhythmic beats the soul must cease to desire its images, and can, as it were, close its eyes.

When all sequence comes to an end, time comes to an end, and the soul puts on the rhythmic or spiritual body or luminous body and contemplates all the events of its memory and every possible impulse in an eternal possession of itself in one single moment. That condition is alone animate, all the rest is fantasy, and from thence come all the passions and, some have held, the very heat of the body.

> Time drops in decay,
> Like a candle burnt out,
> And the mountains and woods
> Have their day, have their day.
> What one, in the rout
> Of the fire-born moods,
> Has fallen away?

XI

The soul cannot have much knowledge till it has shaken off the habit of time and of place, but till that hour it must fix its attention upon what is near, thinking of objects one after another as we run the eye or the finger over them. Its intellectual power cannot but increase and alter as its perceptions grow simultaneous. Yet even now we seem at moments to escape from time in what we call prevision, and from place when we see distant things in a dream and in concurrent dreams. A couple of years ago, while in meditation, my head seemed surrounded by a conventional sun's rays, and when I went to bed I had a long dream of a woman with her hair on fire. I awoke and lit a candle, and discovered presently from the odour that in doing so I had set my own hair on fire. I dreamed very lately that I was writing a story, and at the same time I dreamed that I was one of the characters in that story and seeking to touch the heart of some girl in defiance of the author's intention; and concurrently with all that, I was as another self trying to strike with the button of a foil a great china jar. The obscurity of the 'Prophetic Books' of William Blake, which were composed in a state of vision, comes almost wholly from these concurrent dreams. Everybody has some story or some experience of the sudden knowledge in sleep or waking of some event, a misfortune for the most part, happening to some friend far off.

XII

The dead living in their memories are, I am persuaded, the source of all that we call instinct, and it is their love and their desire, all unknowing, that make us drive beyond our reason, or in defiance of our interest it may be; and it is the dream martens that, all unknowing, are master-masons to the living martens building about church windows their elaborate nests; and in their turn, the phantoms are stung to a keener delight from a concord between their luminous pure vehicle and our strong senses. It were to reproach the power or the beneficence of God, to believe those children of Alexander, who died wretchedly, could not throw an urnful to the heap, nor Caesarion[1] murdered in childhood, whom Cleopatra bore to Caesar, nor the brief-lived younger Pericles Aspasia bore—being so nobly born.

XIII

Because even the most wise dead can but arrange their memories as we arrange pieces upon a chessboard, and obey remembered words alone, he who would turn magician is forbidden by the Zoroastrian oracle to change 'barbarous words' of invocation. Communication with *Anima Mundi* is through the association of thoughts or images or objects; and the famous dead, and those of whom but a faint memory lingers, can still—and it is for no other end that, all unknowing, we value posthumous fame—tread the

[1] I have no better authority for Caesarion than Landor's play.

corridor and take the empty chair. A glove and a name can call their bearer; the shadows come to our elbow amid their old undisturbed habitations, and 'materialisation' itself is easier, it may be, among walls, or by rocks and trees, that bring before their memory some moment of emotion while they had still animate bodies.

Certainly the mother returns from the grave, and with arms that may be visible and solid, for a hurried moment, can comfort a neglected child or set the cradle rocking; and in all ages men have known and affirmed that when the soul is troubled, those that are a shade and a song

> live there,
> And move like winds of light on dark and stormy air.

XIV

Awhile they live again those passionate moments, not knowing they are dead, and then they know and may awake or half awake to be our visitors. How is their dream changed as time drops away and their senses multiply? Does their stature alter, do their eyes grow more brilliant? Certainly the dreams stay the longer, the greater their passion when alive: Helen may still open her chamber door to Paris or watch him from the wall, and know she is dreaming but because nights and days are poignant or the stars unreckonably bright. Surely of the passionate dead we can but cry in words Ben Jonson meant for none but Shakespeare: 'So rammed' are they 'with life they can but grow in life with being.'

XV

The inflowing from their mirrored life, who themselves receive it from the Condition of Fire, falls upon the winding path called the Path of the Serpent, and that inflowing coming alike to men and to animals is called natural. There is another inflow which is not natural but intellectual, and is from the fire; and it descends through souls who pass for a lengthy or a brief period out of the mirror life, as we in sleep out of the bodily life, and though it may fall upon a sleeping serpent, it falls principally upon straight paths. In so far as a man is like all other men, the inflow finds him upon the winding path, and in so far as he is a saint or sage, upon the straight path.

XVI

The Daimon, by using his mediatorial shades, brings man again and again to the place of choice, heightening temptation that the choice may be as final as possible, imposing his own lucidity upon events, leading his victim to whatever among works not impossible is the most difficult. He suffers with man as some firm-souled man suffers with the woman he but loves the better because she is extravagant and fickle. His descending power is neither the winding nor the straight line but zigzag, illuminating the passive and active properties, the tree's two sorts of fruit: it is the sudden lightning, for all his acts of power are instantaneous. We perceive in a pulsation of the artery, and after slowly decline.

XVII

Each Daimon is drawn to whatever man or, if its nature is more general, to whatever nation it most differs from, and it shapes into its own image the antithetical dream of man or nation. The Jews had already shown by the precious metals, by the ostentatious wealth of Solomon's temple, the passion that has made them the money-lenders of the modern world. If they had not been rapacious, lustful, narrow, and persecuting beyond the people of their time, the incarnation had been impossible; but it was an intellectual impulse from the Condition of Fire that shaped their antithetical self into that of the classic world. So always it is an impulse from some Daimon that gives to our vague, unsatisfied desire, beauty, a meaning, and a form all can accept.

XVIII

Only in rapid and subtle thought, or in faint accents heard in the quiet of the mind, can the thought of the spirit come to us but little changed; for a mind that grasps objects simultaneously according to the degree of its liberation does not think the same thought with the mind that sees objects one after another. The purpose of most religious teaching, of the insistence upon the submission to God's will above all, is to make certain of the passivity of the vehicle where it is most pure and most tenuous. When we are passive where the vehicle is coarse, we become mediumistic, and the spirits who mould themselves in that coarse vehicle can only rarely and with great difficulty speak their own thoughts and keep their own memory. They are subject to a kind of drunkenness and are stupefied, old writers said, as if with honey, and readily mistake our memory for their own, and believe themselves whom and what we please. We bewilder and overmaster them, for once they are among the perceptions of successive objects, our reason, being but an instrument created and sharpened by those objects, is stronger than their intellect, and they can but repeat, with brief glimpses from another state, our knowledge and our words.

XIX

A friend once dreamed that she saw many dragons climbing upon the steep side of a cliff and continually falling. Henry More thought that those who, after centuries of life, failed to find the rhythmic body and to pass into the Condition of Fire, were born again. Edmund Spenser, who was among More's masters, affirmed that nativity without giving it a cause:—

> After that they agayne retourned beene,
> They in that garden planted be agayne,
> And grow afresh, as they had never seene
> Fleshy corruption, nor mortal payne.
> Some thousand years so doen they ther remayne,
> And then of him are clad with other hew,
> Or sent into the chaungeful world agayne,
> Till thither they retourn where first they grew:
> So, like a wheele, around they ronne from old to new.

XX

But certainly it is always to the Condition of Fire, where emotion is not brought to any sudden stop, where there is neither wall nor gate, that we would rise; and the mask plucked from the oak-tree is but my imagination of rhythmic body. We may pray to that last condition by any name so long as we do not pray to it as a thing or a thought, and most prayers call it man or woman or child:—

> For Mercy has a human heart,
> Pity a human face.

Within ourselves Reason and Will, who are the man and woman, hold out towards a hidden altar a laughing or crying child.

XXI

When I remember that Shelley calls our minds 'mirrors of the fire for which all thirst,' I cannot but ask the question all have asked, 'What or who has cracked the mirror?' I begin to study the only self that I can know, myself, and to wind the thread upon the pern again.

At certain moments, always unforeseen, I become happy, most commonly when at hazard I have opened some book of verse. Sometimes it is my own verse when, instead of discovering new technical flaws, I read with all the excitement of the first writing. Perhaps I am sitting in some crowded restaurant, the open book beside me, or closed, my excitement having over-brimmed the page. I look at the strangers near as if I

364

had known them all my life, and it seems strange that I cannot speak to them: everything fills me with affection, I have no longer any fears or any needs; I do not even remember that this happy mood must come to an end. It seems as if the vehicle had suddenly grown pure and far extended and so luminous that the images from *Anima Mundi*, embodied there and drunk with that sweetness, would, like a country drunkard who has thrown a wisp into his own thatch, burn up time.

It may be an hour before the mood passes, but latterly I seem to understand that I enter upon it the moment I cease to hate. I think the common condition of our life is hatred—I know that this is so with me—irritation with public or private events or persons. There is no great matter in forgetfulness of servants, or the delays of tradesmen, but how forgive the ill-breeding of Carlyle, or the rhetoric of Swinburne, or that woman who murmurs over the dinner-table the opinion of her daily paper? And only a week ago last Sunday, I hated the spaniel who disturbed a partridge on her nest, a trout who took my bait and yet broke away unhooked. The books say that our happiness comes from the opposite of hate, but I am not certain, for we may love unhappily. And plainly, when I have closed a book too stirred to go on reading, and in those brief intense visions of sleep, I have something about me that, though it makes me love, is more like innocence. I am in the place where the Daimon is, but I do not think he is with me until I begin to make a new personality, selecting among those images, seeking always to satisfy a hunger grown out of conceit with daily diet; and yet as I write the words 'I select,' I am full of uncertainty, not knowing when I am the finger, when the clay. Once, twenty years ago, I seemed to awake from sleep to find my body rigid, and to hear a strange voice speaking these words through my lips as through lips of stone: 'We make an image of him who sleeps, and it is not he who sleeps, and we call it Emmanuel.'

XXII

As I go up and down my stair and pass the gilded Moorish wedding-chest where I keep my 'barbarous words,' I wonder will I take to them once more, for I am baffled by those voices that still speak as to Odysseus but as the bats; or now that I shall in a little be growing old, to some kind of simple piety like that of an old woman.

May 9, 1917

Epilogue

EPILOGUE

M Y DEAR 'MAURICE'—I was often in France before you were born or when you were but a little child. When I went for the first or second time Mallarmé had just written: 'All our age is full of the trembling of the veil of the Temple.' One met everywhere young men of letters who talked of magic. A distinguished English man of letters asked me to call with him on Stanislas de Gaeta because he did not dare go alone to that mysterious house. I met from time to time, with the German poet Dauthendey, a grave Swede whom I only discovered after years to have been Strindberg, then looking for the philosophers' stone in a lodging near the Luxembourg; and one day, in the chambers of Stuart Merrill the poet, I spoke with a young Arabic scholar who displayed a large, roughly-made gold ring which had grown to the shape of his finger. Its gold had no hardening alloy, he said, because it was made by his master, a Jewish Rabbi, of alchemical gold. My critical mind—was it friend or enemy?—mocked, and yet I was delighted. Paris was as legendary as Connacht. This new pride, that of the adept, was added to the pride of the artist. Villiers de l'Isle-Adam, the haughtiest of men, had but lately died. I had read his *Axël* slowly and laboriously as one reads a sacred book—my French was very bad—and had applauded it upon the stage. As I could not follow the spoken words, I was not bored even when Axël and the Commander discussed philosophy for a half-hour instead of beginning their duel. If I felt impatient it was only that they delayed the coming of the adept Janus, for I hoped to recognise the moment when Axël cries: 'I know that lamp, it was burning before Solomon'; or that other when he cries: 'As for living, our servants will do that for us.'

The movement of letters had been haughty even before Magic had touched it. Rimbaud had sung: 'Am I an old maid that I should fear the embrace of death?' And everywhere in Paris and in London young men boasted of the garret, and claimed to have no need of what the crowd values.

Last summer you, who were at the age I was when first I heard of Mallarmé and of Verlaine, spoke much of the French poets young men and women read to-day. Claudel I already somewhat knew, but you read to me for the first time from Jammes a dialogue between a poet and a bird, that made us cry, and a whole volume of Péguy's *Mystère de la Charité de Jeanne d'Arc*. Nothing remained the same but the preoccupation with religion, for these poets submitted everything to the Pope, and all, even Claudel, a proud oratorical man, affirmed that they saw the world with the eyes of vine-dressers and charcoal-burners. It was no longer the soul, self-moving and self-teaching—the magical soul—but Mother France and Mother Church.

Have not my thoughts run through a like round, though I have not found my tradition in the Catholic Church, which was not the Church of my childhood, but where the tradition is, as I believe, more universal and more ancient?

W. B. Y.

May 11, 1917